NOTE

1. All spoon measurements are level. Spoon measures can be bought in both imperial and metric sizes to give accurate measurement of small quantities.

2. All eggs are size 2 or 3 unless otherwise stated.

3. All sugar is granulated unless otherwise stated.

4. Preparation times given are an average calculated during recipe testing.

5. Metric and imperial measurements have been calculated separately. Use one set of measurements only as they are not exact equivalents.

6. Cooking times may vary slightly depending on the individual oven. Dishes should be placed in the centre of an oven unless otherwise specified.

7. Always preheat the oven or grill to the specified temperature.

8. $\boxed{F}$ indicates at which point a dish can be frozen. $\boxed{A}$ indicates up to which point the dish can be prepared in advance. Brief freezing and/or advance preparation details can be found at the end of all recipes in which these symbols have been included. The symbol $\boxed{M}$ precedes information on thawing and reheating dishes in a microwave cooker. The information is based on a cooker having a 650 watt output.

9. If using a fan-assisted oven, follow the manufacturer's instructions for guidance on temperature adjustments.

10. In some menus an asterisk '*' is used to indicate a serving suggestion only. No recipe is given.

11. The countdowns have been worked out by an experienced home economist. Inexperienced cooks may need to allow a little longer.

THE COMPLETE HOSTESS

THE COMPLETE HOSTESS

MAJOR CONTRIBUTORS
ROSEMARY WADEY
AND
PAMELA WESTLAND

FOREWORD BY ARABELLA BOXER

First published in 1987 by Octopus Books Limited
Grosvenor Street, London, England

© 1987 Hennerwood Publications Limited
© 1986 International Wine & Food Society, Vintage Chart
ISBN 0 86273 386 3

Printed in Spain

CONTENTS

*F*OREWORD
BY
ARABELLA BOXER

There are many different styles of entertaining, and each individual must find the one that suits her. For entertaining is no more than the practice of hospitality, and, as such, an extension of your personality. Life goes in seven-year cycles, or so they say, and as one passes through the various stages, different ways of living become appropriate. Perhaps one moves from the city to the country, or from a house to a flat; children grow up and leave home, and what was once a family house often becomes a home for one person. The important thing to remember is that almost every situation has possibilities, which should be exploited. Don't be misled into trying to emulate something that is foreign to your nature, for the strain of trying to live up to a false image is both exhausting and unproductive.

When I was first married, I was keen to experiment, to see what I could do. It amused me to make a four course dinner for ten people, as I once did. Now such a thing would not be possible, for many reasons. Yet I still enjoy entertaining as much as ever, though the scale has changed. Instead of a dinner party for Cecil Beaton, it is more likely to be a tea party for my grandchildren, but no less fun, I assure you. For me, the interest lies as much in the arrangement of the room as in the choice of food. And entertaining should be fun; if it is no more than a chore for the hostess, it will bring little joy to the guests.

I have never thought of myself as a hostess, and am often heard insisting that I rarely entertain. Yet this is not quite true. Although I seldom give dinner parties, I am constantly having friends in for a meal, and this is only another form of entertaining. Looking through my diary, I see that in the last ten days I have cooked for friends on no less than seven occasions: a supper party for four after the ballet, supper for three after an exhibition opening and again for four after a concert, supper for four to watch a programme on T.V., a single friend for lunch on two occasions, and a tea party for my grandchildren.

I have already tried several of the ideas in this book, and find they fit easily into my pattern of informal entertaining. For each reader must be free to use the recipes as they wish, without feeling obliged to stick to the suggested scheme. I have made the deep-fried Potato skins with soured cream dip and Hazelnut and orange tuiles for a children's supper party; a garnish of fried noodles for a creamy vegetable soup after the theatre; Brown rice with courgettes and lemon, Granary soda rolls, and Leek, potato and coriander bake for a series of vegetarian meals. Since I don't much approve the arbitrary mixing of food from different cultures, I particularly liked the suggestions for an Indian dinner, a Creole supper, and the other ethnic meals. My next project will be to make one of these, in its entirety.

Arabella Boxer

PARTY PLANNING

Planning a party combines the joy of anticipation with the down-to-earth business of paying meticulous attention to detail. How to adapt and decorate your home, cope with large numbers, prepare special ingredients, choose the wines, set the table, and, most important, plan your timetable so that you have time to enjoy the party yourself. All these and many other essential details are in this first chapter.

TYPES OF PARTY

Giving a party – any kind of party, for any number of people – is a wonderful way of indulging yourself. It gives you the opportunity to invite the people whose company you most enjoy, and to serve the type of food and drinks that you feel most at home with.

One secret of giving a successful party is to plan it in meticulous detail. Make lists of the guests you will invite, the budget, menu, ingredients, shopping, the containers and appliances you will need, the tasks you can do beforehand, the preparation of the food, and those jobs that have to be left until the last minute. Detailed plans for a party will cover several pages of a loose-leaf notebook but, once the groundwork has been laid, the rest seems easy.

Another secret of success is to plan a party that is well within your resources, your budget and the size of your home. It is all too tempting, weeks ahead of the event, to work out a complicated menu for more guests than your house will comfortably hold. When you review your initial plans for a party, make a careful assessment of how much time you would need to spend away from your guests, stirring and whisking, arranging and garnishing the food. This time factor could be crucial. It is worth remembering that you may well be the only person at the party who knows everyone present, and your ability to introduce guests to others with similar interests, and to bring shy ones into the conversation could truly make all the difference, and make the party go with a swing.

Drinks parties

Drinks parties are the easiest to organise. As they usually last for only a couple of hours, before lunch or dinner, from noon or around 6 pm, there is no need to provide seating for everyone, just a few chairs thoughtfully placed for those who long to take the weight off their feet. This means that you can invite more people – say 20 in a room that would seat only 8 or 10 – and a wider mix of people.

Serving wine, or wine cups can help to keep the drinks party within a reasonable budget. You can decide to provide a great deal of food or none at all, or maybe just a few dips or crisps.

One point to note: do make it clear on the invitation what you will be serving. It is a woeful guest indeed who puts a large casserole in the oven before leaving home, only to be faced with an unexpected spread bordering on a buffet meal.

Kitchen parties can be fun, and have practical advantages for the single-handed host or hostess. If yours is the large, hub-of-the-household type of room, or you have a combined kitchen and dining room, it is a good idea to turn the spotlight on the cooker and have a pancake, waffle or omelette party. The basic ingredients are inexpensive, you can make the batter mixture, the fillings and salads in advance, and the tossing and sizzling becomes part of the cheerful informality of the occasion.

'Self-help' parties of all kinds are well in step with today's relaxed mood. You provide a pile of cooked pancakes, kept warm in a casserole or under a folded cloth, a tray of jacket potatoes, straight from the oven or microwave, or a basket of steaming hot rolls or hunks of French bread and a selection of fillings and toppings for guests to help themselves.

Theme parties

Parties with a special theme give an extra zing to the invitations – somehow a 'French Bistro Evening' holds more promise than just a buffet supper – and they provide a link between the food and any table decorations. Children, particularly, warm to the theme idea, and an invitation to a circus, toy-town, space ships, nursery rhyme, red-white-and-blue, or tramps' party also gives plenty of opportunity for dressing up appropriately.

The timing of your party – not just the season, but the time of day – could well be geared to your own personality. If you are an early riser it could be a good idea to give a weekend breakfast or brunch party of, for example, scrambled eggs, kedgeree, open sandwiches, muffins, poached dried fruits and yogurt. Just think how your incorrigible 'night owl' friends would appreciate having something all ready and waiting, and worth getting up for!

Coffee and tea parties can be the occasion for informal get-togethers to introduce new neighbours or raise money for a good cause. These are perfect occasions, too, to invite guests to contribute by bringing a dish such

as a tray of muesli biscuits or a plate of wholemeal sandwiches.

The best parties are always those at which the host or hostess is most relaxed and confident, so read the relevant sections on the following pages, and judge which type of event is most 'you'.

The size of your rooms may be the deciding factor. Most people are happy to stand for the pre-meal drinks at a buffet party but like to perch, even if it has to be a cushion on the floor, once the food is served. Work out how many people your house will seat and limit your guest list accordingly. Simply by serving the food from the kitchen, thus releasing the dining table for seating and eating, may have a considerable effect on the numbers game.

Summer settings

If your home has a balcony, patio or garden, this can make a charming setting for a summer party – an intimate candlelight dinner on the balcony, a drinks party on the patio or strawberries and champagne, a buffet supper or barbecue party in the garden. With the uncertainties of a northern climate you cannot, unfortunately, allow your mood to become too expansive so make alternative arrangements in the event of bad weather.

Which is it to be, a midsummer night's dream of a supper party, an imaginative 'soup kitchen', or a dinner party with all the trimmings? Take stock of your finances, decide how much you wish to set aside for the occasion and then decide how best to spend it. If you need to cater for large numbers on a low budget it really is no problem. Dips and dunks, pâté and pies, or soup and cheese for 25 may cost no more than a grand dinner for 6 or a buffet for 12. Select your menu – we have a dazzling choice beginning on page 58 – and cost the main ingredients in the shops. Make full use of seasonal fruits and vegetables and promotional offers, list the amounts you need, not forgetting the extras like cheese, coffee, foil and cling film, and then stick rigidly to your shopping list.

Once you have planned your party with this amount of care it only remains for your guests, and you as hostess, to have a thoroughly enjoyable time.

RIGHT: Buffet parties are the time to entertain more guests than you can conveniently invite to dinner

CATERING FOR LARGE NUMBERS

Catering for a crowd is no more complicated than preparing for a much smaller party. It is simply – and we use the word advisedly – a matter of planning every detail with almost military precision, and working methodically through your schedule.

It is crucial to plan a menu that allows you to do most of the food presentation and cooking well in advance, and demands the very minimum of last-minute work in the kitchen. As the day draws near it is comforting to know that casseroles and pies, gâteaux and desserts are ready in the freezer, and long-keeping items like rich cakes and meringues are stored in tins.

Write down a provisional menu and then assess each item, almost on a points system, awarding maximum points to those which can be frozen or stored in advance and minimum points or a black mark to those that involve accurate last-minute timing, lifting large, heavy pans of boiling water and so forth.

Once you are satisfied that your menu is practical from the 'management' point of view, is well balanced in terms of texture, flavour and colour, and will look as well as taste appetizing, work out a time schedule. Divide the menu into cooking stages, deciding when it will be convenient for you to make a start. Then make a detailed shopping list in chronological order for each stage, listing separately the

ingredients for each batch of cooking. This will help to spread the load and chore of shopping and keep the whole task within manageable proportions.

Your work schedule is the key to the smooth running of the party, so it is worth taking time and trouble to make it as accurate and detailed as possible. In the early stages it need be no more specific than, for example, 'Two weeks ahead, make and freeze lasagne and goulash. One week ahead, make and freeze lemon cakes. Make and store salad dressing. Check and wash china

and glasses.' But as the day draws near it is helpful to have a much more detailed plan of action.

List every task you have to do, including arranging the flowers, vacuum-cleaning the floor, dusting the furniture, setting the table, washing and preparing the salad, taking dishes from the freezer in time for them to thaw, putting dishes in the oven to heat, filling meringues, carving meat and decorating desserts. Then arrange the jobs into chronological order, making sure to allow enough time for each. Allow time, too, for a bath or shower, and a leisurely period in which to dress and do your make-up.

Organising your time

Once you have this time plan, the anxiety of the organisation – if indeed you ever experienced any – can be a thing of the past. Each day you just have to work systematically through your allotted tasks, confident that nothing can slip your memory and nothing is left to chance.

Make it an early priority to check how many plates, glasses, serving dishes, chairs and tables you have and will need. Consider improvising serving tables by setting a wallpaper pasting table or an old door on trestles and covering it with first a blanket and then a sheet or cloth. Ask friends to lend you what items they can, and then, if necessary, look in local telephone directories for the names of catering equipment and furniture hire firms.

Plan the arrangement of serving tables carefully to allow guests to move as quickly and easily as possible if they are to serve themselves with food. Remember that the wider the choice you offer, the more slowly the queue will move, as guests ponder over each tempting dish. Wherever possible, divide the food into two separate serving areas – more if you are catering for very large numbers and have the space – and ask someone to 'direct the traffic', in one door and out of another.

If table-top space is limited, you might need to arrange the food a little at a time in small casseroles and dishes, replacing each one as it becomes

LEFT: Tempting nibbles for picnics and buffet parties

empty. This method has the practical advantage in that you can more easily keep food hot or cold, and can perhaps bring it to the table in the quantities and dishes in which it was cooked.

Be prepared for any minor emergencies. Have a dustpan and brush to sweep up a broken glass, a kitchen cloth to wipe up spills and a household cleaner to apply, as quickly and discreetly as possible, to a stain on a carpet.

When the last guests have left, work as methodically through the clearing up and putting away as you did throughout the preparation.

Have a supply of trays to collect empty glasses and used crockery and cutlery. If you are using disposable plates, have a container to collect those and any scraps and a separate one for cutlery to be washed.

Multiplying recipes

One perhaps surprising fact is that a large number of people, whether they are at a buffet meal or tea party, do not eat, in proportion, the same amount as those at a small gathering. This may be accounted for by the fact that when guests have to eat perched on the corner of a chair and juggling with a knife, fork and glass or cup and saucer, they take smaller helpings, and that the food is not the centre of attention for a long time the way it is if people are seated around a table.

If you want to 'multiply' a favourite recipe devised for four people it is not, therefore, just a case of simple arithmetic. Forty people at a buffet will not eat ten times as much as four people at a dinner party. If, for example, you choose a dish which, when cooked for four or six, allows 225 g (8 oz) of boned meat per portion, for a large party you can confidently reduce this to 150 g (5 oz) per person. The capacity of your casseroles and pans may well limit the quantities you can cook at once, but in any case it is never advisable to prepare any recipe in more than times-four the original.

Take special care when you are multiplying dishes which have significant amounts of herbs and spices. These ingredients have the capacity to flavour much larger quantities of meat, fish, sauce and so forth; on no account increase the amount of hot spices in direct proportion to the main ingredients. Add a little, taste the sauce and if necessary add a little more.

FISH

Fish are generally categorised as white or oily, but they may also be divided into freshwater, saltwater (or sea), flat or round.

White fish – a category which includes fish such as cod, plaice, haddock and halibut – have firm white flesh, and a low fat content. Oily fish have a much richer flesh which is darker in colour and has a slightly coarser texture. Fish in this category include herring, mackerel, salmon and trout.

Fish and health

Fish is a valuable source of first class protein, although not as high as meat. Fish is also a useful source of calcium, phosphorus (in the edible bones of whitebait, sardines etc), and many of the B vitamins. Cod liver oil, for instance, is the major source of Vitamins A and D; and D, which occurs in very few foods, is contained in most oily fish. Many fish supply iodine and fluorine.

Fish are also nutritionally important because they contain little fat. Even oily fish seldom have more than a 20 per cent fat content (much less than an equivalent weight of meat). This means that it is more easily digestible and contains few calories. White fish, especially, is valuable for slimmers, and when cooked simply, is an ideal food for the young, the old, and for convalescents.

Buying fish
– Always buy fish on the day it is to be cooked.
– Choose fish that has bright shiny eyes and a plump, firm body.
– The scales and skin should be shiny and moist.
– The flesh should be firm.
– The smell of the fish is an excellent guide to the freshness. It should smell slightly sweet, certainly not unpleasant, nor too fishy.
– Choose a fishmonger who has a good reputation, and take his advice on the freshest fish to choose. The shop itself should not have an unpleasant stale fish smell.
– Allow 175 g (6 oz) fish without bones, 1 large or 2 small fillets per person.

How to skin a sole

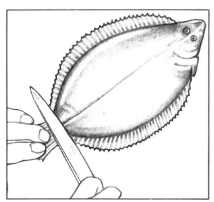
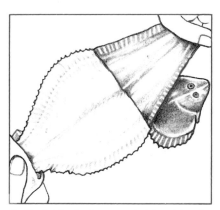
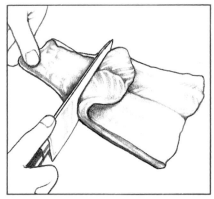

1. Put the sole on a board, dark side up, head away from you, and wipe the skin dry.
2. Using a sharp knife, cut through the skin at the tail. With the point of the knife, loosen and ease up the skin around the cut edge of the tail.

3. Sprinkle the loosened skin with salt, and hold the tail firmly with one hand.
4. With the other hand, very gently lift the skin and pull it upwards towards the head. (The skin may be held with a cloth, to give a firmer grip.) Turn the fish over, and repeat on the other side.

5. Alternatively skin a fish or a fillet by first loosening the skin at the tail end, then grip the loosened skin and ease away the flesh with a knife.

How to fillet a flat fish
To cut 4 fillets from a plaice or sole, lay the fish on a board and cut off the head and fins. Cut along the backbone from the head to the tail. Keeping the knife close to the bone work out from the backbone with long firm strokes. Remove the other fillet in the same way. Turn the fish over and remove the other 2 fillets in the same way.

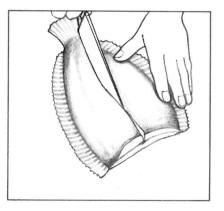
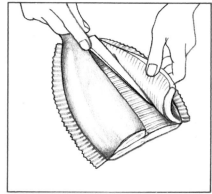

1. Cut along the backbone with a sharp knife.

2. Work the flesh outwards from the backbone.

Bass

Halibut

Bream

Sprat

Carp

Herring

Mackerel

Squid

Cod

Trout

John Dory

Plaice

Turbot

Red Mullet

Dover Sole

Salmon

Flounder

Haddock

Skate

Whiting

How to bone a round fish

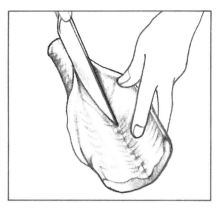

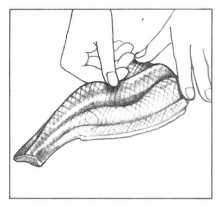

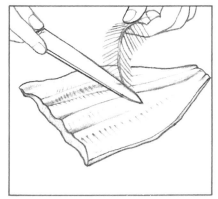

1. To bone a round fish like a herring or a mackerel, first cut off the head and tail and cut down the belly to open it completely. Remove the gut.

2. Lay the fish down flat, skin side up, and press firmly with your thumb along the backbone to loosen it.

3. Turn the fish over use a sharp knife to lift out the backbone.

How to prepare and dress a crab

1. Choose a live crab that is fairly active, has a clean shell and is heavy for its size. (To pick up a live crab, grip it at the tail end.)
2. Put the crab into a large saucepan with a few flavouring vegetables, if liked, cover with cold water, and add a little salt.
3. Cover with a lid, slowly bring to the boil and simmer gently for 10–12 minutes per 450 g (1 lb).
4. Leave to cool in the cooking liquor, which may be used as a base for fish stock or a sauce.
5. When cold, rinse the crab shell under cold water. Place it shell down on a large board, with the legs uppermost.

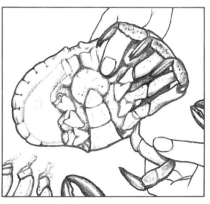

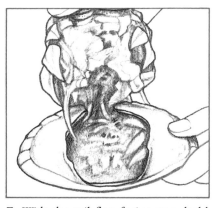

6. Twist off the legs and claws at the joint with the body.

7. With the tail flap facing you, hold the crab firmly with both hands, and using the thumbs push and prise the body section upwards so that it is released from the hard back shell.

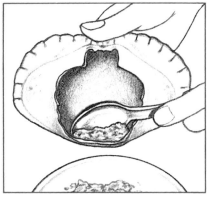

8. Pull away and discard the greyish-white stomach sac (just behind the mouth) and the long white pointed 'dead men's fingers'. These are very obvious and should be removed.

9. Using a small spoon, scoop out all the meat from both shells, keeping white and brown meats separate, in different bowls. Reach in carefully to all the crevices with a lobster pick or metal skewer. Be careful to remove all the little pieces of shell.

10. Crack the claws, using a hammer or shellfish crackers, and remove the white meat. Break the legs at the joints, and extract the meat.
11. Place the empty hard shell on the board, and using the thumbs, or a small hammer, push or tap the shell to remove the thin undershell. This should come away easily, following a visible line on both sides.
12. For dressed crab, wash and dry the hard shell. Mix the brown meat with a little mayonnaise and seasoning and spoon it down the centre of the shell. Season the white meat with salt and white pepper and arrange it on either side of the brown meat. Garnish with finely chopped parsley, paprika and hard-boiled egg. Dressed crab is generally served with a green salad. Minted new potatoes, hot or made into potato salad, also go well.

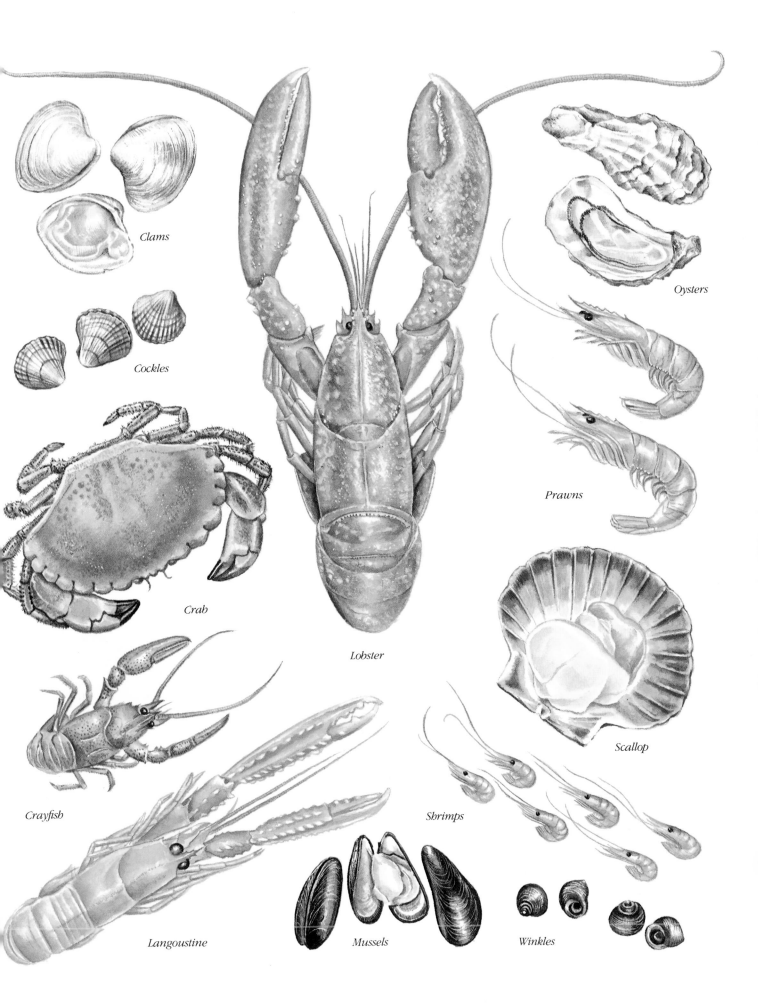

Clams

Cockles

Crab

Crayfish

Langoustine

Lobster

Oysters

Prawns

Scallop

Shrimps

Mussels

Winkles

How to prepare squid

Squid are available frozen all the year round. They are usually about 7.5–15 cm (3–6 inches) in length, but larger ones can be found in fishmonger's shops. The edible parts of squid are the tentacles and body. The head and inner part of the body must be removed and discarded. The body is usually cut into rings and gently fried or stewed, although it can also be stuffed whole.

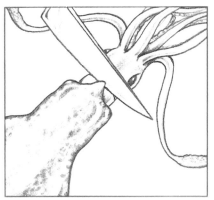

1. Pull the head and tentacles away from the body. Peel the skin from the body and discard. Discard the head.

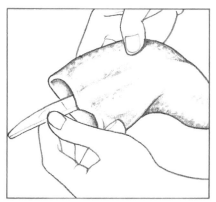

2. Pull out the transparent backbone and remove any remaining innards. Rinse the body cavity, drain and dry.

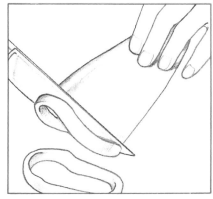

3. Cut the tentacles off the head. Scrape the tentacles free of skin. Cut the body into rings. Wash well and dry.

How to prepare a lobster

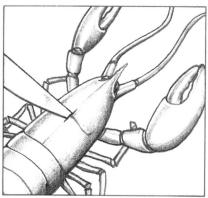

There are two ways of killing a lobster. One (see above) is to pierce its head, at the well-defined cross mark, with a sharp strong knife. This goes straight into the brain, and kills it instantly. The other method is given below.
1. Tie the claws together with string or with a rubber band.
2. Place the lobster, dead or alive, in a large pan of lightly salted water with flavouring vegetables, if liked, and slowly bring to the boil. Cover with a lid and simmer for 15–20 minutes until the dark shell turns bright red.
3. Leave the lobster to cool in the cooking liquor.

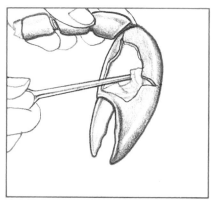

4. Twist off the claws, and remove the legs. Using shellfish crackers, or a hammer, crack the claws, and pull out the meat.
5. Cut away the thin undershell of the tail section, using sharp scissors, and carefully pull out the flesh.

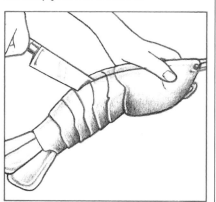

6. Place the lobster on a board and cut in half along its length with a sharp knife.

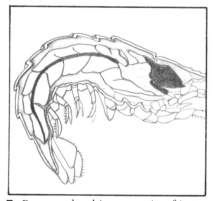

7. Remove the thin grey vein of intestine running along its length.
8. Scrape out the red coral (if present) and reserve.
9. If liked, add the liver to the flesh. This is the grey-green flesh near the head, which is delicious.
10. Carefully lift out the bony part of the head and break it into pieces. Using a lobster pick or skewer pick out the flesh and any remaining liver and roe.
11. Pull away the grey spongy gills and stomach sac from the top of the head and discard.
12. Wash the shell and dry well. This method of preparation means that both the head and tail sections of the lobster may be used to hold and serve the meat.
Note: Crawfish do not have the same large claws as lobsters, but they are prepared and cooked in similar ways. Fresh lobster is delicious hot or cold, but frozen lobster is best served hot in a sauce.

MEAT

Meat has become so expensive nowadays that it is more important than ever to know how to recognize good quality joints, chops and steaks, and to know which cuts to use and how much to buy.

BEEF

When choosing beef, the lean of the meat should be bright to dark red with the fat a creamy white. Small flecks of fat should be visible throughout the lean. Flesh that has a dark red colour indicates that the carcass has been well hung, essential if the meat is to have a good flavour, and be very tender. Bright red meat often indicates that it is very fresh and unhung or not hung long enough for the flavour to develop properly.

In different parts of the country and in other countries such as France the same cuts of beef and other meats are often given a different name. Those used here are generally the most commonly known in Britain.

Sirloin A boned and rolled joint with a good layer of fat to protect it, coming from the back of the animal. It is very suitable for roasting. It is also sold on the bone and can be bought with the 'undercut' on it (fillet).

Ribs come as wing rib, top rib and fore rib joints and they too can be bought on the bone or as boned and rolled joints. The flavour is particularly good when cooked on the bone.

Topside or top round This joint is usually boned and rolled. A very lean cut.

Silverside or round This is a popular joint, always boneless, which can also be bought salted to serve for the traditional boiled beef.

Aitchbone or top rump This is also known as thick flank. These are usually boned and rolled joints, but they can be bought on the bone if you ask your butcher.

Brisket has an excellent flavour, but tends to be fatty so always look for a lean piece.

Stewing meats These include leg and shin which are the cheapest cuts and need the longest and slowest cooking; neck and clod are also good for stews but have less flavour. Skirt and flank are boneless cuts which can be stewed but are normally made into mince. Chuck and blade steak are the best cuts of stewing steak and they require less cooking. These cuts

should not have too much thick fat on the outside, but the flesh of the meat should be well 'marbled' or streaked with flecks of fat. For all stewing steak, either stew, braise or casserole. It can also be used in meat pies, and boiled for stock.

Minced or ground beef Various qualities of mince are available, of which the most expensive are almost fat free. At the other end of the market is the cheapest quality which does contain a lot of fat. The best way to remove any excess fat from mince is to begin cooking in a pan without any extra fat. As it heats gently the fat flows out and can then be spooned off.

Steaks come in several different cuts, and are all suitable to grill or fry. Best known are rump, fillet, entrecôte and Châteaubriand; the sirloin is cut into two parts to give porterhouse and T-bone steaks. Minute steaks also come from the sirloin. Only fillet steaks are completely fat free.

How much to allow
For beef on the bone allow 225–350 g (8–12 oz) raw per person, plus a little extra for some to serve cold. For boned and rolled beef allow about 175 g (6 oz) raw per person, plus a little extra for some to serve cold. For steaks allow 150–175 g (5–6 oz) raw per portion.

GUIDE TO THE CUTS
OF BEEF

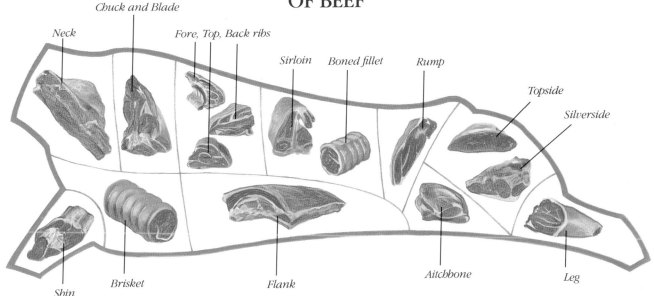

Neck Chuck and Blade Fore, Top, Back ribs Sirloin Boned fillet Rump Topside Silverside

Shin Brisket Flank Aitchbone Leg

LAMB

When you buy lamb, the age of the animal is indicated both by its weight (obviously the heavier a joint, the larger and older the animal), and by the colour of the lean meat. Pale pink flesh denotes young lamb, and this turns to light red as the age of the animal increases. Mutton, once so popular in Britain and one of our traditional dishes, is now hard to obtain; the demand for it has decreased, so lambs are killed very much younger.

Lamb is generally from an animal under a year, mutton from an animal under 2 years, but more often mutton is defined as coming from an animal weighing over 36 kg (79 lb). However, if you can find it, the flavour of mutton is distinctive and extremely good.

The best of the home-produced lamb is obviously the new season or spring lambs which are generally under 6 months old. Welsh lamb, for instance, is renowned for its flavour and tenderness. As the year progresses the price drops and for those interested in buying a whole carcass to freeze, it is worth asking the butcher the best time to buy when it is both good in quality and low in price.

Legs and shoulders of lamb should be plump with a thin layer of fat covering the flesh; this fat should be white to pale cream, not a dark yellow. If you buy New Zealand lamb that is still frozen, do take time to thaw it out very slowly so that the meat is in prime condition when you cook it. If it is thawed fast, the flavour will deteriorate and more often than not it will be tough when cooked.

With lamb the cuts and joints are more universally named than with some of the other meats, apart from the chops which can vary in name from butcher to butcher. There are also some very new and inventive cuts of lamb which are sometimes on display in butchers and supermarkets – if you see something you don't recognise, simply ask the butcher what it is.

Because lamb is young, almost all the cuts are prime, thus suitable for frying and grilling.

Sometimes roast or grilled lamb is served in the French style, with the flesh still pink inside.

Leg This is a prime joint which is quite large and always rather expensive. It is often cut in half and sold as half legs, as the fillet end (or top half) and the shank end (or lower half). The fillet half is sometimes boned out and it is good for kebabs, for casseroling, and it can be cut into leg steaks.

Leg of lamb, whether whole or in halves, is usually roasted although it can also be pot-roasted with great success.

Shoulder One of the sweetest and most tender parts of the animal but it does have a fair amount of fat on it and is one of the most difficult of all joints to carve. It is always succulent and most often roasted either on the bone, or boned and rolled when some of the fat can be discarded. It can also be pot-roasted and boiled to serve with caper sauce. It is a cheaper joint than the leg and, again, can be cut in half to buy as the blade end and knuckle end. Shoulder meat can also be boned to use for kebabs, casseroles, mince and so on, when excess fat can be trimmed off before you begin to cook.

Loin This is a prime cut which is usually roasted on the bone or boned and rolled with or without a stuffing. It can also be pot-roasted. This part of the animal can be cut up and made into an assortment of chops.

Best end of neck This is again a prime roasting joint either on the bone or boned and rolled. It is from this joint that the spectacular crown roast of lamb and guard of honour roasts are made. It can be cut into cutlets which are left as they are or can be trimmed.

Breast of lamb This is a versatile and cheap cut of lamb which is very tasty but also very fatty. It is ideal for casseroling, but should be cooked the day before required, so it can be cooled and the resulting layer of fat on the surface removed before the dish is

GUIDE TO THE CUTS OF LAMB

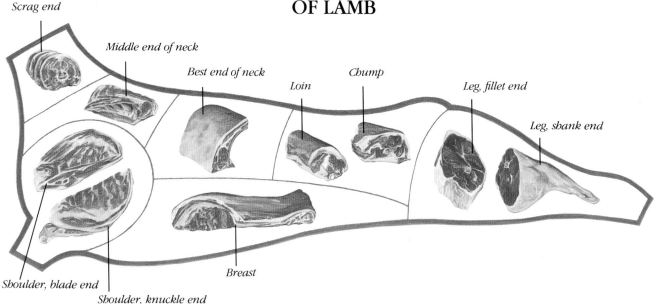

Scrag end

Middle end of neck

Best end of neck

Loin

Chump

Leg, fillet end

Leg, shank end

Shoulder, blade end

Shoulder, knuckle end

Breast

reheated. It can be boned, stuffed, rolled and slow-roasted or pot-roasted with great success.

Middle and scrag end of neck

These are the cheap cuts with a rather high percentage of bone and some fat, but again with a good flavour. Well worth using for casseroles. Chops can be cut from the middle neck.

How much to allow

For leg, loin, shoulder and best end of neck on the bone, allow 350 g (12 oz) raw per portion, with perhaps a little more for the loin and best end joints, plus extra to serve cold.

For boned leg, loin, shoulder and best end of neck, which are rolled (before adding any stuffing), allow 175–225 g (6–8 oz) raw per portion, plus extra to serve cold.

For stewing lamb and breast of lamb, allow 225–350 g (8–12 oz) raw per portion.

For chops and cutlets, allow 1–2 per portion, depending on size, but 1 double loin or chump chop should be sufficient. With noisettes, again allow 1 or 2 depending on size.

VEAL

Veal is the meat from a very young calf and because the calf should be very young, and thus milk-fed (although this is not always so), the flesh should be a very light pink in colour, and soft and moist with only very little fat which should be firm and either white or faintly pink. Do not buy veal that is over-flabby and really wet looking. As the animal ages, the flesh becomes deeper pink, slightly mottled, often taking on a slightly bluish tinge, and more mature veal does not have the melting tenderness of good young veal. If veal looks dry, brownish, or has a very mottled appearance, it is stale.

Veal has a lot of bone in proportion to flesh and these bones make an excellent pale gelatinous stock to use in all sorts of soups, sauces and gravies. Never discard any veal bones that come with the joint; they may be used for stock, either raw or cooked, and the resulting stock will form a really solid jelly. The feet of calves are particularly gelatinous, and are used to make aspic, or the calf's foot jelly that used to be served to invalids in Victorian times.

Because veal has very little fat, great care must be taken during cooking to prevent it drying out, and roasting meat is usually barded with pork fat or fatty bacon. For this reason veal is rarely grilled, unless very carefully moistened by basting. Whatever method of cooking you choose, make sure there is sufficient fat for roasting or frying, and liquid for casseroling or pot-roasting. The meat should not be cooked too fast or over a fierce heat as this would make it dry and tasteless and a waste of money, for all cuts of veal tend to be expensive.

Leg This is a prime cut, and can be subdivided into other cuts, including the knuckle. A leg joint is often boned and rolled, sometimes with a stuffing added before rolling. It is suitable for roasting, pot-roasting, or braising.

Loin Another prime cut for roasting – from the back – which is more often boned and rolled with or without stuffing rather than cooked on the bone. It has more fat on it than most of the other joints. It is also cut into cutlets from the neck end, and chops as you move further down the joint.

Shoulder This is often boned and rolled and roasted or pot-roasted. It is also cut into pieces to use for pies, fricassées, casseroles, etc. It is a more economical joint because of its rather awkward shape.

Fillet This is the prime cut of the calf, from the hindquarters, and is usually sliced into escalopes to fry or grill. However, it can also be used as a very expensive roasting joint or cut into cubes for kebabs.

Knuckle This is a cheaper cut from the end of the leg. It is bony, but is good for stewing, for pies and casseroles and to mince; it is the traditional cut used for the classic Italian dish, Osso buco when it is sawn across into small pieces, each one a ring of bone surrounded by meat. The flavour is good, coming both from the meat and the bone with its marrow. It can also be boned and rolled to pot-roast or braise.

Breast Another fairly cheap cut that is usually boned, stuffed and rolled and then pot-roasted or braised.

Chops These come from the loin. Those from the bottom end, with a small round bone, are known as chump chops, those from the other end are called cutlets although one cutlet is quite large. All chops are suitable for frying, grilling (if basted well) and pan-frying, but need good flavourings or a good sauce as accompaniment.

Veal escalopes These are probably the most popular cut of veal and are the most expensive. The escalopes should be cut from the best part or fillet end of the leg, and they should be cut between 5 mm ($\frac{1}{4}$ inch) and 1 cm ($\frac{1}{2}$ inch) thick. They should always be cut across the grain of the meat, not along it. However, not all veal escalopes are cut from the correct part of the leg.

Once cut, escalopes are usually beaten so they are very much thinner. Usually the butcher will do this for you; if not, put the escalopes, one at a time, between two sheets of damp grease-proof paper and, with a rolling pin, beat out the meat evenly thin. Do not continually beat in one place or the fibres will break.

How much to allow

For roasting joints on the bone, allow 225–350 g (8–12 oz) raw per portion.

For roasting joints, boned and rolled, allow 175–225 g (6–8 oz) raw per portion, plus extra to serve cold.

For fillets or escalopes (boneless) allow 100–150 g (4–5 oz) raw per portion.

For chops allow 1 veal chop taken from the loin; or 1–2 cutlets taken from the neck end or top of loin, depending on the size of the animal.

For breast of veal on the bone, knuckle on the bone, and best end of neck on the bone allow about 450 g (1 lb) raw per portion; or, when boned, allow 100–175 g (6–8 oz) raw per portion.

PORK

When selecting a joint or piece of pork, it should have a good layer of firm white fat with a thinnish elastic skin around the pale pink, smooth and fine-grained lean. A roasting joint should have a good rind that can be scored (cut into narrow parallel lines with a very sharp knife) to give a good crackling when cooked – the butcher should do this.

Leg A large lean joint, often boned and rolled, although excellent when cooked on the bone. It can be cut into joints of various sizes which are usually roasted.

Loin This is a prime roasting joint which can be bought on or off the bone. It sometimes includes the kidney and can be excellent if stuffed and rolled. The loin is also cut into chops and also boneless chops (or steaks as they are often called) which can be grilled or fried.

Spare rib Not to be confused with spare ribs, this joint comes from the shoulder of the pig. A fairly lean joint, but sometimes with more fat than other joints, it should be moderately priced, and has an excellent flavour. Good to roast; and it can be cut up to braise, casserole or stew.

Blade Shoulder of pork is often sub-divided into spare rib and blade. This is a tender cut, available on the bone or boneless. It can be roasted, stuffed, grilled or casseroled.

Fillet or tenderloin A prime piece of meat with very little fat. Very versatile, and excellent for kebabs, escalopes, pan-frying and for grilling or frying. It can also be sliced lengthways and stuffed.

Hand and spring This is the foreleg of the pig and is suitable for roasting, boiling, stewing and casseroling. It is relatively inexpensive so buy if you want to mince pork for meatballs or pâtés.

Belly Cheap and fatty but full of flavour. It can be used on and off the bone, either as a joint or cut into slices. Bone and roll it with a stuffing to roast or pot-roast; or use the slices to grill or fry or casserole or cook on a barbecue. For some recipes it can be salted. The butcher will do this if 3–4 days' notice is given.

Spare ribs Taken from the belly, they are removed in one piece and then cut up into ribs with the meat left around the bones. These are usually barbecued, grilled, or casseroled.

Bacon and ham is the flesh of the pig which has been salted or cured in brine and then smoked. Green or unsmoked bacon is cured, but not smoked and is consequently less strong in flavour and will not keep for the same length of time as its smoked counterpart. Good fresh bacon should have a pleasant aroma with firm, white fat and pink coloured lean, that is firm with a good bloom. The rind should be a good pale cream colour if unsmoked or green; or light to dark golden brown for smoked bacon.

Gammon is the hind leg of the pig which is cured on the side of bacon; if the leg is then cut off and cooked and served cold, it is known as ham. A true ham, however, is the hind leg of the pig, detached before curing, and which is then cured, salted, matured, hung or smoked, depending on the manufacturer's process. Shoulder and collar joints are far less expensive than gammon and they can be served in a similar way and are again called ham.

Methods of cooking

Remember that pork must always be thoroughly cooked – on no account should it be underdone. All pork joints are suitable for roasting – the leg and loin are often boned and stuffed first – while gammon and ham joints can be boiled or baked. Steaks and chops are usually grilled or braised.

GUIDE TO THE CUTS OF PORK AND HAM

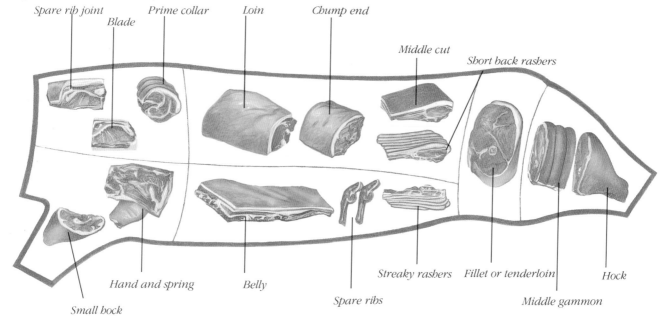

Spare rib joint *Blade* *Prime collar* *Loin* *Chump end* *Middle cut* *Short back rashers*

Hand and spring *Belly* *Spare ribs* *Streaky rashers* *Fillet or tenderloin* *Hock*

Small hock *Middle gammon*

How much to allow

For joints on the bone allow 225–350 g (8–12 oz) raw pork per portion.

For joints boned and rolled allow about 175 g (6 oz) raw pork per portion plus some extra to serve cold.

For chops allow 1 per portion

For cutlets or boneless pork slices allow 1–2 or about 100–175 g (4–6 oz) raw pork per portion.

For hand and spring allow 350 g (12 oz) raw pork per portion.

For tenderloin allow 100–175 g (4–6 oz) per portion.

For belly allow 100–225 g (4–8 oz) raw pork per portion.

For rashers of bacon, allow 2–4 per portion, depending on size and what else is to be served with them.

For bacon chops, allow 1–2 depending on size.

For gammon steaks, allow 1 per portion; for gammon rashers 1–2 depending on size.

Freezing meat

Joints and cuts of meat can be bought ready frozen from a butcher or supermarket to simply transfer to your own freezer. However, if you want to freeze the meat you have just bought, do check with your butcher that it hasn't already been frozen. If it has been frozen, do not refreeze it. Before freezing meat at home, it is important to wrap it very securely with polythene or foil, making sure there are no tears in the wrapping (if there are sharp bones, pad these first with foil before wrapping). Make sure too that all air has been excluded from the pack, then label clearly giving the cut, amount and date of freezing.

Meat keeps well in the freezer, but it must be of top quality and very fresh if pork or veal; lamb or beef should have been hung for the requisite time. The fat on the meat will turn rancid after a time, so it is wise to remove any excess fat visible before freezing. Joints of lamb, beef and veal will freeze well for up to 1 year, steaks and chops are best used within 6–8 months. Boneless braising or stewing meat can be stored in the freezer for about 6 months. Pork can be kept for up to 6 months but the flavour can deteriorate quickly. Because of their high salt and fat content, bacon and sausages should be used within 2 months. Offal and mince should also be cooked and eaten within 2 months. Delicatessen meats can be kept for 1 month.

CARVING

This is a little appreciated culinary art but it is one that may easily be mastered with a little practice.

Good carving should never be underestimated, as without it meat can lack flavour and can be wasted. The first essential is a very good sharp knife with a slightly flexible blade, which is made of best stainless or carbon steel. It should be well balanced and feel 'comfortable' in the hand. It is just as important to have a good carving fork – with a guard for protection in case the knife slips – and a steel for sharpening the knife.

The next essential is some knowledge of the anatomy of the cut that you are to carve. As a general principle, most meat is carved across the grain because this shortens the meat fibres, making each slice more tender. Leg of lamb is an exception as this can be carved either parallel or at right angles to the bone. In general, butchers prepare joints in the easiest way for them to be carved, and they will often give hints on carving if asked.

Always stand up to carve a joint – it is so much easier than sitting down. Let the joint rest for at least 5 minutes and up to 15 minutes before carving, to allow the juices to settle, and make carving very much easier.

Make sure your knife is really well sharpened before carving; the blade will slide through the meat instead of sawing and tearing at the fibres.

Remove any string and/or skewers which will be in the way as you start to carve.

Stand the joint on a flat non-slip surface, such as a wooden board, or on a plate with spikes to hold it in position. A carving fork will help to hold it steady.

Remove any outer bones which will be in the way of carving, but not the main bone to which the flesh is attached.

Don't lose heart if you don't make a wonderful job the first time you try to carve. With a little practice it will soon become much easier. If you feel nervous at your first attempt, carve the joint by yourself in the kitchen and then take it to the dining room.

CARVING BEEF

Beef wing rib

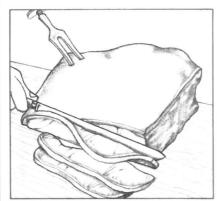

1. Remove the chine bone at the thickest end of the joint.
2. Lay the meat fat uppermost and carve in narrow slices, loosening it from the rib bones as you go.

Beef rib roasts

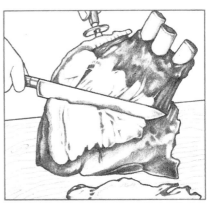

1. Remove any string, and stand the joint on its wide end, holding it securely with a carving fork. If necessary, remove the chine bone with a sharp knife.
2. Cut across the joint in even, fairly thick slices until the blade of the knife reaches the rib bone. Cut down close to the bone to loosen each slice.

CARVING LAMB

Follow the general rules on page 23 and stand the joint neatly and squarely on a board or large plate. Allow to 'set' before carving. Lamb should not be carved too thinly; try to aim for about 5 mm ($\frac{1}{4}$ inch) thick.

The shoulder (below) is probably the most difficult joint to carve. To simplify carving, you can loosen around the blade bone in the raw joint with a small sharp knife, but do not remove it. When cooked, this loosened bone can then be pulled out to make carving easier.

Leg of lamb

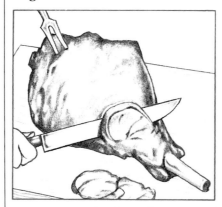

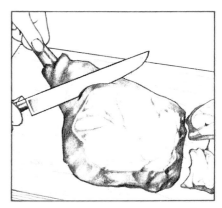

1. Carve a wedge from the centre of the meatiest side. Carve slices from each side of the cut, gradually turning the knife to get larger slices and ending parallel to the bone.

2. Turn the joint over and carve in long horizontal slices.

Shoulder of lamb

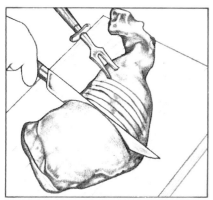

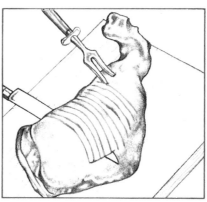

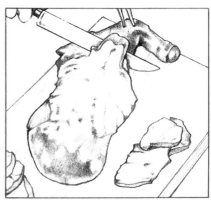

1. Lay the joint skin side uppermost and make a series of parallel cuts, starting at the elbow and ending at the shoulder blade.

2. Run the knife horizontally along the length of the bone so as to free the slices.

3. Turn the joint over, remove any fat, and then carve in horizontal slices.

CARVING VEAL

Veal is similar in shape to beef and therefore is carved in a similar way. However, it is a lot more tender than some meats, so should carve much more easily, providing you have a good sharp knife. Most roasted or pot-roasted veal joints are sold ready-boned and rolled, so all that is necessary is to remove the skewers and the string as each piece is reached. The joint is always carved in fairly thin vertical slices. When tackling joints on the bone, carve them in a similar way to beef or pork (for loin joints). Remember to leave the joint to stand and 'set' for 5–10 minutes before carving.

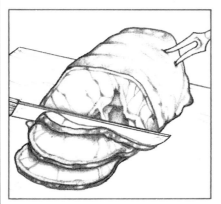

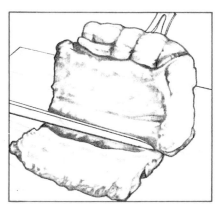

Carve a rolled and boned joint in thin slices.

Carve loin of veal in the same way as beef (page 23).

CARVING PORK

Follow the basic rules on page 23 and allow the meat to stand and 'set' for 5–10 minutes before carving. Stand the joint squarely on a board or large plate. Remove the crackling first to make carving easier, then carve into thin slices. Instructions for loin of pork are given on the right; leg of pork is carved in the same way as leg of lamb, once the crackling is removed.

Loin of pork

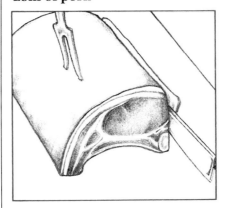

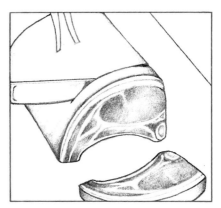

1. Remove the chine bone, after removing the crackling.

2. Carve the loin into chops.

CARVING HAM

All cooked ham and bacon should be carved thinly; thick slices and chunks do not look appetizing and do not do justice to the texture and flavour of the meat. The knife must be very sharp and the experts will use a special ham carving knife which is fairly long and thin, but a good large cook's knife will do just as well.

Prime forehock

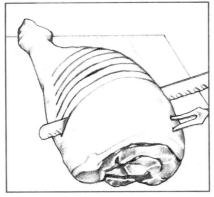

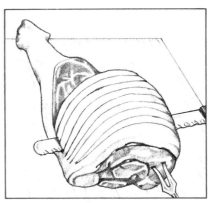

1. This is best carved keeping the fat side underneath. Hold the protruding bone firmly with the fork or a cloth and carve in vertical slices up to the bone, then repeat from the other end.

2. When the bone is reached carve long, downward slanting slices at an angle to the bone. Turn over and carve the remaining slices down to the bone.

Gammon hock

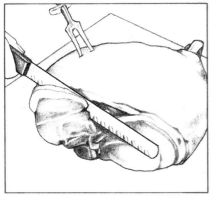

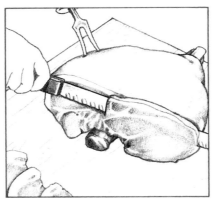

1. Hold the shank end (or bone) firmly with the carving fork or grip it with a clean cloth and carve the joint in thin wedge-shaped slices from one side of the bone. Work down from the knuckle bone to the leg joint.

2. Turn the joint over and repeat, again holding the shank end firmly.

POULTRY AND GAME

Poultry and game were once strictly seasonal, but the advent of freezers means that a wide choice is now available all the year round. However, fresh poultry has a much superior flavour to the frozen variety and game is always best in season.

Choosing poultry

When buying poultry, the larger the bird, the better the value as the proportion of meat to bone is higher. And always make sure you are given the giblets which make an excellent stock for gravy, or can be chopped and added to gravy, stuffings and soups, etc. Wash them carefully before use and cut off any fat and the yellow bits on the liver or gizzard which contain bile. This is very bitter and will spoil the flavour of the stock.

Frozen poultry When cooking poultry that has been frozen it is absolutely essential to make sure it is fully thawed first. You can be sure that it is completely thawed when all the limbs are flexible and there are no ice crystals left in the body cavity. If poultry is cooked whilst still partly frozen, it slows down the cooking and the deepest parts of the body do not get cooked through. Salmonella, a common cause of food poisoning, can lurk in the intestines of all birds, and is normally quickly destroyed by heat. The body cavity, however, is more insulated by the surrounding flesh, and if this is still frozen, the heat may not penetrate enough to destroy the bacteria. It is very important to cool down a bird as quickly as possible and then chill it until needed. It is also possible to cook poultry a second time as a reheated dish, but the important point to remember is that it must be recooked and not just reheated. Put it into a sauce and boil for at least 5 minutes, or put it into the oven in a sauce and make sure it bubbles for at least 5 minutes. Cooked poultry meat can be refrozen even if it was a frozen bird to start with, but again do thaw properly and then recook it before serving. Thaw a frozen bird completely, still in its wrappings, either at room temperature or in a cool place, allowing about 12 hours for a 900 g (2 lb) bird and longer according to size.

To thaw in the refrigerator, the time allowed must be at least doubled and even then you may still find ice crystals present. Chicken portions take about 6–9 hours to thaw depending on size, and longer in the refrigerator.

Fresh poultry is always more expensive than frozen but is thought to have a better flavour. A fresh bird will keep for up to 2 days in the refrigerator before cooking, but remove any tight wrappings, and cover loosely to allow air to circulate. Remove the giblets too, and store separately.

There are several types of chicken and these are given different names mainly to describe the size and age of the bird.

Poussins These are very small chickens weighing from 350–900 g ($\frac{3}{4}$–2 lb) each and are usually only 4–8 weeks old. The larger ones (sometimes called double poussins) are served one per portion, but the really tiny ones may need to be served in pairs. They are very tender and have a delicate flavour so do not cook with overpowering ingredients, or serve with too strong a sauce. Best to roast, pot roast, casserole, or grill.

Broilers These are smallish birds, too, usually about 12 weeks old, and are most often sold ready frozen. They weigh from 1.25–1.5 kg ($2\frac{1}{2}$–$3\frac{1}{2}$ lb), are extremely versatile, and can be cooked by any method. One bird should serve 3–4 portions.

Spring chickens These are small broilers, from 6–8 weeks old, and weighing about 900 g (2 lb). They can be cooked in a variety of ways, and will serve 2–3 people.

Large roasters These are aged about 10–15 weeks, and vary in size from 1.75–2.25 kg (4–5 lb) and should feed 5–6 portions quite easily. Ideal for a family meal, they can be roasted, pot roasted and casseroled.

How to truss a chicken

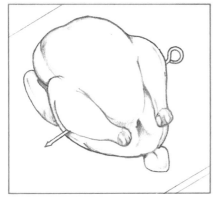

1. Insert a skewer widthwise right through the body of the bird just below the thigh bone so that the ends stick out at either side.

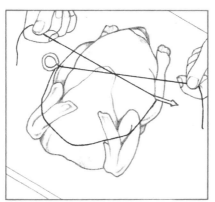

2. Turn the bird over on to its breast. Take a piece of string and first catch in the wing tips, then pass it under the ends of the skewer and cross it over the back.

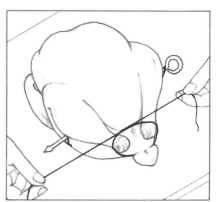

3. Turn the bird over and tie the ends of the string together round the tail, at the same time, securing the legs.

Capons True capons are no longer produced. Capons were roaster cockerels of about 7–10 months old, which were neutered and then specially fattened so they grew much larger than normal chickens. Available now are specially fattened birds, usually called 'capon–style' chickens, and their flavour is always good and the flesh tender. They tend to weigh 3.5–4.5 kg (8–10 lb) and should be sufficient to feed up to 10 portions.

Boiling fowl These are older birds which are much tougher than the others as they are often over 18 months old and may have been former egg-layers. It is essential to remove any fat from inside the cavity before cooking. They usually weigh from 1.75–3 kg (4–7 lb) and should be cooked by boiling (in reality a gentle simmering) or stewing for about 3 hours or until tender.

TURKEY

Turkey is now available all year round. The size varies from mini birds of around 2.25 kg (5 lb) to very large ones of 13.5 kg (30 lb). An average domestic cooker can handle a turkey of about 10.5 kg (23 lb), but not much more. Always buy the giblets with a whole bird. Portions available include wings, thighs (boned and with bone), drumsticks, escalopes, fillets, steaks, etc., as well as the many types of rolled roasts.

Turkeys are available fresh, frozen and chilled as with most other poultry. Both fresh and chilled birds will keep in the refrigerator (out of any wrappings) for about 2 days before cooking. A frozen turkey, however, must be thawed out completely and preferably at room temperature or in a cool place. This should not be done in the refrigerator for, because of the size of the bird, the extra cold will lengthen the thawing process quite dramatically.

When stuffing a turkey, stuff only the neck of the bird and not the body cavity. If the cavity is stuffed, it may mean that the turkey has to be really overcooked to ensure that the stuffing itself is cooked, and this ruins the texture of the flesh.

How to stuff and truss a turkey

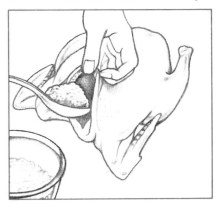

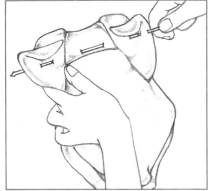

1. Put the stuffing in the neck end only and fold the neck flap over so it completely encloses the stuffing. It can be secured with a small skewer or wooden cocktail sticks.

2. The bird can be trussed in a similar way to a chicken with the wings folded under the body, but do not tie the legs too tightly to the body or the heat of the oven will find it hard to penetrate the deepest part of the body and will increase the cooking time. Put a quartered onion or lemon in the body cavity for flavour and to keep it moist.

How to carve a turkey

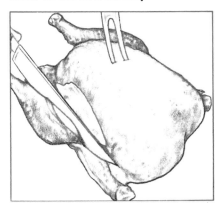

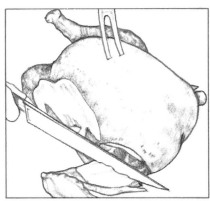

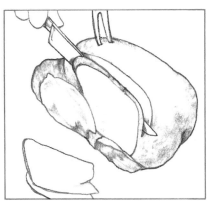

1. Stand the turkey on a board or a large plate with the breast facing upwards. Allow to 'set' for about 10 minutes. Remove a drumstick, leaving the thigh on the bird and slice the meat from the drumstick.

2. Carve slices from the thigh and then remove the wings and strip the meat off neatly.

3. Carve thin slices from the breast, taking in slices from the stuffing as it is reached.

4. Serve a mixture of dark and white meat for each portion plus some of the stuffing. Finish carving one side before turning the bird round to do the other. Stuffing can be sliced or spooned from the breast.

DUCK

The domestic duck is available all year round, both fresh and frozen, as a whole bird and as portions. Duck has dark meat with a good rich flavour, a thick skin and plenty of fat. There is always very much less flesh on a duck than it might appear, thus anything that is less than 1.5 kg (3 lb) in weight is not a good buy for it is likely to be all bone with very little flesh. An average duck will weigh from 1.75–2.25 kg (4–5 lb) and, in general, one duck will feed not more than 4 people, if that. Larger birds are now being bred which will make duck even more popular.

When selecting a duck, it should be young with soft pliable feet, not rough or tough, and the feet and the bill should be yellow; a dark orange indicates age. A duckling is a bird between 6 weeks and 3 months old and the majority of ducks sold are, in fact, duckling. They tend to toughen as they age. Always try to get the giblets, as they can add flavour to the gravy.

Fresh ducks, like chickens, are always better than frozen. As there is so much fat on ducks, this can turn rancid if the bird is frozen for longer than 3 months. The fat content worries many people when cooking duck, but if prepared and roasted carefully, the fat will flow out – and indeed it has a truly wonderful flavour.

Cutting up duck

If you want to cook poultry in portions it is much more economical to cut it up yourself. Individual portions bought in a butcher or even a supermarket are always more expensive, weight for weight, than buying a whole bird. Learn how to do this at home and you will save yourself money.

All you need is a chopping board and a heavy knife. Poultry shears are also useful. The secret is to first find the joints and so cut through the tendons and cartilage, rather than hacking through bones.

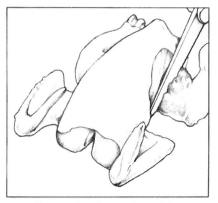

1. Pull one leg from the body. Cut through where the thigh joins the body. Bend the leg and cut between the ball and socket joint. Repeat with the other leg.

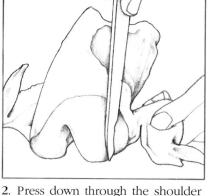

2. Press down through the shoulder joint attaching the wing to the body, then cut down through the skin at the base of the wing. Repeat with the other wing.

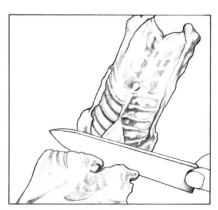

3. Place the knife inside the carcass and carefully slit along the ribs on both sides to separate the breast from the lower carcass. Pull the breast away from the back to expose the shoulder bones and cut down to detach the breast.

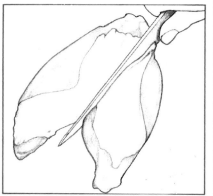

4. Place the breast skin side up on the board and cut down on one side or other of the breastbone to give two breasts. With larger birds the breast portions can then be cut widthways to give 4 or 6 portions.

GOOSE

This is a rather expensive bird which was once rather difficult to obtain. However, it is becoming much more readily available now, both fresh and frozen. It is a large bony bird with a very poor flesh to body size ratio. The flesh, though, has a very fine flavour and texture. It is usually very tender, although it can be a little greasy if insufficient care is taken before and during cooking. Like duck, goose is very fatty and should always be pricked all over with a skewer and then stood on a rack to cook so that it doesn't stew in its own fat.

An oven-ready goose should weigh about 4.5 kg (10 lb) and will feed 6–8 people only, so is an extravagant bird to serve. The bird must be young, preferably under 6 months old, with soft yellow feet, a yellow bill and yellowish fat. A goose for roasting – the best way of cooking them – can be stuffed with a sage and onion stuffing, but the stuffing is more often cooked and served separately. A prune or apple stuffing tastes good, as does a stuffing containing the liver of the bird. A quick and simple way of cutting down on richness and adding flavour is to put some peeled and cored sour apples in the cavity.

How to carve a goose

Follow the general principles for carving meat on page 23 and stand the bird on a board with the breast upwards. Allow to rest and 'set' for about 15 minutes.

1. Place the goose on a rack before roasting.

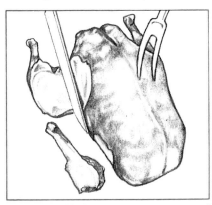

2. Take off the trussing string and remove the skewers and then remove the legs and wings.

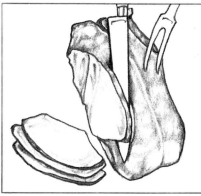

3. Carve thickish slices from either side of the breast bone taking the slices the whole length of the body. Carve the meat off the legs and wings and serve with the breast meat.
4. If the bird is stuffed, carve off the slices with the breast meat and remove the rest with a spoon.

Preparation and selection of game

Game is mainly available fresh, and is displayed by butchers and game dealers as well as some fishmongers whilst it is in season. It is always hung in feather or fur (apart from venison), and undrawn for birds and hares. Hanging is essential to help to tenderize the meat and improve the characteristic flavour associated with game. The length of time required for the hanging varies greatly. Birds are usually ready when one of the tail feathers can be plucked out quite easily.

Some game seasons

Pheasant: October 1 – February 1
Partridge: September 1 – February 1
Red Grouse: Ptarmigan: August 12 – December 10
Black Grouse (Blackcock): August 20 – December 10
Wild Duck: Mainly September 1 – January 31
Pigeon: No close season
Quail: No close season
Hare: No close season
Venison: Some type of venison is available all year

Partridge These are small game birds which will serve only 1 portion. The flavour of partridge is delicate and they are thought to be at their best in October. They are available fresh and frozen. Young plucked birds weigh up to 400 g (14 oz). They are best roasted, but are also good when spatchcocked to cook under the grill or on a barbecue. Older birds will weigh up to 450 g (1 lb) or more.

Wild Duck These birds are frequently not hung at all, but may be hung for about 24 hours. Because of their diet, it is unwise to keep them hanging for longer; the flesh deteriorates very quickly, and the flavour can become rancid. All wild duck have very dry flesh because they are virtually fat-free. When they are roasted, they should be covered liberally with fat to prevent them drying out. A mallard or large wild duck should serve 2 people.

Grouse There are several species of grouse in Britain, the best known being the red grouse – to many, the finest of all game birds. Grouse are usually only available fresh. Young birds are best roasted; older birds can be marinated and casseroled, made into pâtes or pies, or potted. One grouse will usually serve only 1, although sometimes the really large ones will serve 2.

Quail These are the smallest European game birds (like tiny partridges). In the wild they are migratory, so they are only available in Europe during the summer, but they are now bred for the table at rearing farms. As they are so small, 2 can be served for a good portion, but 1 is usually enough, and eating them in the fingers is almost obligatory. Quails must be eaten really fresh – within 24 hours of being killed – and they are most usually roasted. Their meat is soft and tender, with more flavour than chicken.

Pigeon Wood pigeon are in season all year, but are considered best from March to September when birds are young. If plump and young, 1 bird will serve 1 portion; 2 squabs (fledglings) are needed per portion, and an older larger bird will serve 2 portions if casseroled with other ingredients. A roast bird will need to be barded well with streaky bacon.

Pheasant This is probably the best known and most popular of all the game birds. It is available fresh and frozen and now can often be found in larger supermarkets. Birds are often available – and cheaper – by the brace, meaning a cock and a hen. The cock is larger, with brightly coloured plumage, while the dull brown hen is plumper and more succulent, and generally considered the better for eating. Pheasant should be hung for at least 3 days for a good flavour to develop, but it can be as long as 3 weeks if the weather is exceptionally cold.

Young birds are best roasted but more mature birds – which have a better flavour – will be tougher, so need the longer cooking of casseroling, braising or pot-roasting to ensure they are tender. One pheasant will serve 2–3 people when roasted, and larger mature birds may serve up to 4 when casseroled with other ingredients.

CHOOSING AND BUYING CHEESE

There is a vast choice of cheese available throughout Britain, both home produced and imported from the Continent. Always choose a supplier who has a good reputation, so that the cheese is in prime condition. Avoid anything that looks dry, sweaty or has blue mould on the surface.

When choosing soft cheeses such as Brie and Camembert, press the top surface lightly with the fingertips. The cheese should yield slightly. It should be creamy in texture throughout, without any chalkiness in the centre. This chalkiness means that the cheese has not been ripened sufficiently and will remain in this condition. Goat's milk cheeses should be consumed on the day they are purchased, as the flavour soon becomes 'soapy'.

Storing

Ideally, cheese should be stored in a cool, draught-proof larder – the refrigerator is the next best thing. Cheese should be removed from the refrigerator and unwrapped at least 1 hour before it is required so that it has time to come to room temperature.

Most cheeses freeze well. They should be well wrapped and labelled prior to freezing. Hard cheeses tend to become more crumbly but the flavour is good. Soft and cream cheese should not be frozen for more than 6 months. It is not recommended to freeze cottage cheese as it deteriorates. Cheese which has been frozen does not keep as well as unfrozen cheese.

BRITAIN

Blue Dorset

A fairly strong-flavoured cheese with blue veining. Made from skimmed milk, which gives it a sharp flavour. It is a hard, white cheese, with a crumbly texture.

Caboc

A white full-cream soft Scottish cheese. Rolled in toasted oatmeal.

Caerphilly

A semi-hard cheese which has a slightly salty mild flavour. It is crumbly and has a close texture. It is one of the fastest ripening British cheeses. Perfect for a cheeseboard, but can also be used for cooking.

Cheddar

Probably the most popular of British cheeses. Its flavour ranges from very mild to a fully matured strong nutty flavour. Canadian Cheddar has the strongest flavour.

Cheshire

A red or white hard cheese with a crumbly texture and a slightly salty taste. Sometimes Blue Cheshire is available. It is a whitish cheese with blue veining, and has a similar flavour to Stilton.

Cottage cheese

A mild-flavoured cheese, very low in calories as it is made from skimmed milk curds and is therefore low in fat. It is pure white, very moist and lumpy and is sold in cartons. It is often flavoured with herbs or fruit.

Cream cheese

Usually a full fat cheese. It has a rich creamy flavour which is rather bland. Generally sold in small foil containers or from a bulk container.

BELOW: Garnish a cheeseboard with celery, watercress and fresh fruit to make it doubly appealing.

Crowdie

A high protein cottage cheese made from skimmed milk. Made in Scotland. A finer textured cheese than ordinary cottage cheese.

Curd

A soft, unripened, slightly grainy cheese, with a clean acid bland taste. Generally used for cooking.

Derby

A mild-flavoured close-textured hard cheese. The flavour becomes stronger with age.

Sage Derby

This cheese has the same characteristics as Derby, but has layers of chopped fresh sage incorporated during the making. It gives the cheese a green marbled effect.

Double Gloucester

A hard cheese with a close crumbly texture. It is pale orange and has a mild flavour similar to Cheddar.

Dunlop

A moist, soft-textured hard Scottish cheese, pale yellow in colour. Similar to Cheddar, but milder in flavour.

Hramsa

A soft Scottish cheese made from double cream flavoured with wild garlic gathered from the Highlands.

Islay

A miniature Dunlop made in Scotland. Best eaten when it is well matured. It melts easily and is perfect for sauces.

Lancashire

A white open-textured cheese with a crumbly texture. Mild flavoured when new, but becoming fairly strong when fully matured. Use cooked or uncooked. A good grilling cheese and suitable for any cooked dish.

Leicester

A flaky textured cheese. Bright orange in colour. The flavour is fairly strong but sweet.

Lymeswold

A creamy soft cheese similar to Brie in texture and consistency. It has a mild flavour and is one of the newer popular cheeses available.

Morven

A smooth-textured mild-flavoured Scottish cheese. Similar to Dutch Gouda. Sometimes flavoured with caraway seeds.

Orkney

Made in 450 g (1 lb) whole cheeses. A mellow-flavoured close-textured firm cheese made in white or red. Also made with a smoked flavour.

Red Windsor

A fairly rare English cheese with a mild flavour similar to Cheddar. It has red veining throughout, which is caused by the injection of red wine. It has a crumbly texture.

Stilton

The Queen of English cheeses. It should be very creamy and not dry in texture. The blue veining should be evenly distributed throughout the pale cream cheese. If the cheese is white in colour, it is a sign of immaturity.

Wensleydale

A crumbly cheese, varying in colour from white to butter colour depending on its maturity. It has a mild clean and slightly sweet flavour.

Blue Wensleydale

A rich-flavoured creamy cheese with blue veining.

FRANCE

Boursin

A triple cream cheese which is thick and soft, flavoured with garlic, herbs or pepper.

Brie

A soft whitish cheese, made from cow's milk, with a white crust. It should be soft throughout, without any 'chalky' solid centre.

Blue Brie

This is generally a thicker cheese than plain Brie, with blue veining throughout.

Camembert

A stronger flavoured cheese than Brie. Like Brie, it should bulge but not run when the surface is pressed. It is usually about 2.5 cm (1 inch) thick. Fried Camembert is served with gooseberry sauce.

Livarot

A soft, yellow cheese with a reddish-brown rind. Made from skimmed milk, it has a stronger flavour than Camembert.

Munster

A strong-smelling cheese with a sharp flavour. It is semi-soft and has a reddish coloured rind. Sometimes it is flavoured with aniseed or cumin.

Petit Suisse

Made from whole milk with added cream. It has a creamy flavour and texture and is sold in little rolls of paper.

Pont l'Evêque

A semi–soft pale yellow cheese with a yellow crust. It has a rich creamy flavour, stronger than Camembert. Best used uncooked.

Port Salut

A cheese with an orange rind. It is semi-hard and has a creamy bland flavour which gets stronger when it is fully ripe.

Roquefort

Made from ewe's milk curds. It has bluish green veins. A crumbly, semi-soft cheese with a strong flavour.

Saint Paulin

Similar to Port Salut, with a fairly bland flavour.

Tomme au Raisin

A semi-hard cheese, covered with grape pips and skins.

ITALY

Bel Paese
One of the best-known Italian cheeses. A delicately-flavoured cheese with a slightly salty flavour. Close-textured, it is pale yellow in colour, with a dark yellow rind.

Dolcelatte
A creamy white cheese with blue/green veins, a robust strong flavour and a creamy moist texture.

Fontina
One of the few really great cheeses. A soft fat cheese, straw coloured, with a few holes. It has an orange rind. The flavour is nutty and delicate. Variations are called Fontinella and Fontal.

Gorgonzola
A strongly flavoured pale yellow cheese with bluish green marbling and a coarse brown rind. Although it is a semi-soft cheese, it should be firm and fairly dry.

Mozzarella
A soft compact curd cheese, moulded into a ball, egg or flask-shape and tied with raffia. It is also sold in oblong blocks, sealed with plastic. This type is not to be recommended as the texture and flavour are rubbery. It forms long strands during cooking, and becomes rather hard if overcooked.

Parmesan
A very hard cheese, yellowish in colour and fairly grainy. It is strong-flavoured and should be grated just before it is required. When fresh it has a fairly soft texture, similar to Cheddar.

Pecorino
A whole family of ewe's milk cheeses come under this name, the best known being Pecorino Romano. They have a pronounced piquant flavour.

Provolone
A creamy white cheese with a brownish rind. This is a hard curd cheese made in many shapes. When mildly matured, the flavour is delicate and sweet. After further maturing, the flavour becomes sharp and spicy. Usually used for cooking.

Ricotta
Made from ewe's milk, this cheese has a soft bland flavour and texture. It has a low fat content. The rind is distinctively ridged and white.

SWITZERLAND

Emmenthal
A buttery-yellow cheese with large holes. It is slightly rubbery in texture and has a mild to strong nutty flavour.

Gruyère
A pale yellow cheese with small holes, similar in texture to Emmenthal. It has a rich, full flavour with a little sweetness.

Raclette
A pale brown rind encloses a semi-soft cheese which is straw coloured with tiny holes.

Sapsago
A clover-leaf-flavoured cheese which makes the cheese green. This is a very hard cheese.

HOLLAND

Edam
Made from partly skimmed milk, this yellow cheese has a bright red rind and a rubbery texture. It has a mild creamy flavour. Fairly low in calories.

Gouda
A hard cheese with a buttery yellow colour. The rind is fairly thin and a brighter yellow than the cheese itself. It has a slightly rubbery texture, with a fairly mild flavour.

Tilsit
Originally made by the Dutch, this cheese is now made by the Germans and is also produced in Switzerland and Scandinavia. A loaf-shaped cheese, open-textured and straw coloured, it has a sharp, sour flavour.

OTHERS

Bergkase (*German*)
A high-fat content cheese with a mild nutty flavour. It is a pale yellow, with a dark brown rind.

Danbo (*Danish*)
A firm-textured mild cheese with regular, even-sized holes. Sometimes the cheese is flavoured with caraway seeds.

Edelpilz (*German*)
A crumbly textured cheese with blue mottles at the centre and white around the edges. It has a strong flavour.

Feta (*Greek*)
A semi-soft curd cheese made from sheep's milk. Brilliant white in colour, with a flaky texture. It has a salty bland flavour.

Gjetost (*Norwegian*)
A goat's milk cheese with a strong, pungent flavour, with a slight sweetness. A hard, brown cheese.

Jarlsberg (*Norwegian*)
A mild-flavoured cheese, slightly sweet. A semi-hard cheese with irregular holes, pale yellow in colour; similar to Swiss Emmenthal.

Limburger (*Belgian*)
A strong-smelling cheese with a spicy flavour. Made from whole cow's milk. Semi-hard, with a smooth texture. Bright orange/brown rind.

Molbo (*Danish*)
A cheese with a red rind, similar to Edam. Pale yellow cheese with irregular large holes. A mild flavour with an acidic after-taste.

Quarques (*Austrian*)
A piquant-flavoured yellow to white cheese made in small round discs (similar to patties).

Samsoe (*Danish*)
A yellow cheese with a sweet, nutty flavour. It has a firm texture, with irregular holes.

CHOOSING, STORING AND SERVING WINE

Britain has a long history of importing wine from almost every wine-producing country in the world, not only from Europe but from California, Australia, South America, South Africa and Turkey. Add to that list the white wines produced in England and you can see that we are spoilt for choice.

Learning about wine and discovering which ones you like most is a slow and continuing process. Ask your local wine merchant if he organises wine tastings which you could attend. This is a good way of tasting 20 or so wines without cost, noting your comments and then, if you wish, buying some of your favourites.

The chart on page 34 will be a guide to which types of wine best complement various types of food. Do not be afraid to ask the advice of a wine merchant when you are buying, and carefully read the captions in supermarkets. Many wine departments now display informative details about each wine, its characteristics and how to serve it. You may find helpful the numerical ratings some stores give to indicate the dry-to-sweet scale.

Buy one or two bottles of different wines at a time and make a note in an exercise book of the type, date and, most important, your opinion. You can then use your experience to buy gradually, in greater quantity, and build up, if not a cellar, then a selection of wines to suit all occasions.

Storing your wine

The principles of storing your wine vary little, whether you are laying down a case of Grand Cru claret for drinking in a few years' time or a mixed selection of wines to enjoy soon with your family and friends. The ideal conditions are a cellar (which few post-Victorian houses are likely to have), a dark cupboard or the space under the stairs, which is constantly cool – experts advise a temperature of around 10°C/50°F. Avoid any area close to a boiler or heating pipes or where there is a strong draught from an outside door, since wines dislike sudden temperature fluctuations.

All wine in corked bottles should be stored horizontally, so that the liquid is in contact with the cork. This prevents the cork from drying out, contracting, and allowing air to enter the bottle. You can buy purpose-made wine racks in small 8- or 12-bottle multiples which you can build up over the years. Add details of the wines you have in long-term storage to your wine note-book, so you can see at a glance what you have, when you bought it and at what price. Once you have served the wine, do not forget to add your comments.

Bottles of wines with screw caps can be stored upright in the strong cardboard cases in which they are sold.

Generally speaking, all wines benefit to some extent by 'laying down', or storing. This is particularly so of fine clarets and red or white burgundies, some of the best red wines from Italy, Spain, California and South America, and white wines from Bordeaux and the sweeter dessert varieties from Germany. The lighter red wines and light, dry, fruity white wines are really meant to be enjoyed 'young' and do not improve so much with keeping.

BELOW: Château d'Yquem, in the Sauternes region of Bordeaux, home of the world's most famous sweet white wine

	Crisp Dry White	Medium Dry White	Sweet White	Champagne	Light Red	Medium Red	Full-bodied Red	Rosé
Cold hors d'oeuvres	○			○				○
Hot hors d'oeuvres	○	○			○			
Soups (depending on type)	○				○			○
Hot fish dishes	○	○						○
Cold fish dishes	○			○				○
Chicken/turkey	○				○	○		
Duck						○	○	
Game						○	○	
Beef						○	○	
Veal	○				○			○
Lamb/Pork					○	○		○
Cheese	○	○			○	○	○	
Dessert		○	○	○				

LEFT: Blue cheese and full-bodied red wine make perfect partners

Serving wine

There is no mystique about serving wine of whatever quality. Allow yourself time to select suitable ones from your store and, in the case of fine wines, handle them with care. Remove the bottles gently from the rack and slowly raise them to the upright position. If the wine has matured in the bottle, a small, flaky deposit will have formed. This is the process known as 'throwing a sediment'. As you gently pour the wine the deposit will remain in the 'punt', the indentation at the base of the bottle.

All but the youngest red wines should be served at room temperature, which in practice means about 15°C/60°F, so you must allow time for wine, taken from a cool place, gradually to reach this level. All white wines are served chilled. Dry wines are considered best at around 7°C/45°F, sweet dessert ones slightly less chilled.

Most wines benefit from being opened an hour or so before serving and the general rule is that the finer the wine, the more important it is to allow it this time to 'breathe'.

Only the best clarets, burgundies and port need to be decanted, to be sure of separating the wine from the deposit, but of course you may pour any wine into a decanter, jug or flask to serve it. To decant fine wine, hold the bottle at an angle in front of a bright light. Pour off the wine gently, checking all the while that the deposit is not disturbed.

It is largely a matter of personal choice whether you use a simple corkscrew or the more sophisticated butterfly or new pull-screw types. Use a penknife or sharp knife to cut away the plastic capsule covering the neck of the bottle. Insert the sharp point of the corkscrew in the centre of the cork and manipulate the device, according to type. Wipe the neck of the bottle with a clean cloth and carefully remove any small pieces of cork.

You do not need a corkscrew for the joyous task of opening a bottle of sparkling wine. Unless you want to spray yourself and your guests, rally-driver style, hold the bottle steady. Remove the metal foil and untwist to free the wire cover. Firmly hold the round-topped cork in a clean cloth and twist the bottle with the other hand. Have the glasses ready and pour in the wine as soon as the cork is released – with the familiar 'pop'. Tilt each glass towards the neck of the bottle.

Choose glasses to complement your wine and present it in all its brilliant clarity. Glasses should be large enough to capture the bouquet, the enticing aroma of the wine. To enjoy a really fine wine to the full, serve it in plain uncoloured glasses that are only half filled. If guests hold up their glasses to the light, turn the stems in their hands and savour the aroma of the wine, they are paying a compliment to your care and selection.

CHOOSING WINE

This list gives a rough general guide to some of the wines most frequently found on supermarket and off-licence shelves. Some wines are very difficult to classify; Vouvray, Entre-deux-mers and Orvieto, for example, can vary from dry to sweet and Chiantis can range from light to full-bodied. The great thing is to be adventurous and to find out what you most enjoy. Although most of those wines are reasonably priced, a few of them are quite expensive, so check prices when you buy.

Crisp dry white wines
Alsace Sylvaner; Chablis; Gaillac; Mâcon Blanc; Muscadet; Pouilly Blanc Fumé; Rioja; Sancerre; Saumur; Sauvignon; Vinho Verde

Extra dry white wines
Graves; Pouilly Fuissé

Medium dry white wines
Anjou Blanc; Chardonnay; Chenin Blanc; Frascati; Liebfraumilch; Moselle; Piesporter; Riesling; Soave; Verdicchio

Sweet white dessert wines
Barsac; Monbazillac; Muscat de Beaumes de Venise; Sauternes; Tokay; German Beerenauslese and Trockenbeerenauslese wines

Rosé wines
Anjou; Mateus; Tavel

Light red wines
Bardolino; Beaujolais; Lambrusco; Mâcon Rouge; Minervois; Valpolicella

Medium red wines
Beaune; Beaujolais Villages; Cabernet Sauvignon; Côtes du Rhone; Graves; Margaux; Médoc; Pomerol

Full-bodied red wines
Australian Shiraz; Barbera d'Asti; Barbaresco; Barolo; Bordeaux (great growths); older Burgundies; Californian Zinfandel; Châteauneuf-du-Pape; Côte de Nuits; Côte Rotie; Dão; Hermitage; Rioja; South African Pinotage and Roodenberg; St Emilion

VINTAGE CHART

This chart has been prepared by the International Wine & Food Society for the benefit of its members and others interested in good wine. Champagne and port have been restricted to declared vintage years and, in the case of the latter, it should be noted that 1948, 1960 and 1963 were very good. Where older vintages of white wine are concerned the marks are appropriate to high quality and dessert wines. There is insufficient room on this chart to make a detailed assessment of vintages in Spain, California and Australia and, while some wines are obviously made for keeping, the ageing potential for modern wines from these areas is largely untested. Italy is a special case: harvest conditions can vary hugely in the twenty producing areas, each with its own distinctive styles of wine. Most Italian wines sold in Britain are under 6 years old. 1980, 1982, 1983, 1985 and (when available) 1986 should all be of excellent quality. It must also be borne in mind that some years favour one grape more than another and that there are differences between the regions. Every care has been taken to be as accurate as possible but it must be remembered that there are some exceptions to all rules; there are always some very good wines made when a vintage does not deserve the highest marks and there are, unfortunately, some bad wines made in the best vintages.

VINTAGE YEAR	Red Bordeaux	Sauternes	Red Burgundy	White Burgundy	Rhône	Loire	Rhine Moselle Alsace	Champagne	Port
1945	7	6†	6†	—	5†	—	—	4†	7
1947	6†	5†	5†	—	5†	7†	—	4†	6
1949	6†	6†	5†	—	6†	5†	5†	5†	—
1953	6†	5†	4†	3†	6†	—	5†	5†	—
1955	5†	6†	4†	3†	6†	5†	—	5†	7
1959	6	5	6†	3†	6	5†	5†	4†	—
1961	7	5†	5†	3†	7	5†	—	5†	—
1962	5	6	5	4†	5	—	—	5†	—
1964	3/6	2	6	4†	6	4†	—	6†	—
1966	6	5	5	4†	6	—	4†	5†	6*
1967	4	7	4†	4†	6	3†	—	4†	5
1969	2	4	6	5	6	4†	4†	5†	—
1970	6	6	5	3†	6	5†	—	6	6*
1971	5/6	6	6	6	5	6	7	7	—
1972	2	3	5	4†	5	—	—	—	4*
1973	4	3	4	5†	5	4†	4†	6	—
1974	3	—	3	3	4	4†	—	—	—
1975	6*	6	—	4	4	5	5/6	7	6*
1976	5	6	6	5	5	6	7	6	—
1977	3	3	4	5	4	3†	—	—	7*
1978	7*	3	7*	7	7	5	4†	6	6*
1979	6*	5	5*	5	6	5	4/5†	6*	—
1980	4	4	4	3	5*	4†	3†	6	6*
1981	6*	5	3	4*	5*	4	5	6*	—
1982	7*	4	5*	5*	6*	6	4	6*	5*
1983	6*	7*	6*	6*	6*	6*	6*	6*	6*
1984	2/4*	4*	4*	4*	5*	5*	4*	—	—
1985	7*	5*	6*	6*	6*	6*	7*	—	—

7= the best   — = no good   *for laying down   †tiring, drink up

GUIDE TO APERITIFS, SPIRITS AND LIQUEURS

The function of an apéritif, any drink which is served before lunch or dinner, is to freshen the palate, without being so heavy that it dulls the appetite. At one time dry sherry was considered 'the' drink for this purpose, and even now dedicated gastronomes maintain that spirits drunk before a meal destroy the appreciation of the food.

Sherry of all types is a good choice, whether it is a dry fino, medium amontillado or the new, sweeter 'pale cream'. As a general rule, the 'drier' the wine, the more important it is to serve it well chilled; in hot weather it is a good idea to chill the glasses, too, by putting them in the refrigerator for a few minutes. Other fortified wines, from different European wine-growing regions, make pleasant alternatives, and your guests would enjoy the choice of a dry Sercial or Verdelho Madeira, dry Marsala, or white port, all served pleasantly chilled.

The French pre-prandial tradition is for wine-based apéritifs such as Dubonnet, Byrrh and St. Raphael, and the Italians contribute dry and sweet Vermouth, Campari and Punt e Mes. Each of these may be served 'straight', chilled and undiluted; 'on the rocks', which means poured over cracked ice; or diluted with a mixer such as soda water or tonic water. A cube of ice and a twist of thinly sliced orange adds to both the appearance and enjoyment of the drink.

For many people, Champagne is the most festive and special of all apéritifs, to enjoy perhaps before Christmas dinner or a family celebration meal. There is a considerable price difference between fine vintage years and non-vintage wine, and so your exuberant choice need not break the bank. Less expensive sparkling wines, which still give a festive air, include dry ('brut') or medium-dry Saumur or Veuve du Vernay and the sweeter Italian 'sparklers' such as Asti Spumante.

RIGHT: Apéritifs and cocktails to whet the appetite

Remember that all sparkling wines should be served well chilled. You should get six or seven glasses from a standard (75 cl) bottle. Choose long, slender 'flute' glasses and tilt the glass towards the bottle and pour the wine slowly on to the inside of the glass, to make the most of the bubbles.

Buck's Fizz, a mix of Champagne or other sparkling wine with pure orange juice, is specially popular before lunch – and cuts down the alcohol content, a consideration for those who have to drive home. Another delightful wine mix for summer drinking is Kir, made with one part crème de Cassis, a black-currant liqueur, to 8 or 10 parts dry white wine.

In these days of higher hospitality costs and the change in drinking habits, light, fruity still white wines may be served as apéritifs, or you could offer Beaujolais nouveau, one of the few red wines to be served chilled.

Spirits

What you stock in your 'spirits locker' will depend, apart from your bank balance, on your own and your friends' preference. If you enjoy serving cock-tails you will need gin, vodka and white rum, all excellent mixers that form the base of hundreds of tried and tested recipes. Gin, with its unique flavour of juniper berries, is the ideal choice to mix with the less alcoholic ingredients. Bear in mind that, like most other spirits, it has an alcoholic strength of 40°, and is therefore about twice as strong as fortified wines and four times as strong as table wines. For those who like to 'know what they are drinking', serve a measure (about 30 ml) of gin with tonic water, bitter lemon or dry ginger, with crushed ice and a slice of lemon. And with an everlasting bottle of Angostura bitters on the shelf you will be prepared for any ex-naval per-sonnel who ask for a pink gin!

Vodka, colourless and virtually taste-less, is available in a number of strengths. Check the label – and price will be a guide too – if you want one of regular (and not extra) strength. Vodka and tonic is a popular long drink; the spirit is equally refreshing served with lime juice and a splash of soda or with chilled tomato juice.

The dark, Navy-type rum is an ac-quired taste – and it leaves a strong after-taste – but a nip on a cold night does wonders for the circulation. White rum, which retains the sugar-cane flavour without being cloying, may be served with tonic water and lemon and is specially good with pineapple juice.

Purists recommend serving Scotch whisky neat, or simply with water so that the true flavour of the grain is enjoyed, but it may also be served, with or without ice cubes, with soda water, dry ginger, ginger wine (when the mixture is known as Whisky Mac), or as a cocktail. In Whisky Sour, one example, the spirit is mixed with lemon juice, sugar and soda water. The Scots do not have the monopoly on whisky. You can extend your choice with Irish whiskey, American Bourbon or rye, and Canadian whiskey, each of which has a different and distinctive flavour. But it is back to Scotland for the highly individual malt whiskies, made from malted barley and pure stream water, and matured in oak sherry casks. Malt whisky is usually served neat, after a meal.

Digestifs

As an after-dinner drink, or digestif, a popular choice is good French brandy, either Cognac or Armagnac, both of which are distilled from wines, but by different methods. Nearly every wine-producing country makes its own brandy, and holiday-makers may be familiar with Spanish and Cypriot brandies, Metaxa from Greece, Stock from Italy and so forth. Fine brandies deserve fine glasses, not necessarily huge 'balloons' but large enough to release the aroma of the spirit when the glass is gently warmed in the palms of the hands.

Port, another traditional after-dinner drink, is one of the world's finest fortified wines. Few of us can aspire to the luxury of vintage port, wine of a single exceptional year, but there are many other qualities to enjoy. Vintage character types and 'late-bottled vin-tage' are considered worth the extra expense by comparison with the cheaper ruby or tawny types. As a pleasing variation you could offer, both as a dessert wine and digestif, one of the sweeter, richer Madeiras, golden-brown Bual or dark Malmsey, popular even in Shakespeare's day.

Liqueurs offer a bewildering range of after-dinner drinks. They are all spirit based and vary in strength from about 30° to a powerful 55°. Syrup, honey and other sweetening agents are the catalysts used to bring out the individual flavours and aromas from the fruit, berries, flowers, herbs and grains that make up the often secret recipes. It is a good idea to sample a few miniature bottles before you start to build up a selection, choosing per-haps from Bénédictine, Cointreau, Grand Marnier, yellow or green Char-treuse, cherry brandy, the coffee-flavoured Tia Maria, the whisky-based Drambuie, or the cream and whiskey blend of Bailey's Irish Cream.

GLASSES

You may not have a large selection of glassware, but it is worth having one set of rather special glasses, especially for more formal occasions. They can look elegant without being unduly ex-pensive – the glass departments in most large stores stock glassware from several countries that actually looks like crystal, but is not the real thing. For very informal large gatherings, you might well prefer to use plastic 'glasses'; they come in many different shapes and designs and are perfectly adequate.

The thing that confuses most people when planning a fairly formal occasion is which glass to use for a particular drink, and how to arrange the glasses on the table. The answer to the second is simple: glasses are arranged in the same way as cutlery: in the order in which they will be used, working from the outside (on the knife side) inwards to the centre above the plate. As to the first question, common sense can be your guide. Nothing would tempt you to serve hock in a tumbler, because the heat of your skin would warm it too much; for the opposite reason, you would not serve brandy in a long-stemmed glass, when it could not benefit from your body heat.

Here is a brief guide to what glass to use for which drink:

Tall tumbler Ideal for long drinks such as Campari soda and Pimm's, allowing plenty of room for ice and diluting with a 'mixer'. It is also used for some cocktails, such as 'highballs'.
Small stubby tumbler For short drinks, such as whisky 'on the rocks', Bloody Marys, and of course for fruit juices.
Champagne flute A cleverly design-ed shape which helps to retain the bubbles in the wine, unlike the old-

ABOVE: Wine glasses for all occasions. From the left: champagne flute; sherry copita; hock or mosel glass; brandy glass; red wine glass; white wine glass; liqueur glass

fashioned saucer-shaped glass.

White wine glass Generally speaking, the glass should be tall and slender, on a fairly long stem – this prevents the warmth of the hand taking the necessary chill off the wine. Some hock and mosel glasses have a bulbous bowl on a coloured stem, generally green – the idea being that the colour of the stem is reflected in the pale golden hue of the wine.

Red wine glasses The 'Paris goblet' is one of the most popular shapes to use for nearly all red wines, apart from the few that are served chilled. The glass has a wide deep bowl, on a medium-length stem which adds grace to the shape; the wide bowl allows you to appreciate the bouquet or 'nose' of the wine, and you can nestle it in your hand to keep it at the best temperature. Remember that a red wine glass should only be filled to between a third and a half of its depth; you will not be considered mean by your guests! If you are using a flute-shaped glass for red wine you need to fill it to between two-thirds and three-quarters full, as the bowl of this style of glass is not as large.

Sherry glass There are two basic shapes usually used for sherry, the small flute-shaped glass or schooner on a stubby stem, or the more traditional 'copita' – the Spaniards and sherry purists always choose the latter.

Liqueur glass The shape of glass used for serving a liqueur is very similar to that used for sherry, but smaller. You can in fact use any small attractive glass, preferably on a short stem. For liqueurs 'on the rocks' use a slightly larger glass.

Port glass Port is normally served in a larger measure than a liqueur, so the best glass will be a sherry glass.

Cocktail glass Cocktails are as popular now, if not more so, than they were in the '30s. There is a tremendous range of glasses to choose from as far as colour and decorative finish are concerned, but they are mostly the same classic shape – a tall stem, topped with a cone-shaped bowl.

Brandy glass The classic brandy glass or 'balloon' has a short stem with a bowl that is wide at the bottom and gradually tapering in at the top. The shape fits neatly into the palms of the hands, so that you can warm the brandy, and the narrow neck prevents all the delicious aroma from escaping into the air.

Decanters If you have a decanter, use it; a cheap red wine looks much more special if it is decanted, and psychologically it tastes better. Squat, rectangular decanters are usually reserved for spirits.

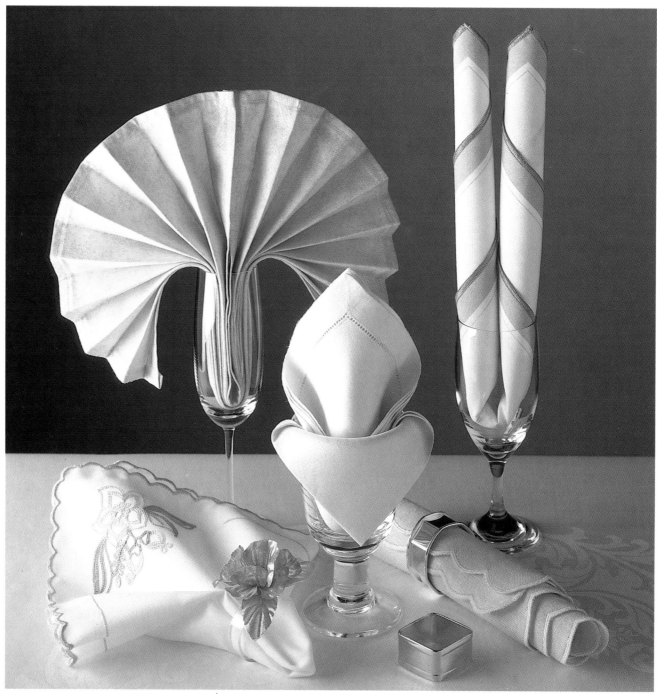

NAPKINS

A table is made by the way it is 'dressed' with napkins and tablecloth. One of the simplest and most fundamental arts of dressing a table is with attractively displayed napkins. Naturally they should tone in with the chosen cloth (or cloths), but the way of folding and presenting them depends very much on the occasion, whether formal or informal.

The following suggestions are for fairly formal place settings, but they can be adapted to suit almost any table or occasion.

Napkins à deux Perfect when laying a table for two. Using lace edged or delicately patterned napkins, pull each napkin casually through a napkin ring. Tuck a rosebud or a stem (or similar bloom) between the ring and the napkin.

Napkin flutes Choose two voile (or similar light-weight fabric) napkins, in harmonizing colours but preferably different patterns. Lay them flat, placing one napkin on top of the other, and gather the napkins together at the centre, shaking them so that they fall in gentle folds. Pull the centre part of the

ABOVE: Novel – and conventional – ways of folding napkins

napkins through a napkin ring, so that the edges of the napkins splay out forming a flute shape.

Chinese napkins Roll a coloured napkin into a thin neat cylinder shape. Tuck it through a napkin ring, together with two chopsticks. Instead of using a napkin ring, you can tie the rolled napkin and chopsticks together with coloured raffia.

FLOWER ARRANGEMENTS

A shallow basket brimming over with wild oats and brilliant blue cornflowers for an autumn celebration; a glistening silver bowl filled with crimson roses to celebrate a wedding anniversary; a copper jug reflecting the glow of hedgerow berries for a kitchen party; a set of eggcups holding precious springtime primroses and violets gathered for Mother's Day – whatever the occasion, and whatever the mood you wish to create, flowers have a complementary part to play.

Flowers for a dining table, when guests will be sitting around it, should be in scale with the size and shape of the table, and never so tall that people have to crane their necks to see and talk over them. A long, slender trailing 'ribbon' or swag of evergreen leaves and silver-sprayed cones or dried flowers looks stunning along the centre of a narrow rectangular table, and a tightly-clustered Victorian-style posy is charming as the centrepiece of a circular one.

A piece of pottery or china from the tableware makes an ideal container, perhaps a spare sauce boat, cream jug, shallow dish or a cup and saucer from the matching tea set. Otherwise, choose a holder that competes with neither the place setting nor the flowers.

Dried flowers and silk 'look-alike' blooms, both of which you can buy in a blaze of pretty colours from most florists and department stores, give you the chance to arrange the design well in advance of the party, one creative task accomplished and ready. Dried flowers, which usually have a matt, almost papery texture, are specially effective in containers that catch every tiny flicker of candlelight. Small wine glasses discreetly packed with a ball of crumpled wire mesh to hold the stems of, say, tiny pink or cream rosebuds, dried everlastings and snippings of pale green lady's mantle make flattering additions to each individual place setting, or a group of glasses makes an eye-catching – and compliment-winning – central feature. Silk flowers take specially well to shallow baskets – wire on a block of florists' dry foam to hold the stems.

Remember that any arrangement for a table centre must be equally pretty from all points of view. If you have a cake-decorating turntable, place the container on that and turn it around as you arrange the flowers, eyeing the design critically – as guests may do – from every angle.

Make sure that all the fresh flowers you use are in the peak of condition. Buy or gather them the day before the party and give them a long drink in tepid water before you arrange them. Highly scented flowers give a romantic air to a room, but you can have too much of a good thing. Flowers with a strong perfume, such as hyacinth, can be overpowering, and mask the subtle flavours of the food, and should be avoided.

The design principles are completely different when it comes to arranging flowers for a buffet table. Here the arrangement needs to be tall enough and dramatic enough to be seen at a distance, and to take over as the centre of attention once the dishes and plates start to empty. If you plan to have a star item in the buffet – perhaps a cold turkey or a decorated dessert – complement it with two matching flower arrangements, one on either side.

Using tall containers as improvised pedestals serves the dual purpose of raising the flowers almost to eye level and taking up the minimum of table space, always an important consideration at a party. Cake stands make pretty holders – you can often find inexpensive ones in junk shops. Tall candlesticks, glass wine carafes, even glass storage jars can all be used as pretend pedestals – you just fix a

BELOW: A dramatic arrangement of lilies for a modern room

ABOVE: A mass of peonies, lilies and sweet peas arranged in a galvanized bucket

saucer or upturned coffee jar lid to the top to hold a piece of foam. Make sure that tall designs are not top heavy and vulnerable. You can weight glass containers with pebbles, gravel or dried beans, which form an attractive part of the design.

Try to have a linking theme for the flowers on the table and elsewhere in the room. A small bowl of sweet peas as a table centre can be echoed with a basket of summer blooms in similar pink-through-to-blue shades in the fireplace or on a side table; a cluster of blazing zinnias or marigolds can give a colour lead for a huge jug of papery, bright orange Chinese lanterns across the room. Plant materials do not have to be expensive to be memorable and effective.

If your numbers of guests have pushed the available space to the limits, and there is scarcely room to place an egg cup of flowers anywhere,

consider the walls. Buy polystyrene rings filled with foam (they are purpose-made for door wreaths at Christmas time), soak the foam and pack the rings with marguerites, spray chrysanthemums, ivy leaves, gypsophila, whatever comes to hand. Snippings, buds and side shoots from large arrangements are ideal to use in this way. Hang a floral ring on a wall, door or even a window – that is a devious way to mask a dreary view! – or fix it with four ribbons and hang it, flower side down, low over the dining table.

Spotlight a buffet table or a small table displaying a celebration cake by trimming the cloth with leaves and flowers. Pin slender trails of ivy all around the table rim; bind short sprays of leaves to thick string, tuck in a few flowers and fix the swags to the vertical surface of the tablecloth, to hang in loops; or pin dainty posies of fresh, dried or silk flowers to the cloth. Clus-

ters of roses, bunches of pink daisies, primulas, marjoram, what you will, they make the prettiest of designs and draw attention to the food.

Do not overlook the possibilities of using flowers to brighten the outdoor scene. A large jug of zingy dahlias on the terrace, buckets of blossom on the balcony, a wooden trug of fruit and flowers on a buffet table, they all bring colour to a 'green' or paved garden. Use wide-based containers and weight them with stones to guard against high winds and the exuberance of children and other guests.

INVITATIONS AND PLANNING

Issuing the invitations is one of the most joyous aspects of giving a party, involving as it does telephoning or writing to friends. It is all too easy to get carried away and invite one or two extra couples at this stage, out of a feeling of anticipation and well-being. Avoid this temptation and stick to your original list, which you carefully compiled with a view to the maximum number of guests you could comfortably entertain, and a good balance of personalities, people you know well and others you may recently have met. Have a 'reserves' list, and then if anyone has to decline your invitation, make up the numbers from that.

Send invitations in plenty of time – book your friends' company early to avoid disappointment, in other words. Six to eight weeks is usual for a wedding invitation, four or six weeks for a large function such as an engagement or birthday party and three or four weeks for a formal dinner party. This does not, of course, preclude the sudden decision to hold a barbecue on a sunny day or to ring up friends for a spur-of-the-moment get-together. Often impromptu parties can be the greatest fun. However, do remember to plan really far ahead and send out your invitations in good time if you plan to give a party during the Christmas season, particularly if you want to entertain on New Year's Eve.

Increased informality

There is an increasing trend towards informality in invitations. The formal type, 'Mr and Mrs John Smyth request the pleasure of your company at the marriage of their daughter ...' is often replaced by a printed or hand-written card announcing that 'Pauline Smyth and John Greene would like you to come to their wedding'. Whether you have invitations printed, choose decorative cards and fill in the details, or telephone your friends, be sure that they have all the information they need. Make it clear whether you are inviting them only for drinks or for a meal, and if there is to be a 'closing time'. In days gone by this somewhat delicate matter was dealt with by the line 'Carriages, 11.30 p.m.' on the invitation. If friends are welcome to stay as long as the party is in full swing, the invitation could say '8 till late'. If not – because of the terms of your lease, or out of consideration for the neighbours – say so. No-one is offended by being asked to a party from '8 o'clock till around midnight', but it can be embarrassing to have to ask happy guests to leave.

There are no longer rigid rules about the right and wrong way to dress on certain occasions, but if you do want your guests to dress up, give them a lead. If you are telephoning the invitation you could say, 'I was thinking of really going to town and wearing a long dress'. If the party is to be held in the garden, make this clear so that guests come well prepared with anoraks or wraps.

There are said to be two major pitfalls for the party-giver – running out of drink, and allowing guests to get cold. Following our quantity guide on page 54 will take care of the first point. To make sure of the second, and avoid a chill setting over the proceedings, make a careful assessment of the heating well in advance of the party. If your normal heating system needs a boost, hire or borrow portable heaters. Protect electric fires with exposed elements by using a guard, or opt for the safer-in-a crowd convector type.

Lighting

Lighting can do a great deal to set the mood of a party. Experiment in advance with different combinations of spotlights and table lamps, consider putting coloured shades around light bulbs or buying coloured light bulbs – though never allow paper or other inflammable materials to come into contact with a bulb – and use fairy lights and candles to add to the party atmosphere. A flat dish with several coloured nightlights (you can buy some which are lightly scented) or a group of tall candles towards the back of a buffet table throws a gentle, flattering light on to the party food. For an even more festive note, you can buy 'holiday tapers', very slender candles about 20 cm (8 inches) long to decorate party cakes and puddings. Although dim lighting is flattering to faces, it is essential to be practical and to provide adequate lighting at the bar and where you will be serving the food.

For an outdoor party, decorate a tree or the balcony with a string of lights specially insulated for use outside, or edge a path or patio with a collection of hurricane lamps, party flares on long poles, or chubby candles protected from the wind in preserve jars. Candles in bottles or jars cast a romantic glow on al fresco tables as dusk falls, but do be sure they are safe, especially if there are children around.

Well before the party, even before you plan the menu, you can work out such logistics as where cars may be parked, where to put wet macs and umbrellas and whether you have enough glasses, ashtrays and so forth.

If parking is difficult, ask your local parish council or friendly neighbours if they can help. Indicate to guests when you invite them, where to park nearby, or have someone on hand to show them into spaces when they arrive.

You can usually put visitors' coats on a spare bed but if it is pouring with rain rig up a line over the bath and hang them there, and stand umbrellas in a large container, such as a preserving pan, in the porch, the kitchen, or just inside the door.

When you check your stocks of glasses, do not count in your 'best' ones for a large party. If you order the drinks from a wine merchant he will usually loan glasses free of charge. Otherwise you can hire them, and any crockery you need, from catering supply firms. Look in local telephone directories for lists of names.

Check that you have enough large casseroles and pans, teapots, crockpots, hot-plates and serving trays. If not, ask friends to help out or if necessary hire them, too, from catering suppliers. Remember to ask what the charge will be and cost it into your budget.

Dinner Parties

Dinner parties offer the most opportunity for in-depth conversation. If you plan to entertain more than just another couple, choose guests who have shared interests, but not necessarily similar lifestyles. A dinner party of computer buffs or people who all work in the health service can turn into a miniature convention! If the occasion is a business dinner, it is a good idea to invite a couple of close friends who have a common bond – perhaps a liking for golf or watersports. They can help to keep the conversation flowing during the inevitable periods when you have to be in the kitchen.

Planning the menu

Plan a menu that is high on style and low on the necessity for last-minute attention. With most of the preparation done in advance you should be able to give your almost undivided attention to your guests.

Decide on the main course first, choosing a dish you know you can cook with confidence, whether it is a roast leg of lamb wrapped in phyllo pastry, a poached salmon or a tasty pie. Make the best possible use of seasonal ingredients – always wise from the budget point of view – and choose at least one vegetable dish that can be cooked in advance. The current trend to serve healthy fresh salads in place of some cooked vegetables is helpful in cutting down on last-minute straining and garnishing.

It is a matter of personal choice whether you serve one or two courses before the main dish, though the tendency now is for smaller meals.

The function of a 'starter' is both to give a good first impression and to stimulate the appetite. Pay special attention to the presentation of this course. If you decide to serve, for example, a vegetable terrine ready sliced on individual plates, garnish each one with decorative salad leaves such as endive, a few tomato slices, and a sprig of fresh herbs.

Soup makes an elegant course if it is well garnished. Spiced courgette soup takes well to a swirl or two of soured cream and a sprinkling of paprika, chilled watercress soup looks appetizing topped with sliced hard-boiled egg and cress leaves, and clear consommé with flower shapes cut from cooked carrot slices. Do not serve soup to accompany a 'liquid' main dish such as a casserole, and avoid creamy soups if you plan to finish the meal with a dairy-based dessert. Fruit makes a light and delicious opening to a meal – though not one which includes fruit salad. Vary the familiar half grapefruit by serving grilled kebabs of orange and grapefruit segments, or cocktails of tiny scoops of melon and contrasting pink watermelon attractively presented in tall-stemmed glasses.

More and more hostesses now follow the French practice of serving the cheese course before the dessert – a good idea if you are serving red wine with the main course and intend to offer a sweet white wine with the pudding. Offer a varied selection of cheeses, including at least one matured English cheese, a blue-veined one, and a creamy one. Decorate the cheese dish with small bunches of black and green grapes, satsuma segments, fresh dates, halved green or black figs or halved kiwi fruits, all tempting accompaniments.

The dessert course presents few management problems, and should be chosen to contrast well with the preceding dishes. Fruit salads, mousses, macerated fruits and gâteaux can all be at the ready in the refrigerator. Remember to transfer ice cream, sorbets and other frozen desserts from the freezer to allow for them to soften slightly and mellow.

A bowl of fresh fruit makes a fine centrepiece for the table. If this is your choice, it is up to you whether you invite guests to 'eat the decorations' or offer a second dish of polished apples and pears, peaches and plums.

You can leave it until the moment of serving to decide whether to hand coffee round at the table. Sometimes moving to another room, or even the other end of the same room, breaks up a good conversation and, at least for a time, destroys the mood of the party. Have the coffee cups, sugar and milk or cream ready on the tray, together with a dish of mints or petits fours, and have the coffee maker ready. It is thoughtful to offer a choice of decaffeinated coffee or tea for guests who cannot enjoy regular coffee late in the evening.

Table setting

The dining table set with glinting glass and cutlery and decorated with fruit or flowers sets the scene for the party. A polished table looks elegant set with just heat-resistant mats, or with place mats concealing cork under–mats. If you have a beautiful lace or fancy tablecloth, now is the time to use it, again with protective mats at each place.

Set cutlery in the order it will be used, working from the outside inwards. The dessert spoon and fork may be placed inside the other items or above the plate, depending on available space, the bread and butter knife may be on the extreme right, across the top of the place setting or placed on the side plate, whichever is the most convenient.

Set the glasses for white wine, red wine and water in a triangle at the top right of each place setting, balancing the side plate on the left. If space is short, port or liqueur glasses may be put in place at the end of the meal.

As this is a special occasion, use cotton or linen napkins to match the cloth or tone with the flowers. If one of the courses involves eating with the fingers you might like to provide extra paper napkins or, preferably, bowls of tepid water with a slice of lemon floating on the top. Finger bowls may seem old-fashioned but they are very practical.

Work out a table plan and either put place cards on the table, or make a note on a card to remind you. Alternate male and female guests, separating couples. Normally the host and hostess sit at each end of a rectangular table but if your party is for eight or twelve this is not possible and one of you will have to forego that honour, and sit one place away.

To ensure that every stage of your dinner party runs smoothly it is important to clear as much space as possible in the kitchen. If necessary, pack away table-top appliances once you have used them, ornaments and spare storage jars to a cupboard or even the garage.

Between courses, rinse plates and cutlery in hot water and pack them in the dishwasher or on the draining board. They will be much easier to wash when the time comes, and look neater if guests catch a glimpse of the room. Unless the kitchen is out of earshot of the dining room do not start the dishwasher. Guests might mistake this as a signal that the party is over.

RIGHT: The scene is set for a sumptuous dinner party

CHILDREN'S PARTIES AND OUTDOOR PARTIES

Children's parties are part of the fantasy world. For two or three hours the youngsters are transported into a wonderland, whether it is toy town, outer space or wherever the theme takes them. The person who has to have her feet firmly on the ground all the time from the moment the invitations are issued, is you.

Be realistic about the numbers you can cope with, be ready to accept offers of help from other parents on the day and organize the food so that you will be completely free to keep things firmly under your control throughout the party.

Luckily, children prefer simple food they can recognize easily, and so it is best to concentrate your creative energies on the cake, always the source of the most delighted oohs and aahs, and the centre of attraction.

Be prepared for the over-enthusiasm and unavoidable clumsiness of very young guests, the under-fives, by providing food that is virtually accident proof. Avoid anything that crumbles easily in the hand – sausage rolls or shortcakes for example – and any cakes and sandwiches that will ooze messy cream and jam if they are squeezed tightly. Serve soft drinks in half portions, and in wide-based unbreakable plastic beakers. Then if there are any spills, at least the mess will be halved.

Use a wipe-down table, or cover your dining table with a large piece of plastic, and set your mind at rest by covering the carpet or rug, too.

It is not really the job of a party hostess to educate the guests into healthy eating, but do your best to provide a wholesome balance. Checkerboard sandwiches alternating wholewheat and white bread, some low-calorie, low-fat fillings including cottage cheese, and sweetness in the form of dried fruits rather than sugar are gaining in acceptability even among the youngest set.

'Grown up' food is the order of the day with the older age groups. It is a good idea to consult the party-giver and take his or her ideas into account, perhaps steering the menu gently away from the seemingly inevitable crisps, sausages and cola. You can buy low-fat crisps now which go some way to reducing the cholesterol content.

Presentation is important – children love to be amused, tempted and flattered. Try wholemeal pizza (or plain scone dough) with funny-face arrangements of tomato, cheese, olives and mushrooms; kebab sticks of fresh orange segments, apple and pear slices (toss them in lemon juice first) and pineapple chunks with cubes of cheese and stoned dates. Open sandwiches with crisp and colourful fruit and vegetable toppings, and bread rolls which older children can fill for themselves from a selection of spreads, cheese, meat and salads are ideas that meet with approval.

If you ask children what is their favourite party drink they will almost certainly reply with a brand name. It is more fun for everyone, however, if you produce exciting and intriguing concoctions, perhaps with slices of fruit bobbing on top, brightly-coloured crazy straws, and imaginative names to fit in with the party theme or just to sound enticing. Orange juice swizzled with mineral water and topped with fruit slices makes a cool Sundance Kid, buttermilk whizzed with banana and honey becomes Pooh Bear's Favourite, and black grape juice and orange juice gently heated with a cinnamon stick and floating with assorted fruits is a passable Mulled Wine taste-alike to appeal to older age groups.

Take evasive action against any unavoidable damage by removing all breakable ornaments and any small pieces of furniture that may get knocked over, and never leave children unsupervised when the birthday candles are alight.

Al fresco entertaining

In an ideal world, perhaps, children's parties would always be held outdoors. Whatever one's age group there is a special magic to eating under the sky, whether it is tea in the garden, a beach barbecue, a lazy meal by a pool or a picnic carried from the car.

Some of the most successful parties are those planned on the spur of the moment, when the barometer is set fair for a fine spell of weather. This is obviously not always possible – in the case of a wedding reception or birthday party, for example. If there is the

space for it, investigate the possibility of hiring a tent from a local scout group or other organisation – cheaper than professional hire – and, in all but high summer, borrow some sturdy portable heaters. At the least, rig up an awning over the barbecue area or where drinks will be served and, if there is no room for guests to crowd indoors, try to clear a space in a garage, car port or shed. If it starts to rain, guests do not mind how cramped the shelter is, as long as there is some!

Looking on the bright side, the choice of barbecue and other cooking equipment will depend on how frequently the mood takes you to give an

outdoor party. Small portable bar-becues which fold up and can easily be packed in the car are versatile and inexpensive. All you need for a more permanent site in the garden is a low brick wall built to form a square, and a grid over the top. An impromptu fire on the beach need be no more than a pile of stones with a wire cover, or a camp fire to heat a frying pan or cooking pot, cowboy style.

If yours is to be a portable feast, a picnic taken in the car, make full use of insulated carriers of all kinds. Vacuum flasks keep soup temptingly hot, and wide-necked ones extend your picnic repertoire to simple casserole dishes –

always welcome on a chilly day. At the other end of the thermometer scale, on a hot day you can use the flasks for iced drinks, ice cream and other chilled desserts. Insulated boxes of both types, made of layers of padded material or rigid plastic, make it easy to transport a whole meal at the right temperature. Jacket potatoes, savoury flans and garlic bread wrapped in foil, or risotto packed into foil dishes, will keep warm; chilled savoury and sweet mousses, cheese and crisp salads and fruits will remain cool.

Take plastic sheeting to spread under rugs or cushions, fold-up chairs for the less agile members of the party,

ABOVE: Simply prepared cold dishes for an al fresco summer lunch

a bright paper tablecloth, matching napkins and disposable plates and cups. Remember to take large plastic bags to carry home litter and washing up, a damp sponge in a polythene bag, a corkscrew and a bottle opener. Make a check list before packing the car, so that you don't forget everyday things like pepper, milk, and the bread knife, and check the picnic site carefully before you go home. 'Leave without leaving a trace' is a good motto for all picnickers to adopt.

BUFFET PARTIES

Buffet parties are an opportunity to entertain more people than you can comfortably seat around a table, but they do have their own special requirements. The most important are that the buffet itself should present a really eye-catching display, that the food should be easy to manage with the minimum of cutlery, and that there are enough places for everybody to be able to sit or, at any rate, perch, to eat it. Younger people are happy with cushions, but the higher the average age of your guests the greater number of comfortable chairs you will need. Remem-

ber, too, to clear ornaments from shelves and side tables so that they can become resting places for plates and glasses.

However informal your party is, the special attention you put into presenting the buffet table attractively will go a long way towards its overall success. Arrange everything within easy reach. Dishes which require spoons are best at the front of the table, as are shallow plates of food. Any taller pedestal dishes should sit further back on the table. You can make a raised section at the back of the table by putting stout boxes under the tablecloth. An old blanket on the table under the boxes will stop them slipping. At a large

gathering, repeat some of the food displays, so that guests can approach from either end of the table, but make sure that there is enough space for people who have filled their plates to be able to leave the buffet table without creating a traffic jam. Arrange meats and fish in the centre of the table, and the salads and side dishes towards the outside edges.

Identification tags are a good idea for foods cooked in pastry and for sandwiches, where the fillings are concealed. Cut a triangular flag from a piece of paper and attach with glue to a cocktail stick, with a handwritten description of the food. To ease crowding, provide separate tables, or a trol-

LEFT: Buffet party food should be easy to manage with the minimum of cutlery

trasts of texture and colour will give visual interest and a brightly coloured dish will liven up a duller one close by. Look into unusual ways to serve foods: a fruit salad in a melon basket, or cocktail bites stuck into a cooking apple, cabbage, or French loaf.

The cheeseboard

If you will be providing a cheeseboard, whole or half cheeses are often more economical than several smaller pieces, and they dry out less quickly. Introduce some green grapes, a jug of celery sticks, or some sprigs of fresh herbs, such as rosemary, as a garnish, and the cheeseboard will look doubly appetizing. Offer a variety of cheese biscuits to accompany. If you can, discreetly remove the cheese course once the guests have finished; you will save it from absorbing other flavours and in particular cigarette smoke, as well as from becoming warm and sweaty.

Curls, pats or balls of butter should be put in iced water before the party and garnished with sprigs of parsley just before setting out on the table. If you are serving plain cuts of bread, warm them first in the oven at a low temperature for 10 minutes, then arrange the pieces in overlapping slices in a basket for an attractive display. If you are serving rolls, mix a variety of shapes and textures in the same selection. Line the bread dish or basket with a napkin, ruffle the edges and even bread takes on a special party style.

One of the easiest ways to guide people on how much to take is to indicate portions by spacing the garnish on the foods at appropriate intervals. Avoid putting a garnish in the centre, though, which is difficult to cut through. Some foods, however, such as terrines, are best pre-cut into slices before serving. Cut through quiches, pies and whole soft cheeses also, so that portions are not left to chance.

ley, for starters, desserts, cutlery, plates and coffee. Wrap each guest's cutlery in a napkin to save time on the day.

Before the party, double-check which foods will be served in which dishes to save yourself a last-minute panic. Larger pastry and more fragile desserts which require slicing should go on flat plates; gravy and sauce boats need a plate under them, and you will want a number of ramekins or glass dishes for individual desserts. Heat foods in a dish you can serve them in wherever possible. To set off a plain china dish, you can place it on top of a large patterned one. Equally important is the arrangement of foods on the table in relation to each other. Con-

Slice a hard cheese such as Cheddar and include individually wrapped cheeses on the cheeseboard. Small individual desserts and decorations on large desserts will give your guests an idea of portions.

Cocktail sticks are indispensable for finger and fork food occasions. You can pierce a selection of sandwich quarters with sticks, to enable a tasty assortment to be picked up in one go. For some parties, such as those where guests have bought tickets, it is more convenient to serve a selection of pre-arranged foods on each plate.

As hostess you want to keep the serving of drinks as easy as you can. Two effort-saving ideas are to serve one type of drink throughout the party and to advise guests to help themselves after the first drink. Don't arrange the bar too near the buffet.

Depending upon the occasion, you can buy wine in a box, decant sherry as the apéritif, top up a large jugful of Buck's Fizz, or have some warming mulled wine at the ready – with a little thought given to it beforehand the bar will run as smoothly as the buffet. Champagne should not be opened until just before it is served, so if it is for a toast enlist some assistance. Keep it chilled until you want to serve it and have a napkin to hand to hold when pouring. Don't forget to offer guests a variety of non-alcoholic drinks.

If your party is fairly informal you can be flexible over the shape of glasses and stick to versatile Paris goblets. However, remember that mulled wine needs special heat-resistant glasses or mugs. Frosting glasses is an imaginative way to decorate a drink – dip the rims into lightly beaten egg white, then into caster sugar. Give non-alcoholic drinks a sophisticated look with fruits on cocktail sticks and fancy straws – thread cocktail cherries, fruits and olives, etc., on to sticks several hours ahead.

SERVING THE FOOD

Many people think that once the food has been cooked and/or prepared in advance, all the entertaining problems are over. One of the greatest problems, however, is how to keep food hot effectively. Nothing is more off-putting than tepid food, and it is something that every hostess wants to avoid. Where appropriate, the recipes in this book give a clear guideline as to how far each dish can be prepared in advance, together with the appropriate tips for finishing off or reheating.

Hostess trolleys These specially heated trolleys, with separate compartments for different foods, are becoming increasingly popular. Most of them have the space for keeping a main course and three vegetables for six people at the correct temperature. The basic idea is that you can put the ready-cooked food into the preheated trolley an hour or so before you plan to eat, giving you the chance to have a relaxed drink with your guests. Remember that foods kept warm in this way dry out slightly, so add a little extra moisture, such as melted butter, to cooked vegetables.

Wrapping food in foil Breads, such as garlic bread and pitta bread, can be wrapped in foil and kept warm in a moderately hot oven, as can jacket potatoes and many firm-textured vegetables. If cooked joints and poultry are wrapped securely in foil once they come out of the oven, they will keep hot enough for 15 to 20 minutes; this 'relaxing period' also makes the meat much easier to carve.

Electric hot trays These are heated trays which can either be placed on the table, or on an adjacent sideboard; the cooked food can be put into the appropriate serving dishes and then placed on the hot tray (do check that the serving dishes are suitable to withstand the heat). They are particularly useful when you are 'keeping back' food for second portions.

COOKING FRESH VEGETABLES IN THE MICROWAVE

FRESH VEGETABLE AND WEIGHT	PREPARATION	WATER TO BE ADDED	APPROX. COOKING TIME ON FULL/MAX. SETTING
Artichokes, 4 medium	Wash and trim	150 ml ($\frac{1}{4}$ pint)	10–20 mins
Aubergines 450 g (1 lb)	Peel and dice	2 table-spoons	5–6 mins
Beetroot 450 g (1 lb)	Wash, skin and cut in half	None	7–8 mins
Broad beans 450 g (1 lb)	Remove from pods and wash	2 table-spoons	7–10 mins
Broccoli 225 g (8 oz)	Prepare, slice into spears	3 table-spoons	4–5 mins
Brussels sprouts 225 g (8 oz)	Trim	3–4 table-spoons	7–8 mins
Cabbage 450 g (1 lb)	Trim and shred	3 table-spoons	7–8 mins
Carrots 225 g (8 oz)	Scrape and slice	2 table-spoons	6–7 mins
Cauliflower 450 g (1 lb)	Trim and cut in florets	4 table-spoons	9–10 mins
Celery, 1 head	Trim and dice	150 ml ($\frac{1}{4}$ pint)	10–13 mins

FRESH VEGETABLE AND WEIGHT	PREPARATION	WATER TO BE ADDED	APPROX. COOKING TIME ON FULL/MAX. SETTING
Corn on the cob (2)	Trim and wash	4 table-spoons	7–8 mins
Courgettes 450 g (1 lb)	Trim, slice, sprinkle lightly with salt	None	7–9 mins
Leeks 450 g (1 lb)	Trim and slice	3 table-spoons	7–9 mins
Mushrooms, button 100 g (4 oz)	Peel or wash, leave whole	2 table-spoons	$2\frac{1}{2}$–3 mins
Parsnips 450 g (1 lb)	Peel and slice	3 table-spoons	6–8 mins
Peas 225 g (8 oz)	Remove from pods and wash	3 table-spoons	6–8 mins
Potatoes, boiled 450 g (1 lb)	Peel and cut into evenly sized pieces	3 table-spoons	6–7 mins
Potatoes, jacket (2) 225–275 g (8 oz–10 oz)	Scrub and prick well	None	9 mins
Runner beans 225 g (8 oz)	String and slice	4 table-spoons	6–7 mins
Spinach 225 g (8 oz)	Wash and shred	None	6–8 mins
Tomatoes 225 g (8 oz)	Slice	None	2–3 mins
Turnips 225 g (8 oz)	Peel and dice	2 table-spoons	6–7 mins

Bains maries (*double saucepans*) This is an excellent way of keeping sauces and soups warm. The top saucepan is covered and placed over a saucepan filled with water. Make sure that the water in the bottom saucepan is kept just at simmering point.

Pressure cookers These can cut cooking times by a third to a quarter of the normal cooking time and will cook foods that use a moist method of cooking, e.g. steaming, boiling, braising, pot roasting.

Microwave cookers These are a great boon to the busy hostess. Not only will they cook items such as jacket potatoes in a matter of minutes, but they can also be used for thawing and reheating prepared frozen foods. Vegetables cook particularly well – and quickly – in a microwave and this method of cooking makes great sense at parties when time and kitchen space are both at a premium. The chart on the right gives a guide to preparation and cooking time of fresh vegetables. In general, the container is covered and very little water used, as the moisture within the vegetable is sufficient. Salt should not be sprinkled directly on to vegetables before cooking as this can result in dehydration and toughness, so add salt to the cooking water or season the vegetable after cooking. Frozen vegetables cook quickly, too, with excellent results, but always refer to the manufacturer's recommended cooking times to ensure the best results.

GARNISHES

Garnishes are the finishing touch – the final embellishment for savoury foods – and one which lifts an attractively presented dish into the professional class. Most garnishes are relatively simple to prepare as you can see from the selection on these two pages.

CROUTONS

1. Use a 1.5 cm ($\frac{1}{2}$ inch) thick slice of day-old bread, remove the crusts and cut into even dice.
2. Heat equal quantities of butter and oil and when very hot fry the dice until golden brown. Alternatively deep fry in oil. Drain immediately on paper towels. Use for soups and salads.

CUCUMBER, LEMON AND ORANGE PEEL SPIRALS AND SLICES

1. For spirals, hold a canelle knife firmly and use the notch to remove a strip of skin or peel. Continue to remove the skin or peel in a spiral fashion. Arrange attractively over the side of a glass or over a dessert.
2. Use cucumber, lemon and orange spirals for drinks and lemon and orange spirals for poached pears.
3 For slices, hold a canelle knife firmly and use the notch to remove strips of skins at regular intervals.
4 Cut into even slices. Prepare orange or lemon slices in the same way, removing any pips when slicing. Use for garnishing fish or for drinks.

POMMES DE TERRE NOISETTE

1. Peel large potatoes and press a parisienne cutter/melon baller right into the potato until a half circle is made. Scoop out small balls.
2. Blanch for 2 minutes then drain and dry thoroughly on paper towels
3. Fry in hot butter in a shallow pan for 5–7 minutes shaking from time to time until golden brown and tender. Drain well. Serve them with steaks or lamb cutlets. Keep uncooked noisettes in water.

GAME CHIPS

1. Peel the potatoes and slice evenly and very thinly using a sharp knife or a mandolin (taking care to keep fingers well away from the blade).
2. Soak in cold water for 10 minutes to remove the starch. Drain and dry thoroughly on paper towels.
3. Fry in hot fat in a chip pan or deep fryer for 3 minutes or until golden brown. Drain well and sprinkle with salt. Serve with roast chicken, game and dips.

ANCHOVY LATTICE

1. Soak the anchovies in milk for about 15 minutes to remove excess salt. Dry well on paper towels.
2. Cut lengthways into thin strips.
3. Arrange in a lattice design and use on egg mayonnaise or tomato salad. This garnish goes well with any bland creamy food.

CUTLET FRILLS

1. For a cutlet or poultry frill, use a piece of plain white paper about 25 cm (10 inches) long and cut a strip 9 cm (3$\frac{1}{2}$ inches) wide.
2. Fold lengthways to within 1.5 cm ($\frac{1}{2}$ inch) of the top of the paper.
3. Make a series of thin cuts 3.2 cm (1$\frac{1}{4}$ inches) in from the folded edge along the length of the paper.
4. Open out the strip and refold inside out, lining up the edges.
5. Fold back 1.5 cm ($\frac{1}{2}$ inch) to form a cuff.

6. Cut to the required length. Roll into a frill with the cuff outside. Cut two nicks and tuck the tab inside to secure. A ham frill is made in the same way but using a much larger piece of paper. Use to decorate any exposed bone such as the end of lamb cutlets on a guard of honour or rack of lamb or the end of the drumstick on poultry. Put the frills on only after cooking.

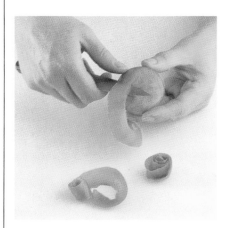

TOMATO ROSE

1. Use a firm tomato. With a sharp knife, remove the skin in a continuous strip about 1.5 cm ($\frac{1}{2}$ inch) wide, starting at the smooth end.
2. With the flesh side inside, start to curl from the base end, forming a bud shape between the fingers.
3. Continue winding the strip of skin into a rose. Use for salads and cold meats.

TOMATO WATER-LILY

1. Hold the tomato between the thumb and forefingers and with a small sharp knife make zigzag cuts around the middle.
2. Carefully separate the two halves and place a small sprig of parsley in the centre of each. Use for salads and cold meats.

TOMATO CUPS

Cut tomatoes in half, scoop out the inside and leave upside down to drain for $\frac{1}{2}$ hour. Fill with peas or sweetcorn and serve, warmed, round a joint.

RADISH ROSE AND RADISH WATER-LILY

1. For a radish rose, remove the stalk and, with the pointed end of a small sharp knife, cut a row of petal shapes round the radish keeping them joined at the base.
2. Cut a second row of petal shapes in between and above the first row and continue cutting rows of petals until the top of the radish is reached.
3. For a radish water-lily, remove the stalks and using a small sharp knife cut through 4–6 times, keeping the radish joined at the base.
4. Place both radish rose and water-lily in iced water for several hours to open out. Use for salads and oriental dishes.

POLONAISE

1. Finely chop some fresh parsley. Chop the white of a hard-boiled egg.
2. Sieve the yolk of a hard-boiled egg.
3. Fry some breadcrumbs in butter.
4. Sprinkle in layers over a vegetable, such as cauliflower, cabbage or Brussels sprouts. Keep ingredients separate, ready to be assembled.

BUTTER CURLS AND BUTTER BALLS

1. For butter curls, using a block of cold butter and a butter curler, draw the curler across the surface.
2. For butter balls, using a block of cold butter press a parisienne cutter, melon or butter baller right into the block and scoop out butter balls.
3. Drop each curl or ball into iced water to keep its shape.

POMMES DE TERRE DUCHESSE BORDER

1 Make a duchesse potato mixture by creaming 450 g (1 lb) mashed boiled potatoes with 50 g (2 oz) butter, 1 beaten egg, salt, pepper, grated nutmeg and a little milk, if necessary. Allow to cool.
2. Fit a nylon piping bag containing a large rosette nozzle with the mixture.
3. For a border, butter the edge of the serving dish and pipe a design round it.
4. Brush lightly with beaten egg and brown in the top of a preheated hot oven (220°C, 425°F, Gas Mark 7) for about 10 minutes. Use the border for lamb or poached fish.

GHERKIN FAN

1. Using a sharp knife slice through the gherkin at regular intervals, keeping it joined at the base.
2. Gently pull the slices apart to form a fan. Use for a cheeseboard or hors d'oeuvre.

FLOWER DESIGN

1. Blanch strips of red or green pepper, carrot or orange or lemon rind for 1 minute. Using an aspic cutter or a small sharp knife cut into petal shapes. Work out a flower design using a strip of tarragon, cucumber skin or chive to make leaves and a stem.
2. Dip in liquid aspic and transfer the design to the food. Use to decorate food in aspic, the base of moulds or terrines which will become the top when turned out, and chaudfroid joints of chicken.

PASTRY FLEURONS

1. Cut a strip of flaky or puff pastry 5 cm (2 inches) wide. Using a 4 cm (1½ inch) diameter fluted cutter start at the base of the strip of pastry and cut out crescent shapes.
2. Brush with beaten egg and bake in a preheated hot oven (220°C, 425°F, Gas Mark 7) for about 10 minutes. Arrange around vegetable and fish dishes or casseroles.

SPRING ONION TASSELS

1. Remove the roots from the spring onions and trim to about 7.5 cm (3 inches). Cut lengthways through the stalk several times to within 4 cm (1½ inches) of the end.
2. Place the tassels in iced water for about 1 hour to open out. Use to garnish dips and oriental dishes.

FLAVOURED BUTTERS

1. Mix softened butter with one or more of the following: chopped fresh tarragon, parsley or another herb; anchovy essence; finely chopped walnuts or hazelnuts; finely grated lemon or orange rind; crushed garlic, paprika.
2. Shape the flavoured butter into a sausage shape on a piece of greaseproof paper and roll up securely, twisting the ends of the paper like a cracker, so as to condense the butter and seal it tightly – ideally the sausage of butter should be about 2 cm (¾ inch) in diameter.
3. Chill in the refrigerator until firm. Serve sliced on top of grilled fish, chops or steaks.

QUANTITY GUIDE

FOR BUFFET PARTIES

	1 PORTION	24–26 PORTIONS	NOTES
SOUPS: *cream, clear or iced*	*200 ml ($\frac{1}{3}$ pint)*	*4.5 litres (8 pints)*	*Serve in mugs or cups garnished with fresh herbs or a swirl of cream.*
FISH COCKTAIL: *shrimp, prawn, tuna or crab*	*25 g (1 oz)*	*750 g (1$\frac{1}{2}$ lb) fish 2–3 lettuces 900 ml (1$\frac{1}{2}$ pints) sauce*	*Serve in stemmed glasses, on a bed of shredded lettuce and garnished with a shrimp or an unshelled prawn.*
MEAT: *with bone* *boneless*	*150 g (5 oz)* *75–100 g (3–4 oz)*	*3–3.5 kg (7–8 lb)* *2.5–3 kg (5$\frac{1}{2}$–7 lb)*	*For roasts or barbecue chops. For casseroles, meat balls, sausages, barbecue steaks and kebabs.*
POULTRY: *turkey* *chicken*	*75–100 g (3–4 oz) boneless* *1 joint* *150–225 g (5–8 oz)*	*7.25 kg (16 lb) dressed* *6 × 1.25–1.5 kg (2$\frac{1}{2}$–3 lb) birds, dressed*	*Serve hot or cold.*
DELICATESSEN: *ham or tongue* *pâté for wine-and-pâté party*	*75–100 g (3–4 oz)* *75–100 g (3–4 oz)*	*2.5 kg–3 kg (5$\frac{1}{2}$–7 lb)* *2.5–3 kg (5$\frac{1}{2}$–7 lb)*	*Halve the amounts if making stuffed cornets. Use half the amount if pâté is a starter course.*
SALAD VEGETABLES: *lettuce* *cucumber* *tomatoes* *white cabbage* *boiled potatoes*	*$\frac{1}{6}$* *2.5 cm (1 in)* *1–2* *25 g (1 oz)* *50 g (2 oz)*	*3–4* *2 cucumbers* *1.5 kg (3 lb)* *750 g (1$\frac{1}{2}$ lb)* *1.5 kg (3 lb)*	*Dress at last minute.* *For winter salads.* *For potato salads.*
RICE OR PASTA	*40 g (1$\frac{1}{2}$ oz) uncooked*	*1 kg (2 lb)*	*Can be cooked a day ahead, refrigerated, then reheated for 5 minutes in boiling water, strained and served.*
CHEESE: *for wine-and-cheese party*	*75 g (3 oz)*	*2–2.25 kg (4$\frac{1}{2}$–5 lb) of at least 4 different types*	*You'll need more if you serve a cheese dip too. This is a good time to buy a whole cheese, e.g. a Brie or a Stilton.*
CHEESE: *for biscuits*	*25–40 g (1–1$\frac{1}{2}$ oz)*	*750–1 kg (1$\frac{1}{2}$–2 lb) cheese plus 450 g (1 lb) butter, 1 kg (2 lb) biscuits*	*Allow the larger amounts for an assorted cheese board, less if portions are plated up.*

	INGREDIENTS	PORTIONS	NOTES
SAUSAGE ROLLS	750 g (1½ lb) shortcrust or flaky pastry 1 kg (2 lb) sausage pork meat	25–30 medium or 50 small rolls	Pastry based on 750 g (1½ lb) flour, 350–450 g (12 oz–1 lb) fat
BOUCHÉES	450 g (1 lb) puff pastry 600 ml (1 pint) thick white sauce 275 g (10 oz) prepared filling	50 bouchées	Pastry based on 450 g (1 lb) flour, 350 g (12 oz) butter. Suitable fillings include chopped ham, chicken, turkey, egg, mushrooms, shrimps and prawns.
CHEESE STRAWS	225 g (8 oz) cheese pastry	100 cheese straws	225 g (8 oz) flour, 100 g (4 oz) fat, 100 g (4 oz) cheese. Make a variety of shapes.
MERINGUES	6 egg whites 350 g (12 oz) caster sugar 450 ml (¾ pint) whipped cream.	50 (small) meringue halves	Allow 2 halves per head with cream and 1 half with fruit and cream, or ice cream. Unfilled meringues can be frozen for 3 months.
JELLY	2.75 litres (5 pints)	25	
TRIFLE	2.25 litres (4 pints) custard 25 sponge fingers 1 large can fruit	25	Decorate a large trifle with whipped cream, glacé cherries, chopped nuts, angelica and ratafia biscuits.
FRUIT SALAD	3 kg (7 lb) fruit 1.75–2.25 litres (3–4 pints) sugar syrup 900 ml (1½ pints) cream	25	Can be prepared a day ahead and left submerged in syrup, covered and chilled, but sliced bananas should be added only just before serving.

PARTY DRINKS

BUFFET PARTIES	DINNER PARTIES	DROP-IN-FOR-DRINKS	DRINKS BY THE BOTTLE
Allow for each person 1–2 shorts and 3–6 longer drinks plus coffee. Allow a half-bottle of wine per person.	One bottle of table wine is sufficient for 2 people.	Allow for 3–5 short drinks each and 4–6 small savouries besides the usual olives and nuts.	Bottles of sherry, port and straight vermouths will make approximately 12–16 glasses. In single nips for cocktails, vermouths and spirits give just over 30 drinks a bottle. You will get 16–20 drinks of spirit from a bottle when serving with soda, tonic or other minerals. Bottles of liqueurs should serve 30. A split bottle of soda or tonic gives 2–3 drinks. A 600 ml (1 pint) can of tomato juice gives 4–6 drinks. Dilute a bottle of fruit cordial with 4 litres (7 pints) water for 20–25 drinks.

APPROXIMATE COFFEE AND TEA QUANTITIES

	1 SERVING	24–26 SERVINGS		NOTES
COFFEE ground, hot	200 ml (⅓ pint)	250–275 g (9–10 oz) coffee 3.5 litres (6 pints) water	1.75 litres (3 pints) milk 450 g (1 lb) sugar	If you make the coffee in advance, strain it after infusion. Reheat without boiling. Serve sugar separately.
ground, iced	200 ml (⅓ pint)	350 g (12 oz) coffee 3.5 litres (6 pints) water	1.75 litres (3 pints) milk sugar to taste	Make coffee (half sweetened, half not), strain and chill. Mix with chilled milk. Serve in glasses.
instant, hot	200 ml (⅓ pint)	50–75 g (2–3 oz) coffee 3.5 litres (6 pints) water	1.2 litres (2 pints) milk 450 g (1 lb) sugar	Make coffee in jugs as required. Serve sugar separately.
instant, iced	200 ml (⅓ pint)	75 g (3 oz) coffee 1.2 litres (2 pints) water	3.5 litres (6 pints) milk sugar to taste	Make black coffee (half sweetened, half not) and chill. Mix with chilled creamy milk. Serve in glasses.
TEA Indian, hot	200 ml (⅓ pint)	50 g (2 oz) tea 4.5 litres (8 pints) water	900 ml (1½ pints) milk 450 g (1 lb) sugar	It is better to make tea in several pots rather than one outsize one.
Indian, iced	200 ml (⅓ pint)	75 g (3 oz) tea 4 litres (7 pints) water	1.2 litres (2 pints) milk sugar to taste	Strain tea immediately it has infused. Sweeten half of it. Chill. Serve in chilled glasses.
China	200 ml (⅓ pint)	50 g (2 oz) tea 5 litres (9 pints) water	2–3 lemons 450 g (1 lb) sugar	Infuse China tea for 2 or 3 minutes only. Put a thin lemon slice in each cup before pouring. Serve sugar separately.

The perfect cup of coffee

Whatever type of coffee and whichever coffee-making method you choose, there are seven golden rules which always apply.
1. Always use fresh cold water.
2. Be generous with the coffee, allowing 1 tablespoon per cup.
3. Boil the water and then let it cool, just slightly, to between 92–96°C before pouring it onto the ground coffee.
4. Always make coffee in a warm dry pot.
5. Drink coffee as soon as it is made.
6. Keep coffee in an airtight container, but do not store opened packages of ground coffee for more than 2 weeks.
7. Keep all coffee-making equipment spotlessly clean.

The perfect cup of tea

To make a good cup of tea, use freshly drawn water from the cold tap and warm the teapot just before the kettle comes to the boil. Add the tea, allowing 1 teaspoon for each person and 1 for the pot and – and this is the golden rule of teamaking – pour on the boiling water straightaway, always taking the teapot to the kettle and not the other way round. Leave the tea to infuse for 5–6 minutes and stir before pouring.

RIGHT: A traditional English tea party

LUNCH & DINNER PARTIES

Whatever the occasion, whether you are planning a romantic meal for two or asking your friends to dress up formally; whether one of your number follows a strict diet regime or you feel like creating a carefree holiday atmosphere over the dining table, our ideas and countdowns will enable you to carry it off with ease – and style.

CLOCKWISE: Meringue baskets with lychee and blueberry ice creams; Fish and vine leaf mousses; Parcelled beef with ginger and walnuts; Rosti potatoes

LOW CHOLESTEROL LUNCH FOR FOUR

Watercress and Cucumber Soup
with Granary Soda Rolls

Sweet and Sour Halibut

Brown Rice with Courgettes
and Lemon

Mange touts*

Caramelized Pineapple

Wine suggestion:
Chablis

COUNTDOWN

Up to 2 days in advance
Make the Caramelized pineapple, cover and chill.

The day before or in the morning
Make the Watercress and cucumber soup, cover and chill.

On the morning
Make the Granary soda rolls.
Prepare the mange touts.

1½ hours before the meal
Complete steps 1 and 2 of the Sweet and sour halibut.
Slice the courgettes and grate the lemon rind for the Brown rice with courgettes and lemon.

40 minutes before the meal
Begin to cook the rice.

15 minutes before the meal
Grill the halibut and boil the marinade. Complete the Brown rice with courgettes and lemon and keep warm. Reheat the Watercress and cucumber soup (if serving hot) and garnish. Warm the Granary soda rolls (if wished).

Just before serving
Cook the mange touts for 3–5 minutes. Dish the Sweet and sour halibut, garnish and keep warm.
Remove the pieces of cinnamon stick from the Caramelized pineapple.

WATERCRESS AND CUCUMBER SOUP

1 small onion, peeled and chopped
½ cucumber, diced
600 ml (1 pint) chicken stock
1 bunch of watercress
2 teaspoons lemon juice
salt
freshly ground black pepper
good pinch of ground coriander
300 ml (½ pint) skimmed milk
2 teaspoons cornflour

Preparation time: about 15 minutes
Cooking time: about 35 minutes

1. Put the onion, cucumber and stock into a saucepan and bring to the boil. Cover and simmer for 15 minutes.
2. Remove a few sprigs of watercress and reserve for garnish and chop the remainder.
3. Add the chopped watercress, lemon juice, salt and pepper and coriander to the saucepan, cover and simmer for a further 10 minutes.
4. Cool slightly, then purée, liquidize or sieve the soup. Return to a clean pan, add the skimmed milk and bring back to the boil.
5. Blend the cornflour with a little cold water, add to the soup and bring back to the boil again. Simmer for 2 minutes, then adjust the seasonings. Serve garnished with the reserved watercress sprigs and the Granary soda rolls.

Variation: Serve the soup chilled.

GRANARY SODA ROLLS

MAKES 8 ROLLS
450 g (1 lb) granary flour
2 teaspoons bicarbonate of soda
2 teaspoons cream of tartar
1 teaspoon salt
50 g (2 oz) sunflower margarine
300 ml (½ pint) skimmed milk
1 tablespoon lemon juice

Preparation time: about 15 minutes
Cooking time: about 30 minutes
Oven: 220°C, 425°F, Gas Mark 7

1. Dredge a baking sheet with flour. Put the flour, sifted soda, cream of tartar and salt into a bowl and mix well.
2. Cut the margarine into pieces and rub in until the mixture resembles fine breadcrumbs.
3. Combine the milk and lemon juice and add sufficient to the dry ingredients to mix to a soft but manageable dough.
4. Turn on to a floured surface and shape into an oblong approx 23 × 10 cm (9 × 4 inches). Transfer to the baking sheet, then, using a sharp knife, mark into 8 fingers.
5. Dredge with a little granary flour

and cook in a preheated hot oven for about 30 minutes or until well risen and golden brown. Cool on a wire rack, then cut or break into finger rolls. Serve the rolls either warm or cold, on the day you make them.

Variation: a mixture of half granary and half plain white flour may also be used.

FROM THE LEFT: Granary soda rolls; Watercress and cucumber soup

SWEET AND SOUR HALIBUT

*4 halibut or cod steaks, about
  175–225 g (6–8 oz) each
4 tablespoons medium sherry
1 tablespoon lemon juice
6 tablespoons unsweetened orange
  juice
3 tablespoons soy sauce
2 tablespoons demerara sugar
salt
freshly ground black pepper
225 g (8 oz) can water chestnuts,
  drained and sliced*

TO GARNISH:
*spring onion tassels (page 53)
sprigs of watercress*

Preparation time: 15 minutes, plus
  marinating
Cooking time: about 15 minutes

1. Lay the halibut steaks in a single
layer in a dish or baking tin.
2. Combine the sherry, lemon juice, 4
tablespoons of the orange juice, soy
sauce, sugar and a pinch of salt and
pepper. Pour over the fish, cover and
leave in a cool place to marinate for
about an hour, turning the fish over
once.
3. Place the drained fish in a foil-lined
grill pan and cook under a moderate
heat for 7–8 minutes on each side until
just cooked through. Remove the skin,
if wished.
4. Meanwhile, transfer the marinade
to a small saucepan, adding the remaining orange juice. Bring to the boil
and simmer for a minute or so. Add the
water chestnuts and continue to simmer gently for 3–4 minutes until the
sauce begins to thicken. Taste and
adjust the seasonings.
5. Serve the fish with the sauce and
water chestnuts spooned over and garnished with spring onion tassels and
sprigs of watercress.

BROWN RICE WITH COURGETTES AND LEMON

*225 g (8 oz) brown rice
salt
grated rind of 1 lemon
juice of 1 lemon
350 g (12 oz) courgettes, trimmed
  and thinly sliced
50 g (2 oz) raisins (optional)
freshly ground black pepper*

Preparation time: 10 minutes
Cooking time: 25–30 minutes

1. Cook the rice in plenty of boiling
salted water for 25–30 minutes, until
tender, stirring occasionally.
2. About 10 minutes before the rice is
ready, put the grated lemon rind, juice
and courgettes into a small pan and
toss over a gentle heat. Add the raisins,
if using, and continue cooking for 1–2
minutes. Season well. The courgettes
should still be crisp, not at all soggy.
3. Drain the rice and rinse under hot
water; drain again very thoroughly, and
then add to the courgettes and toss
together. Turn into a warmed dish to
serve with the fish.

CARAMELIZED PINEAPPLE

*1 medium pineapple
1 cinnamon stick
300 ml ($\frac{1}{2}$ pint) water
225 g (8 oz) white sugar
150 ml ($\frac{1}{4}$ pint) unsweetened orange
  juice
2 tablespoons white rum (optional)*

Preparation time: about 20 minutes,
  plus standing
Cooking time: about 20 minutes

1. Cut the pineapple into 1–2 cm ($\frac{1}{2}$–$\frac{3}{4}$
inch) slices and remove the skin. Cut
each slice into quarters or sixths and
place in a serving bowl.
2. Break the cinnamon stick into 2 or 3
pieces, and put into a heavy-based
saucepan with the water and sugar.
Heat gently until the sugar has dissolved, stirring occasionally, then bring
to the boil.
3. Boil hard, uncovered, and without
further stirring until the mixture
becomes a caramel colour. Remove
immediately from the heat and carefully pour in the orange juice.
4. When all the caramel has dissolved
(heating it again gently, if necessary),
pour it over the pineapple, adding the
rum, if using. Cover and leave to stand
in a cool place for at least 6 hours, and
up to 24 hours before serving. It is a
good idea to give it a stir occasionally
so all the pineapple is evenly coated in
the syrup.
5. Before serving, remove the pieces
of cinnamon stick. This dish will keep
in the refrigerator for several days.

*FROM THE TOP: Caramelized pineapple;
Sweet and sour halibut; Brown rice with
courgettes and lemon*

A Simple Lunch For Four

Leeks in Pastry Cases

Trout with Mushrooms, Cream and Ricard

Sugared Petits Pois

Clementines in Orange Liqueur

Almond Petits Fours

Wine suggestion:
Sauvignon de Touraine

COUNTDOWN

Up to 2 days in advance
Make the Almond petits fours. When cool, pack into an airtight tin.

The day before
Prepare the Clementines in orange liqueur. Cover and chill until 30 minutes before serving.

1 hour before the guests arrive
Coat the trout with seasoned flour. Prepare and bake the puff pastry. Prepare the leeks to the end of step 3. Fry the trout.

Just before serving
As you complete the Leeks in pastry cases, start to cook the Sugared petits pois.
Complete steps 3 and 4 of the Trout with mushrooms, cream and Ricard.

LEEKS IN PASTRY CASES

*1 × 375 g (13 oz) pack frozen puff
  pastry, thawed
1 egg, beaten
50 g (2 oz) butter
350 g (12 oz) white part of leeks,
  thinly sliced
juice of ½ lemon
salt
freshly ground black pepper
1 × 150 ml (¼ pint) carton double
  cream
4 sprigs parsley, to garnish*

Preparation time: 15 minutes
Cooking time: 20 minutes
Oven: 220°C, 425°F, Gas Mark 7

1. Roll out the pastry to a rectangle 26 × 15 cm (10 × 6 inches). Cut into 4 pieces, each 13 × 7½ cm (5 × 3 inches).
2. Score each piece lightly in a diamond pattern and brush the tops with beaten egg. Place on a wetted baking sheet and bake in a preheated oven for 20 minutes.
3. Meanwhile, prepare the filling. Melt the butter in a pan, add the leeks and cook gently for about 10 minutes until soft but not browned.
4. Add the lemon juice, salt and pepper to the leeks, stir well, then add the cream. Bring to the boil, stirring constantly. Cook for 2–3 minutes.
5. When the pastry slices are cooked, remove from the oven and cut each one in half horizontally. Divide the leek mixture between the bottom halves of the pastry slices, then replace the pastry top. Serve immediately, garnished with parsley sprigs.

TROUT WITH MUSHROOMS, CREAM AND RICARD

3 tablespoons plain flour
salt
white pepper
4 trout, about 300–350 g (10–12 oz)
  each, cleaned
75 g (3 oz) butter
1 tablespoon vegetable oil
225 g (8 oz) mushrooms, sliced
2 garlic cloves, peeled and crushed
3 tablespoons Ricard
8 tablespoons double cream
sprigs of watercress, to garnish

Preparation time: 4 minutes
Cooking time: 15 minutes

1. Spread the flour out on a plate and season with salt and pepper. Dip the trout in the seasoned flour, turning to coat on all sides.
2. Heat the butter with the oil in a large frying pan. Add the trout and fry over a moderate heat for 5 minutes on each side, until cooked through and browned. Transfer the trout to a warmed serving dish and keep warm.
3. Add the mushrooms and garlic to the pan and fry over a moderate heat for 5 minutes or until softened, stirring from time to time. Add the Ricard and cream and allow to bubble for 1–2 minutes, stirring. Taste and adjust the seasoning, if necessary.
4. Pour the sauce over the fish and serve at once, garnished with watercress sprigs.

FROM THE LEFT: Trout with mushrooms, cream and Ricard; Sugared petits pois (page 66); Leeks in pastry cases

SUGARED PETITS POIS

40 g (1½ oz) butter
450 g (1 lb) frozen petits pois
2 sprigs fresh mint or 1 teaspoon
 dried mint
salt
freshly ground black pepper
1 teaspoon sugar

Preparation time: 5 minutes
Cooking time: 10–15 minutes

1. Melt the butter in a large saucepan, then add the peas and mint, salt, pepper and sugar.
2. Cover the saucepan and allow the peas to heat gently in the butter over a low heat until tender. It is very important to keep the heat low, otherwise the peas will begin to fry in the butter.
3. Without uncovering, toss the pan from time to time to ensure even cooking.
4. Turn into a vegetable dish and serve.

CLEMENTINES IN ORANGE LIQUEUR

175 g (6 oz) caster sugar
600 ml (1 pint) water
8 clementines, peeled, reserving a
 little rind for decoration, and pith
 removed
2 tablespoons orange liqueur
sprig of mint, to decorate

Preparation time: 10 minutes, plus cooling
Cooking time: 20–25 minutes

1. Put the sugar and water into a pan and bring to the boil, stirring constantly until the sugar has dissolved. Add the fruit, bring to the boil, then simmer for 10 minutes. Leave to cool.
2. Remove the fruit, boil down the syrup until reduced to about 300 ml (½ pint). Cool, then add the liqueur. Pour over the clementines and decorate .

ALMOND PETITS FOURS

MAKES ABOUT 24 BISCUITS
100 g (4 oz) ground almonds
100 g (4 oz) caster sugar
few drops almond essence
2 egg whites, whisked until stiff
flaked almonds or glacé cherries, to
  decorate

Preparation time: 15 minutes
Cooking time: 20–25 minutes
Oven: 150°C, 300°F, Gas Mark 2

1. Stir the ground almonds, caster sugar and almond essence into the egg whites.
2. Line a baking sheet with non-stick silicone or greased greaseproof paper. Place the mixture in a piping bag with a large star nozzle and pipe the mixture into circles, S-shapes and sticks. Put a flaked almond or piece of glacé cherry on to each of the petits fours.
3. Place in a preheated oven for 20–25 minutes. Cool on a wire tray.

FROM THE LEFT: Almond petit fours;
Clementines in orange liqueur

CANDLELIGHT DINNER FOR TWO

Parma Ham with Avocado

Stuffed Chicken Breasts

Pilaf Rice with Cèpe Mushrooms

Green Salad*

Monte Bianco

Wine suggestion:
Fleurie

COUNTDOWN

In the morning
Make the Monte Bianco and chill.
Prepare the chicken breasts up to the end of step 3 and chill.
Prepare the Green salad and the dressing.
Make the dressing for the Parma ham with avocado.

1½ hours before the meal
Soak the saffron threads.
Prepare the mushrooms.
Fry the shallots.

¾–1 hour before the meal
Cook the Stuffed chicken breasts and the Pilaf rice with cèpe mushrooms up to the end of step 4.
Complete the Parma ham with avocado.

15–20 minutes before serving
Complete steps 5 and 6 of the Stuffed chicken breasts.
Toss the salad.
Finish the Pilaf rice with cèpe mushrooms and garnish.
Light the candles.

PARMA HAM WITH AVOCADO

1 ripe medium avocado
6 slices Parma ham, about 75 g (3 oz) total weight

DRESSING:
1 tablespoon olive oil
1 teaspoon lemon juice
1 garlic clove, peeled and crushed
2 teaspoons chopped fresh parsley
salt
freshly ground black pepper

Preparation time: 10 minutes

1. Cut the avocado in half and remove the stone. Peel off the skin and cut each half into 3 thick slices.
2. Wrap each slice of ham around a slice of avocado. Arrange on a serving dish or individual dishes.
3. Place all the dressing ingredients in a screw-topped jar and shake well to mix together.
4. Pour the dressing over to serve.

Variation: Prosciutto di Parma con fichi (Parma ham with figs).

Serve 2 ripe figs per person, cutting each down through the centre in a cross. Open out the figs and arrange on

the plates with the slices of Parma ham. Omit the dressing, but sprinkle with black pepper.

CLOCKWISE FROM THE LEFT: Parma ham with avocado; Pilaf rice with cèpe mushrooms; Stuffed chicken breasts

STUFFED CHICKEN BREASTS

2 chicken breasts
40 g (1½ oz) softened butter
50 g (2 oz) ham, finely chopped
1 garlic clove, peeled and crushed
1 tablespoon grated Parmesan
  cheese
½ teaspoon dried or fresh rosemary,
  chopped
salt
freshly ground black pepper
3 tablespoons dry white wine

Preparation time: 15 minutes
Cooking time: 35–40 minutes
Oven: 200°C, 400°F, Gas Mark 6

1. Wipe the chicken breasts with paper towels. Loosen the skin from the breasts.
2. Beat 25 g (1 oz) of the butter with the ham, garlic, Parmesan cheese, rosemary, salt and pepper.
3. Spread the stuffing under the skin of each chicken breast and secure with cocktail sticks.
4. Place the chicken in a baking dish, dot with the remaining butter, sprinkle with salt and pepper and cover with foil. Bake in a preheated moderately hot oven for 30–35 minutes until tender and golden brown.
5. Place the chicken on a warmed serving dish and pour the cooking juices into a small saucepan. Add the wine and bring to the boil. Simmer for 2 minutes, taste and add more salt and pepper if necessary.
6. Pour the sauce over the chicken.

PILAF RICE WITH CEPE MUSHROOMS

450 ml (¾ pint) hot chicken stock
½ teaspoon saffron threads
3 tablespoons olive oil
2 shallots, peeled and finely chopped
100 g (4 oz) Italian rice
1 bay leaf
salt
freshly ground black pepper
1 garlic clove, peeled and crushed
100 g (4 oz) cèpe mushrooms,
  trimmed and sliced or Italian dried
  mushrooms
2 tablespoons dry white wine
2 teaspoons snipped chives, to
  garnish

Preparation time: 10 minutes, plus soaking
Cooking time: 35–40 minutes

Cèpe (or cep) are delicious wild mushrooms which are occasionally available in specialist greengrocers. They have much more flavour than cultivated ones, but these can be used instead.

1. Pour the hot stock over the saffron threads and leave for about 30 minutes.
2. Heat 2 tablespoons olive oil in a saucepan and fry the shallots for about 5 minutes until softened.
3. Stir in the rice and stir until all the grains are evenly coated with oil. Add the stock together with the saffron threads, bay leaf, salt and pepper. Bring to the boil, reduce the heat, cover and cook gently for 30 minutes, until the rice is tender and the stock absorbed.
4. Meanwhile heat the remaining oil in a small pan, add the garlic and cook for 1 minute. Add the cèpe mushrooms and turn in the oil until coated. Add the wine, salt and pepper and cook gently for 15–20 minutes until the mushrooms are tender.
5. Transfer the rice to a warm serving dish and pour the mushrooms over the top. Sprinkle with chives.

MONTE BIANCO

175 g (6 oz) canned chestnut purée
2 tablespoons dark rum
25 g (1 oz) icing sugar

TOPPING:
4 tablespoons double or whipping
 cream
1 teaspoon caster sugar
1 teaspoon dark rum
little plain chocolate, grated

Preparation time: 15 minutes, plus
 chilling

Any left over chestnut purée can be
used for stuffing or frozen for another
time.

1. Beat the chestnut purée until
smooth. Mix in the rum and icing
sugar. Divide between two glasses.
2. Make the topping. Whip the cream
until it just holds its shape. Fold in the
sugar and rum. Swirl on to the chestnut
purée and chill until ready to serve.
3. Outline the swirl of cream with
grated chocolate.

ABOVE: Monte Bianco

GRAND VEGETARIAN DINNER FOR FOUR

Potato Skins with Soured Cream Dip

Roulade with Wine and Mushroom Filling

Lemon Cabbage with Poppyseeds

Hot Garlic Bread

Melon and Raspberries in Sauternes

Wine suggestion:
Côtes de Duras

COUNTDOWN

In the morning

Prepare the potatoes to the end of step 4, cover and chill.
Make the Soured cream dip, cover and chill.
Prepare the filling for the roulade, cover and chill.
Prepare the Garlic bread and wrap in foil.
Prepare the melon and raspberries, cover and chill.
Line the Swiss roll tin.

1½ hours before the meal

Chill the Sauternes.

1 hour before the meal

Prepare and bake the roulade and reheat the filling.
Fry the potato skins and keep them warm.
Cook the green and white cabbage.

RIGHT: Potato skins with soured cream dip

½ hour before serving

Complete steps 3 and 4 of the Lemon cabbage with poppy seeds.
Complete and garnish the roulade.
Reheat the Garlic bread.
Pour the Sauternes over the melon and raspberries.

POTATO SKINS WITH SOURED CREAM DIP

5 large potatoes, scrubbed and dried
150 ml (¼ pint) soured cream
1 teaspoon snipped fresh chives
salt
freshly ground black pepper
vegetable oil, for frying

Preparation time: 10 minutes
Cooking time: 1½–1¾ hours
Oven: 190°C, 375°F, Gas Mark 5

These golden, crisp potato skins are a North American speciality. The amounts given here are plenty for four but an extra potato jacket or two is usually welcomed. Reserve the insides of the potatoes and use them as a topping for a vegetable pie.

1. Prick the potatoes with a fork and bake for about 1¼ hours until tender; really large potatoes will take about 30 minutes longer.
2. Meanwhile prepare the dip. Mix the soured cream with the chives and salt and pepper to taste. Spoon into a bowl, cover and leave to chill in the refrigerator.
3. When the potatoes are cooked, leave them to cool for a few minutes, then cut each one lengthways into 4 long pieces.
4. Using a teaspoon scoop out most of the potato leaving just a thin layer next to the skin.
5. Pour vegetable oil into a small pan to a depth of 7.5 cm (3 inches). There is no need to use a deep frying pan.
6. Heat the oil to 180°–190°C/350°–375°F or until a cube of bread browns in 30 seconds.
7. Fry 4–5 potato skins at a time for about 2 minutes until brown and crisp. Lift from the oil with a slotted spoon and drain on kitchen paper. Keep the skins hot in the oven while the remaining skins are cooked.
8. Either sprinkle the skins lightly with salt or provide salt for guests to help themselves. Serve with the chilled soured cream dip.

ROULADE WITH WINE AND MUSHROOM FILLING

FILLING:

2 teaspoons vegetable oil
1 shallot or small onion, peeled and finely chopped
225 g (8 oz) button mushrooms, chopped
150 ml ($\frac{1}{4}$ pint) dry white wine and vegetable stock mixed or 150 ml ($\frac{1}{4}$ pint) vegetable stock
salt
freshly ground black pepper
3 tablespoons double or whipping cream
1 bunch watercress, chopped, plus a few sprigs to garnish

ROULADE:

5 eggs, separated
$\frac{1}{2}$ teaspoon made English mustard
1 teaspoon vinegar
100 g (4 oz) grated mature Cheddar cheese
1 tablespoon grated Parmesan cheese

Preparation time: 30 minutes
Cooking time: 20 minutes
Oven: 200°C, 400°F, Gas Mark 6

1. Line a 23 × 33 cm (9 × 13 inch) Swiss roll tin with non-stick silicone paper or greased greaseproof paper.
2. First prepare the filling. Heat the oil in a pan with a lid and fry the shallot or onion for 5 minutes until tender but not brown. Add the mushrooms and cook for 2–3 minutes. Pour in the wine and stock and add a little salt and pepper.
3. Cover the pan and cook for about 5 minutes, then remove the lid and boil rapidly to reduce the liquid to about 2 tablespoons. Stir in the cream and set aside while you make the roulade.
4. Whisk the egg yolks, salt, pepper, mustard and vinegar in a small bowl until light and thick. Fold in the grated Cheddar cheese.
5. In a large bowl whisk the egg whites until they are stiff. Take 2 tablespoons of the whisked whites and fold them into the cheese and yolk mixture to loosen it, then spoon the mixture into the remaining whites and gently fold

CLOCKWISE FROM TOP LEFT: Lemon cabbage with poppy seeds; Hot garlic bread; Melon and raspberries in Sauternes; Roulade with wine and mushroom filling

together until smoothly blended.
6. Pour the mixture into the prepared tin and gently smooth the surface. Bake near the top of the oven for 10–12 minutes until risen and golden brown. Remove from the oven but leave the oven on.
7. Sprinkle a sheet of greaseproof paper with Parmesan cheese and turn the roulade on to it. Peel off the silicone paper.
8. Gently reheat the mushroom filling mixture, but do not allow it to boil, and spoon it evenly over the roulade. Sprinkle the filling mixture with watercress, then roll the roulade up, just like a Swiss roll.
9. Lift carefully on to a warm serving dish and replace in the oven for about 4 minutes to heat through.
10. Serve piping hot, garnished with sprigs of watercress.

LEMON CABBAGE WITH POPPY SEEDS

150 ml ($\frac{1}{4}$ pint) water
$\frac{1}{2}$ teaspoon salt
350 g (12 oz) firm white cabbage,
  shredded
350 g (12 oz) spring greens or green
  cabbage, shredded
25 g (1 oz) butter, cut into small
  pieces
grated rind of 1 lemon
1$\frac{1}{2}$ teaspoons poppy seeds
freshly ground black pepper
2–3 tablespoons soured cream, to
  serve (optional)

Preparation time: 5 minutes
Cooking time: 10 minutes

1. Put the water into a large pan, add
the salt and bring to the boil. Add both
green and white cabbage, cover and
simmer steadily for 7–10 minutes. The
cabbage should be crisply tender and
most of the water absorbed.
2. Take the lid off the pan and boil
quickly to reduce any remaining liquid.

3. Add the pieces of butter, lemon
rind, poppy seeds and lots of black
pepper. Stir briefly until the butter is
melted and the cabbage well coated.
4. Spoon the hot cabbage into a warm
dish and serve with soured cream
spooned over the top if liked.

HOT GARLIC BREAD

150 g (5 oz) butter
$\frac{1}{4}$ teaspoon salt
3 garlic cloves, peeled and crushed
2 wholemeal French loaves

Preparation time: 15 minutes
Cooking time: 10 minutes
Oven: 220°C, 425°F, Gas Mark 7

1. Using a fork, mix together the
butter, salt and garlic cloves.
2. Cut the French loaves through into
5 cm (2 inch) thick slices. Spread the
garlic butter on both sides of each slice
and then put the slices back together to
reshape the loaves. Wrap the loaves in
foil and bake them for 10 minutes.

Unwrap carefully and serve the hot
garlic bread immediately.

MELON AND RASPBERRIES IN SAUTERNES

1 small ripe Galia melon
175 g (6 oz) fresh or thawed frozen
  raspberries
$\frac{1}{2}$ bottle Sauternes, chilled

Preparation time: 5 minutes, plus
  chilling

1. Halve the melon and either scoop
out small balls using a melon baller or
cut the flesh into small cubes.
2. Divide the melon and raspberries
equally between 4 glass dishes. Pour
over any melon juice, cover and chill in
the refrigerator for at least 2 hours.
3. Just before serving, pour the chilled
Sauternes into each dish to almost
cover the melon and raspberries. Serve
immediately.

ELEGANT DINNER FOR FOUR

Prawn Pâté

Duck Breasts with Horseradish Sauce and Country Garden Salad

Rose Petal Tart or *Nid d'Abeilles*

Chocolate Truffles

Wine suggestion:
Pomerol

COUNTDOWN

Up to 2 days in advance
Make the Chocolate truffles, pack in an airtight container and chill.
Make the Crème pâtissière for the Nid d'abeilles, cover and chill.

The day before
Make the Prawn pâté and chill.

In the morning
Complete the Nid d'abeilles.
Make the pastry for the Rose petal tart and prepare the rose petals.
Make the Horseradish sauce.
Prepare the Country garden salad and the dressing to serve with it, but do not combine.
Cook the duck breasts and leave to cool.

Just before serving
Garnish the Prawn pâté and make the toast.
Complete steps 6 and 7 of the Duck breasts with horseradish sauce and Country garden salad.
Complete steps 3 and 4 of the Rose petal tart.

PRAWN PATE

100 g (4 oz) butter
1 garlic clove, peeled and crushed
1 teaspoon crushed coriander seeds
100 g (4 oz) peeled prawns, thawed (if frozen)
3 tablespoons double or whipping cream
salt
cayenne pepper

TO GARNISH:
lemon wedges
sprigs of parsley

Preparation time: 5 minutes, plus chilling

1. Melt the butter in a heavy frying pan over a low heat, then add the garlic and coriander and fry gently for 2–3 minutes.
2. Add the prawns and turn to coat with the butter.
3. Transfer the contents of the pan to a food processor or electric blender and process until smooth. Add the cream and process again briefly. Season to taste with salt and cayenne pepper.
4. Spoon the prawn pâté into individual pots and chill. Garnish with lemon wedges and sprigs of parsley and serve with toast.

DUCK BREASTS WITH HORSERADISH SAUCE AND COUNTRY GARDEN SALAD

4 duck breast portions, boned
1 tablespoon sunflower oil
1 large cooking apple, peeled and thickly sliced
2 tablespoons water
3 tablespoons grated horseradish
65 ml (2½ fl oz) soured cream
65 ml (2½ fl oz) plain unsweetened yogurt
1 tablespoon lemon juice

SALAD:
8 leaves batavia, or curly endive, roughly shredded
8 leaves radicchio, roughly shredded
8 leaves sorrel, cut into strips
8 rosettes lamb's lettuce or mâche, roots removed
8 button mushrooms, trimmed and thinly sliced
8 spring onions, cut into strips and blanched

DRESSING:
1 tablespoon lemon juice
1 tablespoon white wine vinegar
2 tablespoons olive oil
2 tablespoons sunflower oil
salt
freshly ground black pepper

Preparation time: 25 minutes, plus cooling
Cooking time: about 30 minutes

Batavia, radicchio, sorrel and lamb's lettuce can be found in summer in specialist greengrocers and some large supermarkets.

1. Brush the duck breasts with the oil.
2. Make the sauce. Put the apple with the water into a small saucepan, cover and cook for about 15 minutes until soft, stirring from time to time. Pass through a food mill into a bowl and leave to cool.
3. When the apple purée is tepid, stir in the horseradish, soured cream, yogurt and lemon juice.
4. Arrange the duck breasts skin side up on the grill rack. Place under a preheated grill and cook for 10 minutes. Turn and cook for a further 6–8 minutes. Cool.
5. Meanwhile make the salad. Arrange the batavia and radicchio, sorrel, lamb's lettuce, mushrooms and spring onions on 4 plates.
6. Thoroughly combine all the dressing ingredients and spoon over each salad.
7. Using a very sharp knife, cut the cooled duck breasts diagonally into thin slices. Arrange a sliced duck breast in a fan shape on each plate. Spoon a portion of horseradish sauce on to the side of each plate and serve immediately.

FROM THE LEFT: Duck breasts with horseradish sauce and Country garden salad; Prawn pâté

ROSE PETAL TART

1 egg white
rose petals
caster sugar
225 g (8 oz) flaky or puff pastry,
* thawed if frozen*
150 ml (¼ pint) plain unsweetened
* yogurt*
1 egg yolk
2 tablespoons caster sugar
300 ml (½ pint) double or whipping
* cream, whipped*
2 tablespoons rosewater

Preparation time: 20 minutes, plus
  cooling
Cooking time: about 25 minutes
Oven: 200°C, 400°F, Gas Mark 6

1. Whisk the egg white until stiff peaks
form. Gently wipe the rose petals,
brush each one with beaten egg white,
then sprinkle with a little sugar and
leave in a cool place to dry.
2. Roll out the pastry to about 5 mm (¼
inch) thickness and cut out a 25 cm (10
inch) circle. Place on a lightly moistened baking sheet and bake for about
20–25 minutes until the pastry is well
risen, brown and dry underneath.
Leave for at least 1 hour to cool
completely.
3. Fold the yogurt, egg yolk and sugar
into the whipped cream. Whisk in the
rosewater.
4. Spoon the rosewater cream over
the pastry base. Decorate with the
frosted rose petals and serve
immediately.

NID D'ABEILLES

300 g (11 oz) plain flour
100 g (4 oz) butter
120 ml (4 fl oz) milk
10 g (¼ oz) dried yeast
1 egg, lightly beaten
50 g (2 oz) unsalted butter
75 g (3 oz) caster sugar
25 g (1 oz) honey
25 g (1 oz) flaked almonds
1 tablespoon Kirsch

CREME PATISSIERE:
2 eggs
75 g (3 oz) vanilla sugar
25 g (1 oz) cornflour
250 ml (8 fl oz) milk

Preparation time: 35 minutes, plus
  proving
Cooking time: 40 minutes
Oven: 200°C, 400°F, Gas Mark 6

1. Make the crème pâtissière. Whisk
the eggs and sugar in a mixing bowl
until light and creamy, then whisk in
the cornflour.
2. Heat the milk to simmering point,
then pour over the sugar, egg and
cornflour mixture. Stir well.
3. Return the mixture to the rinsed
pan. Stirring constantly, heat until the
sauce thickens.
4. Pour into a clean bowl and whisk
briefly, then cool. To store, rub the
surface with a lump of butter while still
hot as this prevents a crust forming and
cover with an airtight lid.
5. Sift the flour into a mixing bowl and
rub in the butter.
6. Heat the milk to blood heat. Dissolve the yeast in the milk.
7. Add the egg and milk to the flour
and knead to form a smooth dough.
Leave to prove in a warm place until it
doubles its volume. Knock back the
dough. Put it in a buttered 20 cm (8
inch) cake tin. Leave to prove again
until well risen.
8. Melt the butter, sugar and honey in
a saucepan over a gentle heat, stirring
until the sugar dissolves. Spread the
mixture over the risen dough and
sprinkle the almonds on top.
9. Bake in a preheated oven for 30
minutes. After 20 minutes of the cooking time, cover the cake with buttered
foil.
10. Remove the cake from the oven
and turn out on to a wire tray. Leave to
cool.
11. When the cake is cold, split it in
half horizontally.

12. Beat the Kirsch into the cold
crème pâtissière. Spread the cream
over the lower half of the cake and put
the other half back on top.

CHOCOLATE TRUFFLES

MAKES ABOUT 25
100 g (4 oz) plain chocolate, broken
* into pieces*
90 g (3½ oz) unsalted butter
20 g (¾ oz) icing sugar
1 egg yolk
1½ tablespoons dark rum
40 g (1½ oz) cocoa powder

Preparation time: 10 minutes, plus
  cooling
Cooking time: 5 minutes

1. Put the chocolate into a bowl
placed over a pan of simmering water
and leave the chocolate to melt.
2. Beat the butter, icing sugar, egg yolk
and rum into the melted chocolate.
Chill in the refrigerator.
3. Fit a piping bag with a 2 cm (¾ inch)
plain tube and fill it with the mixture.
4. Pipe 25 pieces of truffle mixture on
a baking sheet. Sprinkle cocoa powder
on top and shake the tray until the
truffles are well coated.
5. Shape the truffles roughly into balls.
Shake them in cocoa powder again and
chill until needed.

*CLOCKWISE FROM THE TOP: Rose petal
tart; Chocolate truffles; Nid d'abeilles*

MEDITERRANEAN DINNER FOR SIX

Taramasalata and Melitzano Salata

Lamb stuffed with Pine Nuts and Coriander

Rice *

Orange, Onion and Olive Salad

Baklava

Vanilla Ice Cream

Wine suggestions:
Starter: Retsina
Main course: Penedès

COUNTDOWN

The day before
Make the Taramasalata, cover and chill.
Make the Melitzano salata, cover and chill.
Make the French dressing.
Make the Vanilla ice cream.
Prepare the Baklava up to the end of step 6 and the syrup up to the end of step 9.

In the morning
Cook the Baklava, pour over the syrup and leave to cool.

About 3½ hours before the meal
Prepare, stuff and cook the lamb.

½ hour before the meal
Cook the rice and keep it warm.
Arrange the individual salads.

Just before serving
Warm the pitta bread, garnish the Melitzano salata and the Taramasalata. Transfer the Vanilla ice cream from the freezer to the refrigerator 15 minutes before serving.
Carve the lamb.
Dress the individual salads.
Divide the Baklava into portions.

TARAMASALATA

4 large slices white bread, crusts removed
6 tablespoons cold water
100 g (4 oz) skinned smoked cod's roe or salted tarama (grey mullet's roe)
1 large garlic clove, peeled and crushed
3 tablespoons lemon juice
freshly ground black pepper
150 ml (¼ pint) olive oil

TO GARNISH:
black olives
sprigs of parsley

Preparation time: 20 minutes

The Taramasalata and the Melitzana Salata both serve four, so if you plan to serve just one of them, make a larger quantity.

1. Soak the bread in the cold water for 10 minutes, and then squeeze it lightly, without leaving it too dry.
2. Put the bread into a liquidizer or food processor with the cod's roe or tarama, garlic, lemon juice and black pepper to taste. Blend to a smooth paste.
3. Gradually add the olive oil, as for mayonnaise, blending the mixture thoroughly after each addition.
4. Serve the prepared taramasalata with warmed pitta bread and garnished with black olives and sprigs of parsley.

MELITZANO SALATA
(AUBERGINE PUREE)

2 large aubergines, about 450 g (1 lb) total weight
1 small onion, peeled and roughly chopped
2 garlic cloves, peeled and roughly chopped
4 tablespoons olive oil
2 tablespoons lemon juice
salt
freshly ground black pepper

TO GARNISH:
sprigs of parsley
slices of lime

Preparation time: 10 minutes
Cooking time: about 20 minutes

This Greek dip has a much better flavour if the aubergines are scorched over the barbecue; if this is impossible bake them in a preheated oven (180°C, 350°F, Gas Mark 4) for 45–50 minutes.

1. Thread the aubergines on to a skewer. Place them on the greased grill of a preheated barbecue and cook for 10 minutes, then turn the aubergines over and cook for a further 10 minutes.
2. Leave the aubergines until they are sufficiently cool to handle, then peel them and chop the flesh on a wooden board.
3. Put the aubergine flesh into a liquidizer or food processor with the onion,

garlic, olive oil, lemon juice and salt and pepper to taste; blend until smooth. Cover and chill.
4. Transfer the purée to a bowl and garnish with the sprigs of parsley and slices of lime. Serve with pitta bread.

FROM THE TOP: Melitzano salata; Taramasalata

LAMB STUFFED WITH PINE NUTS AND CORIANDER

2 kg (4½ lb) leg of lamb, boned and
  trimmed of fat
3 tablespoons olive oil
1 tablespoon coriander seeds,
  crushed
4 garlic cloves, peeled and crushed
salt
freshly ground black pepper

STUFFING:
65 g (2½ oz) long-grain rice, cooked
  and drained
50 g (2 oz) currants or seedless
  raisins
50 g (2 oz) pine nuts
½ teaspoon ground cinnamon
salt
freshly ground black pepper
½ egg, beaten

Preparation time: 10 minutes
Cooking time: 2½–3 hours
Oven: 180°C, 350°F, Gas Mark 4

1. Pat the lamb dry with absorbent paper towels. Combine the oil with the coriander seeds, garlic and salt and pepper to taste and rub the lamb inside and out with the mixture.
2. In a bowl combine all the stuffing ingredients and stir well to mix. Spoon into the cavity in the lamb. Roll the lamb and tie in several places with fine string, or secure with meat skewers.
3. Place the stuffed lamb in a large roasting tin and roast in a preheated moderate oven for 2½–3 hours, until done to your liking, basting from time to time.
4. Transfer the lamb to a warmed carving dish and serve carved into slices.

ORANGE, ONION AND OLIVE SALAD

6 seedless oranges, peeled
1 medium red-skinned onion, peeled
100 g (4 oz) black olives, pitted
cos lettuce or chicory leaves, washed
  and dried
sprigs of parsley, to garnish
French dressing (page 121)

Preparation time: 10 minutes

1. Thinly slice the oranges over a plate to catch the juice. Slice the onion paper-thin, separate it into rings and cut the rings in half.
2. Arrange the orange and onion slices alternately, overlapping, on a serving plate and put the olives in the centre of the salad. Tuck the lettuce or chicory leaves around the edge and garnish with the parsley. Immediately before serving, pour over the French dressing.

BAKLAVA

(SPICED PHYLLO PIE)

225 g (8 oz) butter, melted
20–24 sheets phyllo pastry
225 g (8 oz) shelled pistachio nuts,
  chopped
25 g (1 oz) caster sugar
1 teaspoon ground cinnamon

SYRUP:
225 g (8 oz) sugar
150 ml (¼ pint) water
juice and grated rind of ½ lemon
2 tablespoons orange-flower water

TO DECORATE:
1 tablespoon shelled pistachio nuts,
  chopped

Preparation time: about 45 minutes,
  plus chilling
Cooking time: 45–50 minutes
Oven: 180°C, 350°F, Gas Mark 4;
  then: 220°C, 425°F, Gas Mark 7

1. Brush a rectangular dish 30 × 20 cm (12 × 8 inches) with the melted butter.
2. Lay half the sheets of phyllo pastry in the dish, brushing the top of each sheet with melted butter as it is laid down.
3. Mix the chopped pistachio nuts with the sugar and cinnamon and sprinkle over the pastry sheets.
4. Lay the remaining sheets of phyllo pastry on top, brushing each one with melted butter as before.
5. Brush the top of the pie with melted butter.
6. Using a sharp knife, cut lengthways lines in the pastry and cut across these diagonally to make diamond shapes. Cover and chill.
7. For the syrup, put the sugar, water, lemon juice and lemon rind into a pan, and stir over a gentle heat until the sugar has dissolved. Simmer steadily until the syrup is thick enough to coat the back of a spoon.
8. Stir in the orange-flower water and simmer for a further 1–2 minutes.
9. Allow the syrup to cool, then chill in the refrigerator.
10. Place the baklava in a preheated oven and bake for 30 minutes, then raise the oven temperature and bake for a further 10 minutes until the baklava is puffed and golden. Ꞙ
11. Remove from the oven and immediately pour the chilled syrup over. Sprinkle with pistachios and cool.
12. Divide the baklava into portions, along the lines that were cut before baking, and serve.

Ꞙ Freeze cooled baklava without its syrup topping. Reheat from frozen at 190°C, 375°F, Gas Mark 5 for 25–30 minutes. Remove from the oven, prepare the syrup and pour over immediately. Cool.

CLOCKWISE FROM TOP LEFT: Baklava; Vanilla ice cream; Lamb stuffed with pine nuts and coriander; Orange, onion and olive salad

VANILLA ICE CREAM

3 egg yolks
100 g (4 oz) vanilla sugar
250 ml (8 fl oz) milk
300 ml (½ pint) double cream

Preparation time: 20 minutes, plus
   cooling and freezing
Cooking time: 2 minutes

1. Whisk the yolks and sugar until pale and creamy. Heat the milk to simmering point and pour over the yolks and sugar. Blend well.
2. Pour the mixture into the rinsed pan and heat until it coats the back of a wooden spoon. Pour into a bowl and cool.
3. Whisk the double cream until it thickens, then fold into the custard.

4. Pour the mixture into a freezer container and place in the freezer. Freeze for about 2–3 hours or until it begins to set at the edges.
5. Remove the ice cream from the freezer and whisk thoroughly to break down the ice crystals. Return to the freezer for 1–2 hours or until firm. F

F Can be frozen for up to 3 months.

BIRTHDAY DINNER FOR SIX

Avocado and Mango Salad with Raspberry Vinaigrette Dressing

Parcelled Beef with Ginger and Walnuts

Braised Red Cabbage with Apples

Green and White Broccoli*

Rosti Potatoes with Parmesan Cheese

Coffee and Vanilla Mousse

Wine suggestions:
Starter: dry Champagne
Main course:
Château-bottled Médoc

COUNTDOWN

The day before
Make the Coffee and vanilla mousse.

Up to 12 hours before the meal
Make the Raspberry vinaigrette dressing for the Avocado and mango salad. Thaw the puff pastry for the Parcelled beef with ginger and walnuts if it is frozen.

3 hours before the meal
Brown the beef and leave it to cool. Make the sauce for the beef (step 8). Prepare the broccoli.

1¼ hours before the meal
Make the stuffing for the beef (steps 2 and 3).
Complete steps 4 to 6 of the Parcelled beef with ginger and walnuts.
Cook the Braised red cabbage with apples.

50 minutes before the meal.
Cook the beef.

40 minutes before the meal
Complete steps 1 and 2 of the Rosti potatoes with Parmesan cheese.

30 minutes before the meal
Cook the Rosti potatoes with Parmesan cheese and keep warm.

20 minutes before the meal
Complete steps 3 and 4 of the Avocado and mango salad with Raspberry vinaigrette dressing.

10 minutes before the meal
Cook the broccoli.
Reheat the sauce for the Parcelled beef with ginger and walnuts.

AVOCADO AND MANGO SALAD WITH RASPBERRY VINAIGRETTE DRESSING

3 ripe avocados
1 large ripe mango
little extra lemon juice
sprigs of dill or continental parsley, to garnish

DRESSING:
100 g (4 oz) raspberries, fresh or frozen
150 ml (¼ pint) sunflower or vegetable oil
2 tablespoons white wine vinegar
3 tablespoons lemon juice
1½ teaspoons caster sugar

Preparation time: about 20 minutes, plus marinating

1. Make the dressing. Put the raspberries into a bowl then add the oil, vinegar and 1 tablespoon of the lemon juice and mash well together. If using frozen raspberries allow them to thaw partially before mashing. Leave to stand for 30 minutes.
2. Liquidize or purée the raspberry mixture then sieve to remove all the pips. Put into a clean bowl and beat in the sugar.
3. Just before serving, peel, quarter and slice the avocados and the mango and dip the avocado slices in the remaining lemon juice.
4. Spoon 2–3 tablespoons of the raspberry vinaigrette on to 6 side plates. Arrange slices of drained avocado and mango over the sauce, and garnish with a sprig of dill or continental parsley. Serve within an hour to prevent the avocados from discolouring.

RIGHT: *Avocado and mango salad with Raspberry vinaigrette dressing*

PARCELLED BEEF WITH GINGER AND WALNUTS

65 g (2½ oz) butter
1 kg (2 lb) fillet of beef
2 onions, peeled and thinly sliced
2–3 pieces stem ginger, finely
  chopped
50 g (2 oz) walnut halves, roughly
  chopped
2 tablespoons chopped fresh parsley
¼ teaspoon dried thyme
salt
freshly ground black pepper
350 g (12 oz) puff pastry
beaten egg, to glaze
sprigs of chervil, to garnish

SAUCE:
1 tablespoon plain flour
300 ml (½ pint) ginger wine
300 ml (½ pint) beef stock
1 tablespoon lemon juice

Preparation time: about 20 minutes
Cooking time: about 1 hour
Oven: 220°C, 425°F, Gas Mark 7

Make sure you buy the thick end of the fillet for this recipe. The cooking time is for rare cooked beef, so increase it by 15 to 30 minutes if you want the meat medium or well cooked. This dish is also excellent served cold with salads.

1. Melt the butter in a frying pan and fry the piece of beef all over until it is well sealed and browned. Remove the beef from the pan and leave to cool.
2. Fry the onions in the same fat until golden brown. Remove them to a bowl with a draining spoon, leaving the excess fat in the pan.
3. Add the ginger, walnuts, parsley, thyme and salt and pepper to the onions and mix well. Cool.
4. On a lightly floured surface roll out the pastry thinly until it is large enough to enclose the beef. Spoon the onion mixture over the centre of the pastry and place the beef on top.
5. Wrap the beef in the pastry, sealing the edges with beaten egg and keeping the joins underneath. Place on a well greased baking sheet.
6. Glaze all over with beaten egg. Roll out the pastry trimmings and cut out 6 or 8 leaves. Arrange the leaves over the centre of the joint and glaze again. Make a hole in the centre of the pastry for the steam to escape.
7. Cook in a preheated hot oven for 50 minutes for rare beef, increasing the time by 15–20 minutes for medium beef and by 30–40 for really well cooked beef. When it is sufficiently browned, lay a sheet of greaseproof paper over the pastry.
8. Meanwhile make the sauce. Stir the flour into the pan juices and cook for a minute or so. Gradually add the ginger wine and stock and bring to the boil. Season well, then add the lemon juice

and simmer for about 5 minutes until the sauce is slightly reduced and thickened. Strain into a jug or sauce boat and keep warm.

9. Remove the beef carefully to a serving dish, taking care not to break the pastry case, and garnish with the sprigs of chervil. Cut into thick slices and serve with the sauce.

BRAISED RED CABBAGE WITH APPLES

1 kg (2 lb) red cabbage
2 tablespoons oil
1 onion, peeled and thinly sliced
3 tablespoons wine vinegar
3 tablespoons water
salt
freshly ground black pepper
¼ teaspoon ground cinnamon
3 tablespoons demerara sugar
2 dessert apples, cored and chopped

Preparation time: about 10 minutes
Cooking time: about 1¼ hours
Oven: 180°C, 350°F, Gas Mark 4

1. Quarter the cabbage, remove the core and shred finely.
2. Heat the oil in a flameproof casserole or saucepan and fry the onion gently until soft but not coloured.
3. Add the cabbage and mix until covered in oil. Add the vinegar, water, salt and pepper, cinnamon and sugar and bring to the boil, stirring occasionally.
4. Add the apples, mix well and cover the pan, if it is a flameproof one. Otherwise transfer the mixture to a casserole and cover.
5. Cook in a preheated moderate oven for about 1 hour. Give a good stir, adjust the seasonings and serve.

FROM THE LEFT: Parcelled beef with ginger and walnuts; Braised red cabbage with apples; Rosti potatoes with Parmesan cheese; Coffee and vanilla mousse

ROSTI POTATOES WITH PARMESAN CHEESE

1 kg (2 lb) potatoes
1 medium onion, peeled
3 tablespoons grated Parmesan
  cheese (preferably freshly grated)
salt
freshly ground black pepper
good pinch of grated or ground
  nutmeg
2 tablespoons oil
25 g (1 oz) butter, melted

Preparation time: about 10 minutes
Cooking time: about 25 minutes

1. Peel the potatoes and grate fairly coarsely with the onion.
2. Put into a bowl with 2 tablespoons of the Parmesan cheese, salt, pepper and nutmeg and mix well.
3. Heat the oil in a heavy-based frying pan about 25 cm (10 inches) in diameter. Add the potato mixture and press well down to make an even cake.
4. Cook over a gentle heat for about 20 minutes, until the underside of the cake is golden brown and the potato almost tender. Loosen occasionally with a palette knife.
5. Brush the top of the potato cake lightly with melted butter and sprinkle with the remaining cheese. Put under a moderate grill and cook until a good golden brown.
6. Slide the potato cake carefully on to a warmed serving plate and keep warm until ready to serve.

COFFEE AND VANILLA MOUSSE

4 eggs, separated
175 g (6 oz) caster sugar
6 tablespoons warm water
4 teaspoons powdered gelatine
½ teaspoon vanilla essence
2 tablespoons coffee essence or very
  strong black coffee
300 ml (½ pint) double cream
2 tablespoons milk
about 40 g (1½ oz) ratafia biscuits
25 g (1 oz) luxury plain chocolate,
  coarsely grated

Preparation time: about 30 minutes
Cooking time: 5 minutes

Once the gelatine is mixed into the two separate mousse mixtures, you must work very quickly before it sets, for if it begins to set too firmly it will not swirl easily and evenly and will not give such an attractive and smooth effect.

1. Put the egg yolks, sugar and 4 tablespoons of the warm water into a large mixing bowl and whisk until very thick and creamy and the whisk leaves a heavy trail when lifted. This may be done in a large electric mixer or with a hand-held mixer over a pan of very gently simmering water.
2. Meanwhile put the remaining 2 tablespoons of water, 2 teaspoons of the gelatine and the vanilla essence into a small bowl or jug and dissolve over a pan of gently simmering water. Put the remaining gelatine and the coffee essence into another small bowl or jug and dissolve in the same way. Allow to cool a little.
3. Whip the cream and milk together until thick but not too stiff. Whisk the egg whites until very stiff.
4. Roughly crumble the ratafia biscuits, reserving a few for decoration.
5. Put half the creamed mousse mixture into a separate bowl. To one portion, fold in first the vanilla gelatine liquid, followed by half the cream and half the egg white, until evenly blended.
6. Then, to the other portion, fold in the coffee gelatine liquid followed by the remaining cream and finally the remaining egg white,
7. Put alternate large spoonfuls of the mousse mixtures into a glass serving bowl, sprinkling with the ratafias and most of the grated chocolate as you go. Then quickly take a knife and swirl it around in the bowl to give a marbled effect by partly mixing the two colours together. Do not overmix. Allow the top to settle and sprinkle with the remaining chocolate.
8. Top with the reserved ratafias and chill until set.

FISH DINNER FOR EIGHT

Vine Leaf and Fish Mousses

Sea Trout en Croûte with Tomato Basil Sauce

Braised Fennel with Yogurt

French Beans*

Riced Sweet Potatoes

Green Fruit Salad with Hazelnut and Orange Tuiles

Wine suggestion:
Pouilly Blanc Fumé

COUNTDOWN

Up to 2 days before
Make the Hazelnut and orange tuiles and store in an airtight container.

24 hours before the meal
Make the Vine leaf and fish mousses, cover and chill.

In the morning
Fillet and skin the sea trout and chill. Prepare the stuffing for the sea trout. Thaw the puff pastry if it is frozen. Make the Green fruit salad, cover and chill.

2 hours before the meal
Complete steps 4–7 of the Sea trout en croûte.
Make the Tomato basil sauce.
Prepare the fennel.

1¼ hours before the meal
Cook the fennel.

1 hour before the meal
Cook the Sea trout en croûte.
Prepare the Riced sweet potatoes.
Prepare the French beans.
Turn out the Vine leaf and fish mousses and garnish.

15 minutes before the meal
Cook the Riced sweet potatoes.
Complete steps 3 and 4 of the Braised fennel with yogurt.
Reheat the Tomato basil sauce.

Just before serving
Cook the French beans for 5 minutes.
Complete step 11 of the Sea trout en croûte with Tomato basil sauce.
Garnish the Braised fennel with yogurt and the Riced sweet potatoes.

VINE LEAF AND FISH MOUSSES

approx. 100 g (4 oz) vine leaves in
* brine (canned or in packets)*
100 g (4 oz) smoked salmon
1 kg (2 lb) plaice fillets, skinned
4 eggs
3 tablespoons dry white wine
5 tablespoons double cream
1 teaspoon lemon juice
salt
freshly ground black pepper
good pinch of ground coriander
lemon slices, to garnish

Preparation time: about 30 minutes, plus chilling
Cooking time: 40 minutes
Oven: 160°C, 325°F, Gas Mark 3

1. Rinse the vine leaves in water, as directed on the can or packet, to remove excess brine. Drain well.
2. Lightly grease 8 individual ramekin dishes and completely line the inside of each one with a double layer of vine leaves.
3. Cut the salmon into strips and roll into 8 larger and 8 smaller rolls.
4. Purée, mince or liquidize the plaice and beat in the eggs, followed by the wine, cream, lemon juice, salt and pepper and ground coriander.
5. Put a spoonful of the fish mixture into each ramekin, place one of the larger smoked salmon rolls on each and cover with the remaining fish purée.
6. Stand the ramekins in a roasting tin with water to come at least half way up the sides of the dishes. Cover with foil and cook in a preheated moderate oven for about 40 minutes or until set and cooked through.
7. Leave to cool, then chill. Turn out carefully and serve each one topped with a smoked salmon roll and a lemon slice. Serve with thinly sliced brown bread and butter.

Variation: If preferred, the mousses may be served warm (but not hot) rather than chilled. In this case, leave them to stand for 10 minutes before turning out.

RIGHT: Vine leaf and fish mousses

SEA TROUT EN CROUTE WITH TOMATO BASIL SAUCE

1.5–1.75 kg (3½–4 lb) sea trout or salmon, cleaned and head removed

STUFFING:
40 g (1½ oz) butter
1 onion, peeled and finely chopped
100 g (4 oz) button mushrooms, chopped
finely grated rind of 1 lemon
2 tablespoons freshly chopped basil leaves or 1 tablespoon dried basil
salt
freshly ground black pepper
¼ teaspoon ground coriander
100 g (4 oz) fresh white breadcrumbs
1 egg yolk
1 tablespoon lemon juice
450 g (1 lb) puff pastry, thawed if frozen
beaten egg, to glaze

TOMATO BASIL SAUCE:
25 g (1 oz) butter or margarine
1 onion, peeled and finely chopped
2½ tablespoons tomato purée
450 g (1 lb) tomatoes, peeled and chopped
250 ml (8 fl oz) dry white wine
4 tablespoons water
1 tablespoon freshly chopped basil or 1½ teaspoons dried basil
1 tablespoon lemon juice
1 teaspoon light soft brown sugar

TO GARNISH:
cherry tomatoes
sprigs of fresh basil or watercress

Preparation time: 45–60 minutes
Cooking time: about 1 hour
Oven: 200°C, 400°F, Gas Mark 6
then: 190°C, 375°F, Gas Mark 5

1. Fillet the fish and remove the skin (page 16).
2. Make the stuffing. Melt the fat in a frying pan and fry the onion until it is soft but not coloured, then add the chopped mushrooms and fry gently for a few minutes. Turn the mixture into a bowl and mix in the lemon rind, basil, salt, pepper and coriander, followed by the breadcrumbs.
3. Add the egg yolk and lemon juice and bind together, then leave until cold.
4. Lay one fillet of fish on a board and spread the stuffing over it. Cover with the second fillet to reassemble into a fish shape.
5. Roll out about three-quarters of the pastry thinly and use to enclose the fish, keeping to the shape as much as possible and sealing the edges with beaten egg.
6. Place the fish carefully on a greased baking sheet and brush all over with beaten egg.
7. Roll out the remaining pastry and the trimmings very thinly and use to cut into 'scales'. Arrange all over the fish, working from tail to head and glazing each one with beaten egg as it is added. Cut out an enlarged piece for the tail and an eye for the head. Position these, glaze, and then glaze the whole fish again.
8. Cook in a preheated moderately hot oven for about 30 minutes. Reduce the oven temperature and cook for a further 25–30 minutes until a good golden brown. When the pastry is sufficiently browned, cover it with a sheet of greaseproof paper.
9. Make the sauce. Melt the fat in a pan and fry the onion slowly until soft but not coloured. Add the tomato purée and cook for a minute or so. Add the tomatoes, wine and water and bring to the boil. Season, cover and simmer for 15 minutes.
10. Liquidize or purée the sauce and then sieve to remove the seeds. Return to a clean pan and add the basil. Adjust the seasonings, add the lemon juice and sugar and simmer for a minute or so. Reheat when required to serve with the fish.
11. Carefully transfer the sea trout en croûte to a large serving dish and garnish with basil leaves and cherry tomatoes. Serve the sauce separately in a sauce boat or jug.

FROM THE LEFT: Riced sweet potatoes; Braised fennel with yogurt; Sea trout en croûte with Tomato basil sauce

BRAISED FENNEL WITH YOGURT

3–4 small bulbs fennel
450 ml (¾ pint) chicken or vegetable
  stock
salt
freshly ground black pepper
good pinch of ground coriander
4–6 tablespoons plain unsweetened
  yogurt
1 tablespoon cornflour

Preparation time: about 15 minutes
Cooking time: 1–1¼ hours
Oven: 190°C, 375°F, Gas Mark 5

1. Trim the fennel and reserve any feathery leaves for garnish. Cut each bulb into quarters or sixths depending on its size and lay them in a shallow ovenproof dish in a single layer.
2. Bring the stock to the boil, season well with salt, pepper and coriander and pour over the fennel. Cover tightly with a lid or foil and cook in a preheated moderate oven for 45–60 minutes or until tender.
3. Drain the cooking juices into a saucepan and boil hard, uncovered, until reduced by half; meanwhile keep the fennel warm in a serving dish.
4. Blend the yogurt with the cornflour and add to the juices. Bring back to the boil and simmer for a minute or so. Adjust the seasonings and pour back over the fennel. Garnish with the fennel leaves and serve immediately.

RICED SWEET POTATOES

1 kg (2 lb) sweet potatoes
50 g (2 oz) butter
150 ml (¼ pint) water
salt
freshly ground black pepper
grated or ground nutmeg
chopped fresh parsley, to garnish

Preparation time: 20 minutes
Cooking time: about 12 minutes

1. Peel the potatoes and grate coarsely either in a food processor or by hand.
2. Melt the butter in a pan, add the potatoes and toss until evenly coated in butter.
3. Add the water, salt, pepper and a touch of nutmeg and bring to the boil. Cover the pan and simmer gently for 5–10 minutes until the potatoes are tender but not soggy. Taste and adjust the seasonings including the nutmeg.
4. Drain the potatoes, place in a warmed serving dish and sprinkle liberally with parsley.

GREEN FRUIT SALAD

2 limes
300 ml (½ pint) water
175 g (6 oz) caster sugar
150 ml (¼ pint) white wine
1 small green-fleshed melon (e.g.
  Ogen or Honeydew)
225 g (8 oz) green grapes
  (preferably small seedless variety)
1 firm pear, peeled, cored and sliced
2 grapefruit or sweeties
3 kiwi fruit
1 ripe avocado
2 green-skinned dessert apples

Preparation time: about 40 minutes,
  plus chilling
Cooking time: about 9 minutes

The sweetie is one of the newest of the exotic fruit imports from Israel and is available from specialist greengrocers. A cross between a grapefruit and a pomelo, it has a greenish skin and is extremely juicy. As its name implies, it is very much sweeter than ordinary grapefruit.

1. Using a potato peeler pare the rind thinly from the limes, and cut it into julienne strips. Put them into a sauce-pan with the water, bring to the boil and simmer for 5 minutes.
2. Strain the lime rind; reserve the cooking liquor and make it up to 300 ml (½ pint). Add the sugar, heat slowly until it has dissolved, then boil for 2–3 minutes. Add the wine and pour the syrup into a glass serving bowl.
3. Halve the melon, remove the seeds, then scoop out the flesh with a melon baller. The flesh can also be cubed, if you prefer. Add the melon to the syrup in the bowl.
4. Wash the grapes, removing any stalks, and add them to the syrup. If you are using a seeded variety, either scoop out the seeds or if they are large grapes, cut them in half and take out the seeds. Do not remove the skins as they are required for colour.
5. Peel, core and slice the pear; cut away the peel and pith from the grape-fruit or sweeties and ease out the segments from between the mem-branes, cut in half if large and add both to the syrup.
6. Peel and slice the kiwi fruit and add to the salad. Cover, then chill for 2–3 hours.
7. Squeeze the juice from the limes into a bowl. Quarter, peel and dice the

avocado and toss it in the lime juice. Drain the avocado and add it to the salad, then quarter, core and slice the apples and toss them in the lime juice. Add the apples to the salad with the remaining lime juice from tossing the fruit.

8. Mix gently and sprinkle with the reserved julienne strips of lime peel. Chill before serving with the Hazelnut and orange tuiles.

HAZELNUT AND ORANGE TUILES

MAKES ABOUT 20
1 egg white
50 g (2 oz) caster sugar
25 g (1 oz) plain flour, sifted
25 g (1 oz) toasted hazelnuts, finely
  chopped
finely grated rind of ½ orange
25 g (1 oz) butter, melted

Preparation time: 10 minutes
Cooking time: about 30 minutes
Oven: 190°C, 375°F, Gas Mark 5

1. Line 2 baking sheets with non-stick silicone paper. Lightly grease a rolling pin and stand it on a wire rack.

2. Whisk the egg white until very stiff and then fold in the sugar, flour and hazelnuts and finally the orange rind. Mix gently but thoroughly.

3. Finally fold in the cooled but still runny butter.

4. Put teaspoons of the mixture on to the baking sheets, keeping them well apart and spread out thinly. 4 or 5 per sheet is ample.

5. Cook in a preheated moderately hot oven for about 8 minutes or until browned around the edges and a very

pale brown in the centre.

6. Cool only very briefly and then remove from the paper, using a palette knife, and lay over the rolling pin so they form a curl as they cool and set. When cold and firm, remove and store in an airtight container.

7. Use the rest of the mixture to make further tuiles in the same way.

FROM THE LEFT: Hazelnut and orange tuiles; Green fruit salad

BLACK TIE DINNER FOR EIGHT

Pink Trout Fillets in Aspic

Cream of Carrot and Dill Soup

Roast Goose with Damson Sauce

Fantail Potatoes

Celeriac Purée

Wedges of Cabbage*

Meringue Baskets with Lychee and Blueberry Ice Creams

Wine suggestions:
Starter:
Gewürztraminer Prince d'Alsace
Main course:
Clos du Roi
Dessert:
Johannisberger Riesling Spätlese

COUNTDOWN

Up to 2 days in advance
Make the Meringue baskets and store in an airtight container.
Make the Lychee ice cream.
Make the Blueberry ice cream.
Prepare the spiced damsons for the Damson sauce.

1–2 days before
Make the Cream of carrot and dill soup, cover and chill.

24 hours before
Make the Pink trout fillets in aspic, cover and chill.

In the afternoon
Prepare the goose.
Peel the potatoes.

Prepare the cabbage wedges.
Make the Melba toast to serve with the Cream of carrot and dill soup.

3 hours before the meal
Cook the goose.

1 hour before the meal
Put out the Meringue baskets.
Transfer the ice creams from the freezer to the refrigerator.
Cook the Fantail potatoes.
Prepare the celeriac.

30 minutes before serving
Cook the celeriac.

15 minutes before serving
Reheat the Cream of carrot and dill soup.

Just before serving each course
Complete steps 3 and 4 of the Celeriac purée.
Cook the cabbage wedges.
Make the Damson sauce for the roast goose.
Garnish the goose.
Fill the Meringue baskets with the ice creams.

PINK TROUT FILLETS IN ASPIC

4 small pink rainbow trout, filleted or 8 fillets pink rainbow trout
900 ml (1½ pints) water
1 small onion, peeled and sliced
few parsley stalks
pared rind of ½ lemon
salt
¼ level teaspoon black peppercorns
2 tablespoons lemon juice (optional)
150 ml (¼ pint) dry white wine
1 tablespoon powdered gelatine
1 egg white
2 egg shells, crushed

TO GARNISH:
few black olives cut into small strips
fresh tarragon leaves
little chopped aspic

Preparation time: about 40 minutes
Cooking time: about 35 minutes
Oven: 160°C, 325°F, Gas Mark 3

1. If using whole fish, reserve the heads and bones and put them into a pan with the water, onion, parsley stalks, lemon rind, salt and peppercorns. Bring to the boil, then cover and simmer for 20 minutes. If you use fillets of fish make the stock as above but add 2 tablespoons of lemon juice instead of the fish heads and bones.
2. Strain the stock into a shallow oven-proof container, then add the fillets of trout, skin side downwards, in a single layer. Cover with foil and cook in a preheated moderate oven for 5 minutes. Remove from the oven and leave undisturbed until cold.
3. Strain the liquor and boil until it has reduced to 350 ml (12 fl oz). Put the wine into a bowl or pan, sprinkle over the gelatine and heat gently to dissolve. Add to the fish stock with the egg white and crushed shells.
4. Bring to the boil, whisking all the time. Allow the foam to rise to the top of the pan, without further stirring, then remove and allow to subside. Bring to the boil again, and then pour through a scalded jelly bag. The aspic should come through clear. Cool, then chill until thickening up.
5. Meanwhile carefully remove the skin from each trout fillet and place each fillet on an individual plate, or one large dish, if preferred.
6. Spoon or brush a thin layer of aspic over each fillet of fish. Garnish each with an attractive pattern of tarragon leaves and strips of olive. Dip each into aspic before attaching to the fish. Add a little more aspic to give a second thin layer to the fish and if liked to flood the plate. Extra decorations may be added to the aspic on the plate, e.g. a small border of chopped aspic. Chill until set. May be served with mayonnaise, if wished.

CREAM OF CARROT AND DILL SOUP

50 g (2 oz) butter or margarine
1 onion, peeled and chopped
450 g (1 lb) carrots, peeled and diced
100 g (4 oz) peeled potatoes, diced
900 ml (1½ pints) chicken stock
2 tablespoons lemon juice
salt
freshly ground black pepper
good pinch of ground coriander
150 ml (¼ pint) unsweetened orange juice
300–450 ml (½–¾ pint) milk or skimmed milk or part milk and part single cream
2 tablespoons chopped fresh dill
Melba toast, to serve (optional)

Preparation time: 25 minutes
Cooking time: 45 minutes

1. Melt the fat in a pan, add the onion and fry very gently until it begins to soften.
2. Add the carrots and potato and continue frying very gently for 4–5 minutes, without allowing the vegetables to colour, stirring occasionally.
3. Add the stock, lemon juice, salt, pepper and coriander and bring to the boil. Cover the pan and simmer gently for 30 minutes until tender.
4. Cool slightly, then purée, liquidize or sieve the soup and return it to a clean pan with the orange juice and 300 ml (½ pint) of the milk. ⅋F⅋
5. Bring the soup back to the boil and add the dill and sufficient extra milk to give the desired consistency. Simmer for 2–3 minutes then adjust the seasonings and serve with Melba toast if wished.

F Can be frozen for up to 3 months.

FROM THE TOP: Pink trout fillets in aspic; Cream of carrot and dill soup

ROAST GOOSE WITH DAMSON SAUCE

5.5 kg (12 lb) oven-ready goose
salt
freshly ground black pepper

DAMSON SAUCE:
400 ml (14 fl oz) red wine
200 ml (7 fl oz) red wine vinegar
6–8 whole cloves
2 cinnamon sticks, halved
½ teaspoon ground ginger
75 g (3 oz) light soft brown sugar
thinly pared rind of ½ lemon
450 g (1 lb) damsons
300 ml (½ pint) chicken stock

TO GARNISH:
sprigs of parsley
wedges of lemon

Preparation time: about 30 minutes, plus marinating
Cooking time: about 3 hours
Oven: 200°C, 400°F, Gas Mark 6

A goose is a very bony bird with very little flesh in proportion to the size of its carcass. The size suggested is the smallest which will yield sufficient flesh to feed 8 people. If you can get a larger one, it would allow for a little extra. Make the spiced damsons at least 24 hours in advance, they will keep for several weeks in a cool place and can be used for several sauces.

1. For the spiced damsons, put the wine, wine vinegar, cloves, cinnamon sticks, ginger, sugar and lemon rind into a saucepan and heat gently until the sugar dissolves, then bring to the boil and simmer for 10 minutes.
2. Meanwhile, prick each damson and put it into a bowl, then pour the boiling liquid over. Leave until cold.
3. Drain the liquid into a saucepan, bring back to the boil, then pour again over the damsons. Cover and leave for at least 24 hours in a cool place.
4. Prick the goose all over and sprinkle it lightly with salt. Put it into a roasting tin, standing on a wire rack. Lay a sheet of greased greaseproof paper over the bird.
5. Cook in a preheated moderately hot oven allowing 15 minutes per 450 g (1 lb). Baste once or twice during cooking and remove the paper for the last 30 minutes of cooking time to brown the bird. When the goose is ready, transfer to a serving dish and keep warm.
6. Pour off almost all the fat from the pan, but leave any juices. Add 300 ml (½ pint) of the spiced damson liquid and the stock and bring to the boil. Simmer for about 10 minutes until reduced by about a third. Add about 24 drained damsons to the sauce, adjust the seasonings and simmer for a minute or so, taking care not to break up the fruit. Serve the sauce with the goose, which should be garnished with parsley and lemon wedges.

Variation: If damsons are not available you can use either small very dark plums with lemon juice added for they are not so tart as damsons; or you can use blackcurrants, which, of course, do not need to be pricked.

FANTAIL POTATOES

8 potatoes, about 175–225 g (6–8 oz)
  each
4 tablespoons oil or dripping
salt (optional)

Preparation time: 10 minutes
Cooking time: about 1 hour
Oven: 200–225°C, 400°–425°F, Gas
  Mark 6–7

1. Peel the potatoes and take a thin slice off the base of each one so they stand evenly.
2. Using a sharp knife make cuts at 5 mm ($\frac{1}{4}$ inch) intervals along the length of each potato almost through to the base, just leaving a hinge to hold them together.
3. Heat the oil in a roasting tin in the oven until hot. Add the potatoes and spoon fat evenly over each one.
4. Cook in a preheated moderately hot oven for 30 minutes. Baste well and sprinkle with a little salt, if liked.
5. Cook for a further 30 minutes or so until golden brown and crisp and the

cuts have opened out a little. Drain and serve with the goose. The potatoes may be cooked around the goose if there is sufficient room in the tin.

CELERIAC PUREE

1.25 kg (2$\frac{1}{2}$ lb) celeriac
1 tablespoon lemon juice
salt
freshly ground black pepper
25 g (1 oz) butter
2 tablespoons single or whipping
  cream (optional)
chopped fresh parsley, to garnish

Preparation time: 20 minutes
Cooking time: about 35 minutes

1. Peel the celeriac and cut it into cubes. Place in a saucepan of water, to cover, with lemon juice added to prevent discoloration.
2. Bring to the boil, add a little salt and cover the pan. Simmer for about 30 minutes until tender.

FROM THE LEFT: Celeriac purée; Roast goose with Damson sauce; Fantail potatoes

3. Drain the celeriac very thoroughly and mash or purée it in a food processor.
4. Beat in the butter, plenty of pepper, and salt to taste until the mixture is quite smooth, then beat in the cream, if using. Turn the purée into a warmed dish and fork up the surface. Sprinkle with chopped parsley before serving.

MERINGUE BASKETS WITH LYCHEE AND BLUEBERRY ICE CREAMS

BLUEBERRY ICE CREAM:
225 g (8 oz) blueberries
1 tablespoon lemon juice
3 tablespoons caster sugar
250 ml (8 fl oz) double cream
1 egg white

LYCHEE ICE CREAM:
350 g (12 oz) fresh lychees (or a
1 × 225 g (8 oz) can of lychees,
drained)
1 tablespoon lemon juice
finely grated rind of ½ lemon
2 level tablespoons caster sugar
250 ml (8 fl oz) double cream
1 egg white

MERINGUE CUITE:
6 egg whites
400 g (14 oz) icing sugar, sifted
twice

TO DECORATE:
tiny sprigs of mint

Preparation time: about 50 minutes,
plus freezing
Cooking time: about 2–2½ hours
Oven: 110°C, 225°F, Gas Mark ¼

1. Make the blueberry ice cream. If you are using frozen blueberries allow them to thaw almost completely, then purée or liquidize them with the lemon juice until smooth. Add the sugar and purée again.
2. Whip the cream until thick, but not too stiff. Fold the blueberry purée evenly through the cream and turn it into a freezer container.
3. Cover with foil and freeze until slushy with ice crystals forming around the edge, but not completely solid.
4. Make the lychee ice cream. Peel the lychees, remove the stones, then purée or liquidize the flesh adding the lemon juice, rind and sugar.
5. Whip the cream until very thick but still not too stiff, and fold the lychee purée through the cream. Turn the mixture into a freezer container, cover and freeze as for blueberry ice cream.
6. Whisk the two egg whites until stiff. Beat each ice cream separately until smooth. Fold half the egg white through each one.
7. Return the ice creams to their containers and freeze until firm – preferably for at least 24 hours. [F]
8. Make the meringue baskets. Cover 1 or 2 baking sheets with non-stick silicone paper or greased greaseproof paper and draw 8 ovals of about 13 cm (5 inches) in length on the paper.
9. Put the egg whites and sifted icing sugar into a heatproof bowl and mix together lightly. Stand the bowl over a saucepan of very gently simmering water and whisk the mixture until stiff and white and standing in firm peaks.
10. Transfer the meringue to a piping bag fitted with a large star vegetable nozzle and pipe baskets to cover the patterns. First cover each shape, then pipe another ring around the outer edge on top of the base and finally pipe a row of small stars on top of this, to complete the basket.
11. Cook in a preheated very cool oven for 2–2½ hours until firm and crisp. Reverse the position of the trays in the oven after 1 hour, if using 2 trays.
12. Cool on the paper, then remove carefully and store in an airtight container until required. The meringue baskets will keep for up to 2 weeks.
13. To serve, remove the ice creams from the freezer to the refrigerator about 1 hour before serving, then place the baskets, one on each of 8 side plates or on one large serving dish. Just before serving fill the baskets with alternate spoonfuls of the blueberry and lychee ice creams. Serve at once.

[F] The ice creams can be kept in the freezer for up to 3 months.

ABOVE: Meringue baskets with lychee and blueberry ice creams

MALAYSIAN DINNER FOR FOUR

Chicken, beef or pork saté

Laksa Lemak

Kambing Korma

Gado–Gado

Nasi Goreng

Tomato and Onion Sambal

Tropical Fruit*

Drink suggestions:
Lager or jasmine tea

This menu provides a taste of a few of the most characteristic dishes of southeast Asia. Favourite spices and flavourings include familiar ones like garlic, ginger, cumin, cinnamon, cardamon; less well-known are blachan (also known as *balachong* and *terasi*) and tamarind water. Blachan is a pungent mixture of salted, pounded and dried shrimps (it is always used in small quantities and never eaten raw) while tamarind, which has a sweet-sour flavour, is a fibrous, sticky pulp of dark brown partly dried pods and seeds which are compressed into a block. To prepare tamarind water, steep a little of the pulp in boiling water, then allow the water to cool and rub the mixture to a purée. Sieve to remove the seeds and the fibre. Blachan and tamarind are available in oriental shops and both should be tightly wrapped and stored in the refrigerator. Use a mixture of vinegar and orange juice if you cannot find tamarind.

A Malay meal usually ends with fresh fruit, so make a selection from whatever exotic fruit is in season, mangoes, pineapples, rambutans, paw paws, oranges and bananas, for example.

COUNTDOWN

The day before
Prepare and marinate the meat for the satés and make the peanut sauce. Cover and chill.
Cook the rice for the Nasi goreng. Cover and chill.
Complete steps 1 and 2 of the Laksa lemak.

In the morning
Prepare all the vegetables for the Gado-gado, cover and chill.
Prepare the vegetables for the Tomato and onion sambal. Cover and chill.
Complete steps 1 and 2 of the Kambing korma.

1½ hours before the meal
Complete step 3 of the Kambing korma.
Complete step 3 of the Laksa lemak.

¾ hour before the meal
Complete step 4 of the Laksa lemak.
Complete the Gado-gado.
Cook the Nasi goreng.
Cook the satés.

Just before serving
Finish the peanut sauce and garnish the satés.
Garnish the Nasi goreng.
Make the Tomato and onion sambal.
Complete the Laksa lemak.
Complete step 4 of the Kambing korma.

CHICKEN, BEEF OR PORK SATE

450 g (1 lb) lean steak, lean pork or chicken breasts, skinned
8 bamboo skewers, soaked in water for 30 minutes to prevent burning

MARINADE:
1 small onion, peeled and grated
2 garlic cloves, peeled and finely chopped
2.5 cm (1 inch) piece of fresh ginger, peeled and finely chopped
65 ml (2½ fl oz) soy sauce
2 tablespoons clear honey
2 tablespoons cooking oil
1 tablespoon rice wine or sherry

PEANUT SAUCE:
1 tablespoon cooking oil
1 tablespoon grated onion
1 red chilli, seeded and finely chopped
1 garlic clove, peeled and finely chopped
1 tablespoon clear honey
½ tablespoon soy sauce
½ tablespoon lemon juice
¼ teaspoon ground coriander
¼ teaspoon ground cumin
75 g (3 oz) crunchy peanut butter

TO SERVE:
250 ml (8 fl oz) coconut milk
salt (optional)
1 spring onion
2 lemon twists (optional)

Preparation time: 30 minutes, plus marinating
Cooking time: 12–19 minutes

Choose whatever meat you like for this recipe. Try just one or a mixture of all three. If you use a mixture, marinate the beef, chicken and pork separately, then thread each on its own individual skewer. Remember to make sure the pork is thoroughly cooked before serving.

1. Trim any fat from the meat and cut it into 1.5 cm (1 inch) cubes. Set the meat aside.
2. In a bowl, mix together the marinade ingredients, then add the meat. Toss well to coat with the marinade. Cover with cling film and chill for at least 1 hour.
3. To make the peanut sauce, heat the oil in a small saucepan, then add the onion and cook for 5 minutes, or until tender and golden. Add the chilli and garlic, then cook for 1 minute. Reduce the heat, then blend in the honey, soy sauce, lemon juice, coriander and cumin. Stir well, then add the peanut butter and set aside.
4. Remove the meat from the marinade and thread onto the skewers, making sure the meat is not packed too tightly. Cook under a preheated grill, turning frequently. Allow 5 minutes for rare beef, 7 minutes for chicken and 12 minutes for pork.
5. To serve, stir the coconut milk into the peanut sauce and keep warm over a low heat. Taste and add salt if necessary. Arrange on a warm platter and garnish with the spring onion and lemon twists, if wished. Hand the peanut sauce separately.

LAKSA LEMAK

(PRAWN AND NOODLE SOUP)

600 ml (1 pint) water
100 g (4 oz) pork fillet or chicken
salt
freshly ground black pepper
175 g (6 oz) thin rice noodles
1½ tablespoons vegetable oil
5 shallots, peeled and finely sliced
4 spring onions, cut into 1 cm (½
   inch) lengths
2 garlic cloves, peeled and crushed
1 teaspoon ground ginger
1 teaspoon ground coriander
½ teaspoon ground turmeric
175 g (6 oz) peeled prawns
300 ml (½ pint) thick coconut milk
2 blocks bean curd, cut into thick
   strips
75 g (3 oz) bean sprouts

Preparation time: 15 minutes
Cooking time: 1¼–1½ hours

1. Bring the water to the boil in a large
pan. Add the pork or chicken and salt
and pepper to taste. Cover and simmer
for 40 minutes.
2. Strain and reserve the cooking liquid. Cut the meat into small cubes.
3. Put the rice noodles into a pan and
cover with boiling water. Cover and
leave to stand for 5 minutes. Drain
thoroughly.
4. Heat the oil in a wok or deep frying
pan, add the shallots and fry for 1
minute, then add the spring onions,
garlic and spices. Fry for 30 seconds,
stirring constantly, then add the reserved cooking liquid and simmer for
25 minutes.
5. Add the rice noodles and coconut
milk and bring very slowly to the boil,
stirring gently to prevent the coconut
milk from curdling. Add the bean curd
and bean sprouts and simmer for 5 to 8
minutes, stirring occasionally. Pour
into a warmed soup tureen and serve
hot.

KAMBING KORMA

(SPICED LAMB)

4 shallots, peeled
3 garlic cloves, peeled
6 macadamia nuts or blanched
   almonds
450 ml (¾ pint) thick coconut milk
500 g (1¼ lb) boned leg of lamb, cut
   into small cubes
salt
3 tablespoons vegetable oil
1 small onion, peeled and finely
   sliced
1½ teaspoons ground coriander
½ teaspoon ground cumin
1 teaspoon ground ginger
pinch of laos powder (optional)
4 cloves
2.5 cm (1 inch) piece of cinnamon
   stick
3 cardamon pods
1 bay leaf
1 stalk lemon grass, bruised or 1
   small piece thinly pared lemon rind
3 tablespoons tamarind water
½ teaspoon freshly ground white
   pepper
lemon grass, to garnish (optional)

Preparation time: about 30 minutes
Cooking time: about 1 hour

1. Chop the shallots, garlic and nuts
very finely, then add 2 tablespoons of
the coconut milk and work to a
smooth paste.
2. Put the mixture into a bowl, add the
lamb and a little salt and mix well.
Leave to marinate for 30 minutes.
3. Heat the oil in a pan, add the onion
and fry gently until soft. Add the spices,
bay leaf and lemon grass or lemon
rind. Stir-fry for a few seconds, then
add the meat and the marinade and fry
for 2 minutes. Add the tamarind water,
salt and pepper. Cover and cook gently
for 15 minutes, stirring every 5 minutes
to prevent burning. Stir in the remaining coconut milk and simmer for 40
minutes or until the meat is tender and
the sauce is quite thick.
4. Discard the bay leaf, lemon grass
stalk, if using, cloves, cinnamon stick
and the cardamon pods. Taste and
adjust the seasoning if necessary. Garnish with lemon grass, if wished.

*CLOCKWISE FROM THE TOP: Kambing
korma; Laksa lemak; Chicken, beef or
pork saté with peanut sauce (page 97)*

GADO-GADO
(COOKED MIXED SALAD)

225 g (8 oz) green beans, topped,
  tailed and halved
225 g (8 oz) white cabbage, shredded
225 g (8 oz) carrots, scraped and
  finely sliced
225 g (8 oz) waxy potatoes, peeled
  and diced
225 g (8 oz) beansprouts
1 cucumber, quartered lengthways
  and sliced
2 hard-boiled eggs, shelled and sliced
1 tablespoon oil
5 fresh chillies, seeded
3 garlic cloves, peeled and crushed
1 teaspoon blachan
1 × 225 g (8 oz) jar crunchy peanut
  butter
450 ml (¾ pint) coconut milk
2.5 cm (1 inch) piece of fresh ginger,
  grated
1 stalk lemon grass or 1 small piece
  thinly pared lemon rind
2 teaspoons light soft brown sugar
1 teaspoon lemon juice

Preparation time: 30 minutes, plus
  standing
Cooking time: 30 minutes

1. Put all the vegetables, except the
cucumber, into a steamer and steam
for about 15 minutes or until just
tender, removing the beansprouts
after 5 minutes.
2. Arrange all the vegetables in bands
on a large flat dish and garnish with
hard-boiled eggs.
3. Heat the oil in a frying-pan and fry
separately first the chillies, and then the
garlic, then the blachan. Transfer the
chillies, garlic and blachan to a blender, add the peanut butter and coconut
milk and process until smooth. Return
the mixture to the pan with the ginger,
lemon grass, sugar and lemon juice
and slowly bring to the boil uncovered.
Stir and pour over the salad. Serve at
once with prawn crackers.

NASI GORENG
(SPECIAL FRIED RICE)

6 tablespoons vegetable oil
2 eggs, lightly beaten
225 g (8 oz) lean beef, trimmed of fat
  and cut into matchstick pieces
50 g (2 oz) peeled prawns
2 fresh green chillies, seeded and
  finely chopped
1 onion, peeled and finely chopped
1 garlic clove, peeled and crushed
350 g (12 oz) cold cooked rice
1 peanut sized piece of blachan,
  crushed
1 tablespoon dark soy sauce
salt

TO GARNISH:
7.5 cm (3 inch) piece cucumber,
  diced
2 tomatoes, quartered

Preparation time: 10 minutes
Cooking time: 12 minutes

1. Heat 1 tablespoon of the oil in a
frying pan, add the eggs and cook over
a moderate heat for 2–3 minutes to
make a thin, flat omelette. Remove
from the pan, cut into thin strips and
reserve.
2. Heat the remaining oil in the pan,
add the beef, prawns, chillies, onion
and garlic, and fry over a moderate heat
for about 5 minutes, stirring all the time

with a wooden spoon.

3. Add the rice, and stir until well mixed and warmed through. Add the blachan and soy sauce, and turn until the rice is evenly browned. Add salt to taste.

4. Pile onto a warmed serving dish, arrange the sliced omelette on top and garnish with diced cucumber and tomato wedges. Serve at once.

TOMATO AND ONION SAMBAL

2 large tomatoes, peeled and chopped
4 spring onions, finely chopped
1 green chilli, seeded and finely chopped
2 tablespoons lemon juice
2 tablespoons unsweetened desiccated coconut
½ teaspoon ground cumin

Preparation time: 10 minutes

FROM THE LEFT: Nasi goreng; Tomato and onion sambal; Gado-gado

A fresh-tasting, crunchy side dish, which needs to be prepared just before you are ready to serve the meal.

1. Mix together the tomatoes, spring onions and chilli in a medium bowl.
2. Add the lemon juice, coconut and cumin, then toss well. Serve the sambal immediately.

INDIAN DINNER FOR SIX

Murgh Pasanda

Poppadums*

Kofta

Baigan Tamatar

Aviyal

Basmati Rice

Sewaian

Drink suggestion:
Lager

COUNTDOWN

In the afternoon
Cook the Baigan tamatar.
Fry the poppadums, allowing 2 per person.
Prepare and cook the Sewaian if you are serving it chilled. Allow to cool, then chill until required.
Prepare the vegetables for the Aviyal and the Baigan tamatar, place in separate containers, cover and chill.

2 hours before the meal
Prepare and cook the Kofta.
Prepare and cook the Murgh pasanda.

1 hour before the meal
Make the Aviyal.

45 minutes before the meal
Cook the Basmati rice.

15 minutes before serving
Reheat the Baigan tamatar.

MURGH PASANDA
(CHICKEN CURRY WITH YOGURT)

6 tablespoons oil
450 g (1 lb) onions, peeled and thinly sliced
12 pieces of chicken, total weight about 1.5 kg (3 lb), skinned
10 cardamom pods
$\frac{1}{2}$ teaspoon ground cinnamon
6 cloves
25 g (1 oz) piece of fresh ginger, peeled and finely chopped
5 garlic cloves, crushed
2 teaspoons ground cumin
$\frac{1}{2}$ teaspoon hot chilli powder
$1\frac{1}{2}$ teaspoons salt
1 teaspoon garam masala
150 ml ($\frac{1}{4}$ pint) plain unsweetened yogurt
300 ml ($\frac{1}{2}$ pint) single cream or milk
225 g ($\frac{1}{2}$ lb) tomatoes, peeled and cut into sixths

TO GARNISH:
25 g (1 oz) flaked almonds, toasted
fresh coriander leaves

Preparation time: about 20 minutes
Cooking time: about 45 minutes

1. Heat the oil in a flameproof casserole. Fry 225 g (8 oz) of the onions until golden brown, then, using a spoon, remove from the pan and keep warm.
2. Fry the pieces of chicken in the same fat until golden brown all over, then remove from the pan and keep warm.
3. Add the cardamom pods, cinnamon, cloves, ginger, garlic, cumin, chilli powder, salt and garam masala and cook for 2–3 minutes, stirring all the time.
4. Add the yogurt, 1 tablespoon at a time, stirring it in well and cooking for about 30 seconds each time before adding more. Add the cream or milk and bring to the boil.
5. Add the remaining onion and simmer for 5 minutes.
6. Return the chicken and onions to the pan, cover and simmer for 20 minutes.
7. Add the tomatoes and continue cooking for a further 15 minutes.
8. Remove the cardamom pods, then transfer to a serving dish and serve sprinkled with toasted almonds and coriander leaves.

FROM THE TOP: Murgh pasanda; Poppadums

KOFTA

(MEATBALLS)

450 g (1 lb) onions, peeled
6 garlic cloves, peeled
25 g (1 oz) chopped fresh parsley
500 g (1¼ lb) minced beef
4 tablespoons oil
½ teaspoon hot chilli powder
½ teaspoon freshly ground black
 pepper
1 teaspoon ground cumin
2 teaspoons garam masala
2 teaspoons paprika
1 teaspoon turmeric
1½ teaspoons salt
50 g (2 oz) piece of fresh ginger,
 peeled and finely chopped
150 ml (¼ pint) plain unsweetened
 yogurt
150 ml (¼ pint) beef stock or water

Preparation time: about 40 minutes
Cooking time: about 1 hour
Oven: 180°C, 350°F, Gas Mark 4

1. Place 225 g (8 oz) of the onions and 3 garlic cloves in a food processor and chop finely. Add the parsley and minced beef and continue processing until finely mixed.
2. Divide the mixture into 24 pieces and shape into even-sized balls.
3. Heat the fat in a large heavy-based pan and fry the meatballs until evenly browned all over. Using a slotted spoon, transfer the meatballs to a casserole.
4. Slice the remaining onions and crush the remaining garlic cloves and add them to the fat in the pan. Fry for 3–4 minutes until lightly browned.
5. Add the chilli powder, pepper, cumin, garam masala, paprika, turmeric, salt and ginger and cook gently for 5 minutes, stirring frequently. Add the yogurt and stock and bring to the boil, stirring continuously to loosen all the sediment on the base of the pan.
6. Pour over the meatballs, cover the casserole and cook in a preheated oven for 45 minutes. Stir well before serving.

BAIGAN TAMATAR

(AUBERGINES AND TOMATOES)

6 tablespoons oil
225 g (8 oz) onions, peeled and
 chopped
1 garlic clove, crushed
½ teaspoon hot chilli powder
1 bay leaf
1 cinnamon stick, halved
1½ teaspoons salt
¼ teaspoon freshly ground black
 pepper
450 g (1 lb) tomatoes, peeled and
 quartered
450 g (1 lb) aubergines, trimmed
 and cubed
2 tablespoons tomato purée

Preparation time: about 20 minutes
Cooking time: about 40 minutes

1. Heat the oil in a large heavy-based pan, then fry the onions gently until they are a light golden brown. Add the garlic, chilli powder and bay leaf, cinnamon, salt and pepper. Add 2 tablespoons water and bring the mixture gently to the boil.
2. Add the tomatoes and cook gently for 2–3 minutes.
3. Add the aubergines and the tomato purée and mix well. Cover and simmer gently for 25–30 minutes, giving an occasional stir but trying not to break up the vegetables too much.

AVIYAL

(MIXED VEGETABLES WITH COCONUT)

225 g (8 oz) desiccated coconut
600 ml (1 pint) water
100 g (4 oz) ghee or clarified butter
25 g (1 oz) piece of fresh ginger,
 peeled and finely chopped
3 garlic cloves, crushed
½ teaspoon mustard seeds
175 g (6 oz) onions, peeled and
 chopped
2 teaspoons ground coriander
1 tablespoon garam masala
1 teaspoon turmeric
2 teaspoons salt
225 g (8 oz) broccoli, separated into
 florets
2 green peppers, seeded and sliced
225 g (8 oz) carrots, peeled and
 sliced
100 g (4 oz) French beans, trimmed
 and cut into 2.5 cm (1 inch) lengths
1 green chilli, seeded and chopped

Preparation time: about 20 minutes
Cooking time: about 30 minutes

1. Put the coconut and water into a food processor or blender and process until smoothly mixed.
2. Heat the ghee in a pan and add the ginger, garlic, and mustard seeds and fry for about 1 minute.
3. Add the onions and continue frying until they are a light golden brown.
4. Add the coriander, garam masala, turmeric and salt and simmer for about 5 minutes.
5. Add the broccoli, peppers, carrots, French beans and chilli and cook gently, stirring continuously, until they are thoroughly coated with the spice mixture. Pour on the coconut milk and bring to the boil.
6. Cover the pan and simmer for about 10 minutes, giving the vegetables an occasional stir. Serve hot.

BASMATI RICE

350 g (12 oz) basmati rice
600 ml (1 pint) water
¾ teaspoon salt
25 g (1 oz) butter

Preparation time: about 10 minutes,
 plus soaking
Cooking time: about 30 minutes

1. Soak the rice in a large pan of cold
water for 30 minutes.
2. Drain the rice thoroughly, then put
it into a heavy-based saucepan with the
water, salt and butter and bring to the
boil.
3. Cover the pan tightly, lower the heat
and cook very gently for 20 minutes,
stirring the rice after 15 minutes.
4. Stir the rice again, replace the lid
immediately and continue cooking for
about 5 minutes or until all the liquid is
absorbed.
5. To serve, fork up the rice and turn
into a warm serving dish.

SEWAIAN

(VERMICELLI WITH NUTS AND ROSEWATER)

8 whole cardamom pods
50 g (2 oz) ghee or clarified butter
8 cloves
225 g (8 oz) vermicelli
750 ml (1¼ pints) milk
175 g (6 oz) caster sugar
50 g (2 oz) blanched almonds,
 roughly chopped
50 g (2 oz) pistachio nuts, blanched
2 teaspoons rosewater

Preparation time: about 20 minutes
Cooking time: about 20 minutes

1. Slit open the cardamom pods and
crush the seeds with a heavy rolling pin
or a pestle and mortar. Melt the butter
in a heavy pan and fry the ground
cardamom and the cloves gently for 2
minutes.
2. Add the vermicelli and fry it very
gently and carefully, if possible without

*CLOCKWISE FROM TOP LEFT: Baigan
tamatar; Kofta, Aviyal; Basmati rice;
Sewaian*

breaking, until it is a light golden
brown.
3. Add the milk and bring it slowly to
the boil, stirring gently. Cover the pan
and simmer very gently for 10 minutes,
giving an occasional stir to prevent the
vermicelli from sticking.
4. When the milk is almost all absorbed, add the sugar, almonds, pistachio
nuts and rosewater. Stir until well
mixed then remove from the heat.
5. If liked, remove the whole cloves
before serving. This dessert may be
served warm or chilled.

SUPPER PARTIES

Match your mood – and the time you have available – to our selection of supper party menus. Take your guests on a culinary trip to a French bistro, the heart of Italy or the Caribbean; delight unexpected visitors with your ingenuity; or prepare a stunning spread for a crowd of teenagers – all these plans of action (and more) are here for you.

CLOCKWISE FROM THE LEFT: Nectarines in Grand Marnier; Mixed salad with sesame seed dressing; Cannelloni Abruzzi; Goat's cheese and tomato hors d'oeuvre

AFTER THEATRE SUPPER FOR TWO

Fennel Soup with Garlic Croûtons

Pan-Fried Calves' Liver with Thyme

Potato, Orange and Olive Salad

Spinach Salad

Hot French Bread*

Nectarines in Grand Marnier

Wine suggestion:
Fitou

COUNTDOWN

The day before
Make the Nectarines in Grand Marnier, cover and chill.
Make the Fennel soup, cover and chill.

In the morning
Make the Potato, orange and olive salad, cover and chill.
Prepare the Spinach salad, cover and chill.
Make the dressing for the Spinach salad.

Just before going out
Put the Fennel soup into a saucepan.
Fry the Garlic croûtons for the Fennel soup (step 5).

Just before serving
Reheat the Fennel soup and garnish.
Toss the Spinach salad.
Heat the French bread.
Slice the liver and toss in seasoned flour.
Cook the Pan-fried calves' liver and garnish.
Warm the Garlic croûtons.

FENNEL SOUP WITH GARLIC CROUTONS

1 small bulb fennel, weighing about 200 g (7 oz)
1 small onion, peeled and chopped
300 ml (½ pint) chicken stock
salt
freshly ground black pepper
150 ml (¼ pint) milk
1 teaspoon lemon juice
3 tablespoons plain unsweetened yogurt or single or soured cream
1 egg yolk

GARLIC CROUTONS:
25 g (1 oz) butter
2 tablespoons oil
2 garlic cloves, peeled and sliced
3 slices white bread, crusts removed and diced, or cut into shapes

Preparation time: about 30 minutes
Cooking time: 40 minutes

1. Cut any sprigs of green from the fennel and reserve for garnish; chop the remainder of the bulb. Place in a saucepan with the onion, stock and seasonings.

2. Bring to the boil, cover the pan and simmer gently for 30 minutes until tender.

3. Leave to cool a little, then purée, liquidize or sieve the soup and return to a clean pan. Add the milk and lemon juice and bring to the boil.

4. Blend the yogurt with the egg yolk, add a little of the soup then whisk back into the pan of soup. Heat gently without boiling.

5. Make the croûtons. Melt the butter and oil in a frying pan with the garlic. Heat gently until the garlic sizzles and begins to colour, then remove from the pan. Add the croûtons and fry gently until golden brown all over, stirring frequently. Drain on absorbent paper towels.

6. To serve, taste and adjust the seasoning of the soup and reheat without boiling. Garnish with the reserved sprigs of fennel and serve with the croûtons.

BELOW: Fennel soup with garlic croûtons

PAN-FRIED CALVES' LIVER WITH THYME

2 slices calves' liver, about 75–100 g
  (3–4 oz) each or 4 very thin slices
2 tablespoons seasoned flour
40 g (1½ oz) butter or margarine
¼ level teaspoon dried thyme or ½
  teaspoon freshly chopped thyme
3 tablespoons dry sherry
grated rind of ½ lime or lemon
1 tablespoon lime or lemon juice
salt
freshly ground black pepper

TO GARNISH:
slices of lime or lemon, optional
sprigs of fresh thyme, optional

Preparation time: 10 minutes
Cooking time: about 10 minutes

1. If the liver is thick, cut each piece carefully into two thinner slices. Toss the liver in the seasoned flour.
2. Melt the fat in a frying pan, add the thyme and then the liver. Fry gently for 2–4 minutes on each side until well sealed and just cooked through, but in no way overcooked. Transfer to 2 plates and keep warm.
3. Add the sherry to the pan juices, followed by the lime rind and juice. Heat gently until it bubbles well. Taste and adjust the seasoning and pour over the liver.
4. Garnish with slices of lime and sprigs of thyme placed beside the liver if wished.

POTATO, ORANGE AND OLIVE SALAD

175–225 g (6–8 oz) tiny new
  potatoes
salt
1 large orange
10–12 black olives, halved and
  stoned

DRESSING:
2 tablespoons safflower oil
2 teaspoons wine vinegar
1 tablespoon orange juice
½ teaspoon caster sugar
½ teaspoon French mustard
2 tablespoons finely chopped spring
  onions or 1 tablespoon freshly
  chopped parsley
freshly ground black pepper

FROM THE LEFT: Spinach salad; Pan-fried calves' liver with thyme; Nectarines in Grand Marnier

1. Wash the spinach very carefully, removing any tough stalks; then dry well. Tear the leaves (do not cut them) and put them into a bowl.
2. Add the onions, tomatoes and cucumber and mix well. Cover with cling film and chill.
3. Put all the dressing ingredients into a bowl and whisk together thoroughly. Add the salad only just before serving.

NECTARINES IN GRAND MARNIER

3–4 ripe nectarines or peaches
250 ml (8 fl oz) water
2 pieces thinly pared lemon rind
2 pieces thinly pared orange rind
100 g (4 oz) caster sugar
4 tablespoons Grand Marnier

Preparation time: about 30 minutes, plus chilling
Cooking time: about 10 minutes

1. Nectarines do not need to be peeled, but peaches do. If using peaches, dip them briefly in boiling water, then plunge them into cold water to loosen the skins. Make a small cut in the skin and peel it off.
2. Quarter the nectarines and remove the stones. Place in a bowl. They may be left whole but it is more difficult to flavour the whole fruit quickly.
3. Put the water, lemon and orange rind and sugar into a saucepan and heat gently until the sugar dissolves, then boil hard until reduced by just over a third. Remove from the heat and stir in the Grand Marnier.
4. Pour the syrup over the nectarines, cover and chill for at least 12 hours and up to 36 hours, turning the fruit once or twice.
5. Remove the pieces of orange and lemon rind and cut into julienne strips. Divide the nectarines and juice between 2 glass dishes and sprinkle with a little of the strips of citrus rind. Serve as they are or with cream.

Preparation time: 15 minutes
Cooking time: 10 minutes

1. Wash the potatoes but do not peel, and cook in boiling salted water for 8–10 minutes until just tender. Drain, and if too large cut in half. Put into a serving bowl.
2. Finely grate a quarter of the rind from the orange and put it into a bowl.
3. Cut away the rest of the peel and pith from the orange and ease the segments from between the membranes and add them to the potatoes with the olives.
4. Add the dressing ingredients to the orange rind with salt and pepper and whisk together thoroughly. Pour over the potatoes whilst they are still warm and mix evenly. Cover with cling film and cool and chill until required.

SPINACH SALAD

75 g (3 oz) fresh young spinach leaves or spinach beet leaves, trimmed
3 spring onions, trimmed and sliced
3 tomatoes, each cut in half or 8 cherry tomatoes
4 cm (1½ inch) piece of cucumber, diced

DRESSING:
2 tablespoons plain unsweetened yogurt
1 teaspoon wine vinegar
½ teaspoon caster sugar
pinch of dry mustard
salt
freshly ground black pepper

Preparation time: 15 minutes

STORE CUPBOARD SUPPER FOR SIX

Egg and Walnut Pâté

Macaroni and Tuna Fish Layer

Mixed Salad*

Guava and Mandarin Syllabubs

Wine suggestion:
Settesoli bianco
a firm Sicilian white

COUNTDOWN

1–2 hours beforehand
Hard-boil the eggs. Make the Egg and walnut pâté, cover and chill.
Cook and drain the macaroni.
Make tuna fish mixture and the sauce for the Macaroni and tuna fish layer.
Assemble the Macaroni and tuna fish layer.
Make the dressing for the salad.

1 hour beforehand
Prepare the Guava and mandarin syllabubs.
Make the syllabubs and decorate.
Prepare the salad.

30 minutes before serving
Cook the Macaroni and tuna fish layer.
Garnish the Egg and walnut pâté.
Make the toast, if required.
Toss the salad.

EGG AND WALNUT PATE

1 small onion, peeled and chopped
1–2 garlic cloves, crushed
25 g (1 oz) butter or margarine
175 g (6 oz) full fat soft cheese
100 g (4 oz) shelled walnuts, roughly chopped
1 tablespoon chopped fresh parsley
½ teaspoon dried thyme
salt
freshly ground black pepper
2 tablespoons lemon juice
3 eggs, hard-boiled

TO GARNISH:
walnut halves
spring onion tassels (page 53)

Preparation time: about 20 minutes
Cooking time: 5 minutes

1. Fry the onion and garlic gently in the melted fat until soft and lightly browned. Leave to cool.
2. Soften the cheese in a bowl and beat in the onion mixture followed by the walnuts, parsley, thyme, salt and pepper and lemon juice.
3. Finely grate or chop the eggs and mix evenly through the pâté.
4. Turn into a dish, level the top and chill until required. Garnish with walnut halves and spring onion tassels, if available, and serve with hot toast or crackers and butter.

MACARONI AND TUNA FISH LAYER

350 g (12 oz) short cut macaroni
salt
1 tablespoon oil
40 g (1½ oz) butter or margarine
1 large onion, peeled and sliced
1 garlic clove, crushed
100 g (4 oz) mushrooms, chopped (optional)
1 teaspoon dried marjoram or oregano
2 × 200 g (7 oz) cans tuna fish in brine, drained and roughly flaked
4–6 tablespoons plain unsweetened yogurt or top of the milk

SAUCE:

50 g (2 oz) butter or margarine
3 tablespoons plain flour
600 ml (1 pint) milk or chicken or
  vegetable stock
1 teaspoon dry mustard
freshly ground black pepper
75 g (3 oz) mature Cheddar cheese,
  grated
3 tablespoons grated Parmesan
  cheese
2–3 tomatoes, peeled and sliced

Preparation time: about 25 minutes
Cooking time: about 50 minutes
Oven: 220°C, 425°F, Gas Mark 7

1. Cook the macaroni in plenty of boiling salted water with the oil added for about 10 minutes or until barely tender. Drain, rinse under hot water and drain again thoroughly.

2. Meanwhile melt the butter in a pan and fry the onion and garlic gently until soft but not coloured. Add the mushrooms, if using, and continue frying for a few minutes. Stir in the herbs, tuna fish and yogurt or milk and heat through until really hot. Season well.

3. Put half the macaroni into a greased ovenproof dish. Spoon the tuna fish mixture in an even layer over the macaroni and cover with the remaining macaroni.

4. Make the sauce. Melt the butter in a pan, stir in the flour and cook for a minute or so. Gradually add the milk or stock and bring to the boil. Stir in the mustard and plenty of salt and pepper and simmer for 2 minutes.

5. Remove the sauce from the heat and stir in 50 g (2 oz) of the grated Cheddar cheese and 1 tablespoon of the Parmesan until melted, then pour over the macaroni.

6. Cover with sliced tomatoes, then sprinkle with the remaining Cheddar and Parmesan cheeses.

7. Cook in a preheated hot oven for 25–30 minutes until golden brown and bubbling. Serve at once.

FROM THE LEFT: Macaroni and tuna fish layer; Egg and walnut pâté

GUAVA AND MANDARIN SYLLABUBS

1 × 425 g (15 oz) can guavas
1 × 300 g (11 oz) can mandarin
  oranges
grated rind of 1 lemon
4 tablespoons lemon juice
100 g (4 oz) caster sugar
2 tablespoons brandy
2 tablespoons sherry
300 ml (½ pint) double cream
4 tablespoons thick set plain
  unsweetened yogurt (optional)

Preparation time: about 15 minutes,
  plus standing

Any type of canned fruit can be used for this dessert depending on what is available in the store cupboard. Alternatively use sliced bananas, grapes, oranges or crushed biscuits in the base. The brandy and sherry may be replaced with sweet white wine.

1. Drain the guavas and roughly chop; drain the mandarins and put 18 aside for decoration if wished. Mix the remainder with the guavas and divide between 6 wine glasses.
2. Make the syllabub. Put the lemon rind, juice, sugar, brandy and sherry into a bowl and, if you have time, leave it to stand for at least 15 minutes and up to 1 hour.
3. Add the cream to the mixture and whip until it is thick and stands in soft peaks. Add the yogurt, if using, and continue to whip until it is completely mixed in.
4. Spoon or pipe the syllabub over the fruit in the glasses and decorate each one with 3 mandarin orange segments if wished. Serve within an hour, or chill and serve within 2 or 3 hours.

ABOVE: Guava and mandarin syllabubs

ITALIAN SUPPER FOR SIX

COUNTDOWN

Up to a week beforehand
Make the Mango sorbet, cover and freeze.

Up to 24 hours beforehand
Make the Chick pea soup, cover and chill.

In the morning
Prepare the pasta for the Cannelloni.
Make the filling for the Cannelloni.
Assemble the Cannelloni, cover and chill.
Prepare the Mixed salad, cover and chill.
Make the Sesame seed dressing.

30 minutes before serving
Transfer the Mango sorbet from the freezer to the refrigerator.
Cook the Cannelloni.
Reheat the Chick pea soup for 5 minutes.
Boil and fry the noodles for the Chick pea soup.

Just before serving
Toss the salad.

CHICK PEA SOUP WITH FRIED NOODLES

100 g (4 oz) chick peas, soaked overnight
2 onions, peeled
2 rashers lean bacon, rinded
1–2 garlic cloves, crushed
2 tablespoons oil
2 tablespoons tomato purée
1 tablespoon plain flour
1 × 425 g (15 oz) can peeled tomatoes, puréed
1 litre (1¾ pints) chicken, beef or vegetable stock or water
salt
freshly ground black pepper
1 teaspoon light soft brown sugar
2 bay leaves
50 g (2 oz) noodles
fat or oil, for frying

Preparation time: 20 minutes, plus soaking overnight
Cooking time: about 1¼ hours

Chick peas with their nutty, earthy flavour, have always been popular in the countries bordering the Mediterranean; in fact, there is evidence that they were being cultivated in Palestine as long ago as 4000 BC. Although they are best known as the prime ingredient of the Middle Eastern dip, Hummus, they are also a favourite item in Italian peasant cooking and the inspiration for dishes like this one. If you do not have time to soak the chick peas overnight, cook them, unsoaked, in boiling water for 1 hour and then drain them.

1. Drain the chick peas.
2. Chop the onions and bacon in a food processor, or mince them finely. Put them into a pan with the garlic and oil and cook gently, stirring frequently, for 5 minutes.
3. Add the tomato purée and flour and cook for a minute or so, still stirring. Gradually add the puréed tomatoes, followed by the stock, stirring all the time, and bring to the boil.
4. Season well, then add the brown sugar, bay leaves and the drained chick peas and cover the pan. Simmer for about 50 minutes, giving the mixture an occasional stir, until the chick peas are very tender.
5. Meanwhile, prepare the noodles. Break them into lengths, about 2.5 cm (1 inch) long, and cook in boiling salted water for 6 minutes. Drain well and dry on paper towels.
6. Heat the oil to about 160°C/325°F and fry the noodles, a few at a time, for about 1 minute until they are very pale brown and crispy. Drain on absorbent paper towels.
7. Remove the bay leaves from the soup, taste and adjust the seasoning, pour into a tureen and serve sprinkled with fried noodles.

CANNELLONI ABRUZZI

75 g (3 oz) plain flour
pinch of salt
4 egg yolks
2 eggs
250 ml (8 fl oz) milk
lard, butter or oil, for frying
50 g (2 oz) freshly grated Parmesan
  cheese

FILLING:
2 tablespoons oil
1 onion, peeled and very finely
  chopped
1 carrot, peeled and coarsely grated
1 celery stick, very finely chopped
2 garlic cloves, crushed
225 g (8 oz) chicken livers, chopped
1½ tablespoons tomato purée
4 tablespoons chicken, beef or
  vegetable stock or water
salt
freshly ground black pepper
2 courgettes, total weight about 225 g
  (8 oz), trimmed and coarsely
  grated
100 g (4 oz) cooked ham, chopped
½ teaspoon Worcestershire sauce
½ teaspoon dried oregano

SAUCE:
40 g (1½ oz) butter or margarine
40 g (1½ oz) plain flour
150 ml (¼ pint) dry white wine
300 ml (½ pint) milk
½ teaspoon made mustard

Preparation time: about 50 minutes
Cooking time: about 1 hour
Oven: 200°C, 400°F, Gas Mark 6

This dish comes from the Abruzzi region of central Italy. The pasta is like a cross between an omelette and ordinary pasta and it simply melts in the mouth. It can also be used for lasagne.

1. Make the cannelloni. Sift the flour and salt into a bowl, make a well in the centre and add the egg yolks and the eggs. Gradually beat them together until they are smooth, adding the milk a little at a time. Beat the mixture until it is very smooth and, if necessary, strain it into a jug.
2. Heat a little lard, butter or oil in a 20 cm (8 inch) frying pan. Pour in sufficient batter to cover the base of the pan and cook undisturbed until just set. Do not turn it over. Carefully slide the pancake on to a plate and cook 11

more in the same way, placing a piece of greaseproof paper or foil between each one.
3. Make the filling. Heat the oil in a pan and fry the onion, carrot, celery and garlic until they are soft, stirring the mixture occasionally.
4. Add the livers and cook until they are well sealed. Stir in the tomato purée, cook for 1 minute, then add the stock and bring to the boil. Season with salt and pepper, then add the courgettes, ham, Worcestershire sauce and oregano and simmer for 3–4 minutes.
5. Spread a little filling on to each pasta circle and roll up to form cannelloni. Place in a single layer in a greased shallow ovenproof dish, seam side down.
6. Make the sauce. Melt the fat in a pan, stir in the flour and cook for 1 minute. Gradually add the wine, and then the milk and bring to the boil. Stir in the mustard, season with salt and pepper and simmer for 2 minutes.
7. Pour the sauce over the cannelloni and sprinkle with the Parmesan cheese. Cook in a preheated moderately hot oven for about 25 minutes until lightly browned.

MIXED SALAD WITH SESAME SEED DRESSING

100 g (4 oz) lamb's lettuce
2 heads chicory
1 bunch watercress, trimmed
½ small curly endive
½ bunch spring onions, sliced

DRESSING:
6 tablespoons safflower oil
1 tablespoon wine vinegar
1 tablespoon lemon juice
1 garlic clove, crushed
½ teaspoon dry mustard
½ teaspoon French mustard
salt
freshly ground black pepper
½ teaspoon caster sugar
1½ tablespoons sesame seeds

Preparation time: 20 minutes

1. Wash the lamb's lettuce, dry it thoroughly and put it into a bowl. Slice the chicory and add it to the bowl with the watercress and sprigs of endive. Add the onions and mix well together.

2. Put all the ingredients for the dressing into a bowl and whisk thoroughly or put them into a screw-topped jar and shake until thoroughly emulsified.
3. Just before serving shake the dressing again and spoon it over the salad. Toss lightly and serve.

MANGO SORBET

400 ml (14 fl oz) water, plus 4
  tablespoons
thinly pared rind of 1 lemon
175 g (6 oz) caster sugar
1 mango
3 tablespoons lemon juice
3 egg whites

Preparation time: about 30 minutes,
  plus chilling
Cooking time: about 10 minutes

1. Put the water, lemon rind and sugar into a pan and heat gently until the sugar dissolves. Bring to the boil and boil gently for 10 minutes. Cool, then remove the lemon rind.
2. Peel the mango and chop the flesh. Put the flesh into a pan with the lemon juice and 4 tablespoons of water. Simmer gently for 5 minutes. Cool, then purée or sieve the fruit. Leave until cold.
3. Combine the syrup and mango purée and pour the mixture into a shallow container or ice tray. Freeze until almost firm but not too hard.
4. Turn the mixture into a chilled bowl, break down the ice crystals and beat until smooth and mushy. Whisk the egg whites until very stiff and fold them evenly through the mixture.
5. Return the mixture to the freezing container and freeze until firm. Remove the container from the freezer about 20 minutes before you are ready to serve and put it in the refrigerator. Serve the sorbet slightly soft rather than rock hard.

FROM THE TOP: Mango sorbet; Chick pea soup with fried noodles (page 115); Mixed salad with Sesame seed dressing; Cannelloni Abruzzi

TEENAGE PARTY FOR TEN

Crudités with Three Dips

Turkey Jessica

Baked Potatoes with Herb Butter

Curly Salad

Almond Choux Puffs with
Raspberry Sauce

Cinnamon Cheesecake with Kiwi
Fruit

COUNTDOWN

The day before
Prepare the Cinnamon cheesecake up
to the end of step 5.

In the morning
Make the three dips, cover and chill.
Make the Herb butter for the baked
potatoes, cover and chill.
Make the Almond choux puffs and
leave to cool.
Make Raspberry sauce, cover and chill.

2 hours before the party
Prepare the Curly salad and the French
dressing to serve with it, but do not
combine.
Prepare the Crudités and put out the
three dips.
Bake the potatoes.
Prepare the Turkey Jessica to half way
through step 5.

1 hour before serving
Cook the Turkey Jessica.
Turn out the Cinnamon cheesecake
and decorate with kiwi fruit.

30 minutes before serving
Fill and assemble the Almond choux
puffs.

Just before serving
Complete step 6 of Turkey Jessica.
Complete step 3 of the Curly salad.

CRUDITES WITH THREE DIPS

SMOKED MACKEREL DIP:
1 smoked mackerel fillet, weighing
  about 150 g (5 oz)
4 tablespoons soured cream
1 garlic clove, crushed
grated rind of $\frac{1}{4}$ lemon
salt
freshly ground black pepper
1–2 tablespoons lemon juice
paprika, to garnish

CHEESE AND ONION DIP:
100 g (4 oz) full fat soft cream cheese
2 tablespoons salad cream
75 g (3 oz) mature Cheddar cheese,
  finely grated.
$\frac{1}{2}$ bunch spring onions, trimmed and
  sliced or chopped

CURRIED EGG DIP:
2 tablespoons soured cream
2 tablespoons mayonnaise
1 teaspoon curry powder
2 hard-boiled eggs, finely grated
1 tablespoon chopped fresh parsley,
  plus some for garnish
1–2 teaspoons lemon juice
little curry powder, to garnish

CRUDITES:
2 large carrots, peeled and cut into
  sticks
$\frac{1}{3}$ cucumber, cut into sticks
2 courgettes, trimmed and sliced
100 g (4 oz) button mushrooms,
  halved
1 bunch radishes, trimmed
1–2 packets tortilla crisps

Preparation time: about 45 minutes

1. Make the smoked mackerel dip.
Skin the mackerel and mash it
thoroughly. Beat in the soured cream,
garlic, lemon rind and add salt and
pepper to taste. Add sufficient lemon
juice to give a dipping consistency. Put
the dip into a small bowl, and cover
with cling film.
2. Make the cheese and onion dip.
Beat the cream cheese until soft, then
beat in the salad cream and season
with salt and pepper, then beat in the
Cheddar cheese and the spring onions,

reserving a few for garnish. Turn into a
small bowl and cover with cling film.
3. Make the curried egg dip. Beat together the soured cream, mayonnaise
and curry powder; then beat in the
eggs and parsley, season with salt and
pepper to taste and add sufficient
lemon juice to give a dipping consistency. Turn the dip into a small bowl
and cover with cling film.
4. Leave the dips to stand in a cool

place or chill in the refrigerator for at least 2 hours and up to 12 hours before serving.

5. To serve, select one or two large platters and place the bowls of dips in the centre. Sprinkle a little paprika over the smoked mackerel dip and a little curry powder over the curried egg dip and garnish the cheese and onion dip with the reserved spring onions. Arrange sections of the different vege-tables and crisps attractively around the bowls.

6. Everyone helps themselves to some of each dip and a selection of veg-etables and crisps to use for dipping.

CLOCKWISE FROM THE LEFT: Curried egg dip; Smoked mackerel dip; Cheese and onion dip; Crudités

TURKEY JESSICA

1.5 kg (3 lb) raw turkey (thigh,
* breast or a mixture), skinned*
100 g (4 oz) butter or margarine
225 g (8 oz) onions, peeled and
* sliced*
2 garlic cloves, crushed
175 g (6 oz) lean bacon, rinded and
* chopped*
6–8 celery sticks, sliced
50 g (2 oz) plain flour
900 ml (1½ pints) apple juice
2 chicken stock cubes
salt
freshly ground black pepper
½ teaspoon ground coriander
225 g (8 oz) button mushrooms,
* quartered*
6 tablespoons thick set plain
* unsweetened yogurt, soured cream*
* or single cream*

Preparation time: about 25 minutes
Cooking time: 1 hour
Oven: 180°C, 350°F, Gas Mark 4

1. Cut the turkey into 2.5 cm (1 inch) cubes.
2. Melt 50 g (2 oz) of the fat in a flameproof casserole and fry the turkey in two batches until well sealed. Remove the turkey from the casserole.
3. Add the remaining fat to the casserole and fry the onion and garlic gently until soft. Add the bacon and celery and continue frying for 3–4 minutes, stirring frequently.
4. Stir in the flour and cook for about 2 minutes, stirring continuously, then gradually add the apple juice and stock cubes and bring to the boil. Season well and add the coriander.
5. Stir in the mushrooms and return the turkey to the casserole. Cover tightly and cook in a preheated moderate oven for 50 minutes.
6. Taste and adjust the seasoning and stir in the yogurt or cream. Reheat gently and serve.

BAKED POTATOES WITH HERB BUTTER

10 medium to large baking potatoes,
* well-scrubbed*
fresh herbs, to garnish

HERB BUTTER:
175 g (6 oz) butter
1 garlic clove, crushed
2 tablespoons chopped fresh parsley
1 teaspoon dried mixed herbs
grated rind of ½ lemon
salt
freshly ground black pepper

Preparation time: about 20 minutes, plus chilling
Cooking time: 1½–2 hours
Oven: 180°C, 350°F, Gas Mark 4

Normally potatoes are baked in a hot oven (200–220°C, 400–425°F, Gas Mark 6–7) for 1 hour but on this occasion they are cooked for a longer time at a lower heat to allow the

casserole to cook in the oven at the same time.

1. Either prick the potatoes all over or cut a cross in each one.
2. Cook the potatoes at the top of a preheated moderate oven for $1\frac{1}{2}$–2 hours until tender.
3. Meanwhile make the herb butter. Cream the butter until soft, then beat in the garlic, herbs, lemon rind and season with salt and pepper. Form the mixture into a roll, wrap it in cling film or foil and chill until firm.
4. To serve, make a cut or cross in each potato and press to open it out. Put a slice of herb butter in each potato, garnish with fresh herbs and serve immediately.

CURLY SALAD

1 small endive, trimmed
1 head radicchio, roughly shredded
1 bunch watercress, trimmed
1–2 heads chicory, sliced
$\frac{1}{4}$–$\frac{1}{3}$ cucumber, thinly sliced

FRENCH DRESSING:
1 garlic clove, crushed
150 ml ($\frac{1}{4}$ pint) olive, sunflower or safflower oil
2 tablespoons wine vinegar
1 tablespoon lemon juice
$\frac{1}{2}$ teaspoon caster sugar
salt
freshly ground black pepper
1 teaspoon French mustard

Preparation time: about 25 minutes

1. Tear up the endive and put it into a salad bowl with the radicchio, watercress sprigs, chicory and cucumber. Mix all the items together thoroughly, then cover and chill until required.

2. Put all the dressing ingredients into a screw-topped jar and shake until thoroughly emulsified. (This dressing will keep for up to 2 weeks in a cool place.)
3. Just before serving either add a little of the dressing to the salad and toss well; or put the dressing into a bowl with a spoon for each person to help themselves.

FROM THE LEFT: Baked potatoes with herb butter; Turkey Jessica; Curly salad

ALMOND CHOUX PUFFS WITH RASPBERRY SAUCE

CHOUX PUFFS:
100 g (4 oz) butter
300 ml (½ pint) water
150 g (5 oz) plain flour
pinch of salt
4 eggs, beaten
50 g (2 oz) blanched almonds,
 chopped

RASPBERRY SAUCE:
225 g (8 oz) raspberries
1 tablespoon arrowroot
2 tablespoons caster sugar

FILLING:
300 ml (½ pint) double cream
2 tablespoons milk
few drops of almond essence
2 tablespoons sifted icing sugar

TO DECORATE:
sifted icing sugar
fresh flowers (optional)
large fresh raspberries

Preparation time: 35–40 minutes
Cooking time: about 40 minutes
Oven: 220°C, 425°F, Gas Mark 7

For a more sophisticated version of the choux puffs, substitute 2 tablespoons of Amaretto di Saronno liqueur for the milk and almond essence.

1. Make the choux puffs. Place the butter in the water in a large saucepan, heat gently until the butter melts, then bring to the boil.
2. Sift together the flour and salt and add to the pan all at once. Beat the mixture until it is smooth and forms a ball. Remove the pan from the heat immediately.
3. Spread the paste over the base of the pan and leave to cool for about 10 minutes.
4. Gradually beat in the egg, a little at a time, until the mixture is smooth and glossy. A hand-held electric mixer is best for this as it incorporates the most air.
5. Beat in the chopped almonds and put the paste into a piping bag fitted with a 2 cm (¾ inch) plain vegetable

FROM THE LEFT: Almond choux puffs with Raspberry sauce; Cinnamon cheesecake with kiwi fruit

CINNAMON CHEESECAKE WITH KIWI FRUIT

400 g (14 oz) full fat soft cheese
½ teaspoon ground cinnamon
150 ml (¼ pint) soured cream
grated rind of 1 lemon
50 g (2 oz) caster sugar
15 g (½ oz) powdered gelatine
2 tablespoons lemon juice
1 tablespoon water
75 g (3 oz) butter
225 g (8 oz) digestive biscuits, crushed
25 g (1 oz) unsalted peanuts or
  cashew nuts, chopped
1 kiwi fruit
fresh mint, to decorate

Preparation time: about 40 minutes, plus chilling
Cooking time: about 5 minutes

1. Line a 23 × 13 cm (9 × 5 inch) loaf tin with non-stick silicone paper or greased greaseproof paper.
2. Beat the cream cheese until it is soft, then beat in the cinnamon, soured cream, lemon rind and sugar.
3. Put the lemon juice and water into a small bowl, sprinkle over the gelatine and heat over a pan of gently simmering water until the gelatine dissolves.
4. Leave to cool a little, then mix evenly through the cream cheese mixture. Pour into the lined tin and chill until almost set.
5. Place the butter in a saucepan and heat gently until it has melted. Stir in the crushed biscuits and chopped nuts and mix until evenly blended. Spoon the mixture in an even layer over the cheesecake. Press down lightly and chill until firm.
6. To serve, turn out the cheesecake on to a serving dish or board and peel off the paper. Decorate with overlapping slices of kiwi fruit along the top of the dessert in two or three rows and a few fresh mint leaves. Serve the cheesecake cut in slices.

nozzle. Pipe small balls the size of a walnut on to greased baking sheets leaving plenty of space to allow for spreading.
6. Cook in a preheated moderate oven for about 25 minutes until well risen, firm and golden brown. Make a small hole in each puff to let the steam escape and return them to the oven for 2–3 minutes to dry out. Cool on a wire tray.
7. Make the raspberry sauce. If you are using frozen fruit make sure it has thawed completely before you start to make the sauce, then liquidize or purée the raspberries and rub through a sieve into a saucepan. Bring the raspberry purée just to the boil.
8. Blend the arrowroot with 8 tablespoons of water, add to the purée, bring back to the boil and simmer gently until thickened and clear. Stir in the sugar and leave to cool. Pour into a serving jug and cover with cling film.
9. When you are ready to serve, whip the cream with the milk until stiff, then fold in the almond essence and the icing sugar. To fill the choux puffs, either place the mixture in a piping bag fitted with a small plain nozzle and insert the filling through the steam escape hole; or cut each puff in half and spoon in the cream.
10. Arrange the choux buns in a pile on a flat dish and dredge them lightly with sifted icing sugar. A few tiny fresh flowers may be dotted over the choux puffs for decoration or, if they are in season, add a few large fresh raspberries.

WARMING WINTER SUPPER FOR FOUR

French Onion Soup

Pork Chops with Juniper

Cabbage with Soured Cream

Baked Potatoes*

Treacle Tart

Wine suggestion:
Dão, a full-bodied Portuguese red

COUNTDOWN

The day before
Make the shortcrust pastry for the Treacle tart, cover and chill.

In the morning
Complete steps 1 and 2 of the French onion soup.
Grate the Gruyère cheese.
Chop the cabbage.
Complete steps 3 and 4 of the Treacle tart.

1 hour before the meal
Cook the baked potatoes.
Prepare the vegetables for the Pork chops with juniper.
Complete steps 5 and 6 of the Treacle tart and keep it warm.

½ hour before the meal
Start to cook the Pork chops with juniper, leaving them to simmer as you serve the French onion soup.
Complete step 1 of the Cabbage with soured cream.

Just before serving
Reheat the French onion soup and make the cheese toast. Complete the Cabbage with soured cream.

FRENCH ONION SOUP

50 g (2 oz) butter
750 g (1½ lb) onions, peeled and thinly sliced
2 teaspoons sugar
2 teaspoons plain flour
1 litre (1¾ pints) beef stock
salt
freshly ground black pepper
½ French loaf, sliced
50 g (2 oz) Gruyère cheese, grated

Preparation time: 15 minutes
Cooking time: 50 minutes – 1 hour

1. Melt the butter in a pan, add the onions and sugar. Lower the heat and cook the onions slowly for 20–30 minutes, until they are an even chestnut brown. Take care to cook them slowly, so that they brown evenly and to a good colour without burning.
2. Add the flour and cook for about 5 minutes, stirring well. Add the stock, salt and pepper. Bring to the boil and simmer for 15–20 minutes.
3. Meanwhile, place the slices of French bread under a preheated grill and toast on one side. Cover the other side with the grated cheese and toast until golden brown.
4. Taste and adjust the seasoning, then pour the soup into a hot tureen. Place a piece of toast in each serving dish and pour the soup over.

PORK CHOPS WITH JUNIPER

4 tablespoons olive oil
4 pork chops, about 225 g (8 oz) each
2 shallots, peeled and chopped
1 garlic clove, peeled and chopped
8 juniper berries, roughly crushed
225 g (8 oz) tomatoes, skinned and roughly chopped
4 tablespoons gin or vodka
120 ml (4 fl oz) chicken stock
½ tablespoon chopped fresh thyme
salt
freshly ground black pepper
fresh thyme, to garnish

Preparation time: 10 minutes
Cooking time: 30 minutes

1. Heat the oil in a deep frying pan with a lid. Add the pork chops and fry over a brisk heat for 3–4 minutes on each side to brown, then remove and keep warm.
2. Add the shallots to the pan and fry over a gentle heat for 2 minutes, then add the garlic and cook for 1 further minute.
3. Stir in the juniper berries and tomatoes and cook for 2–3 minutes, stirring. Then add the gin or vodka and boil rapidly over a brisk heat until reduced by half. Pour in the stock and stir in the thyme. Season to taste with salt and pepper.
4. Return the pork chops to the pan, cover and simmer for 15–20 minutes, adding a little extra stock if necessary, until the chops are cooked through. Serve garnished with fresh thyme.

CABBAGE WITH SOURED CREAM

salt
1 large green cabbage, about 750 g (1½ lb), roughly chopped
50 g (2 oz) butter
½ teaspoon caraway seeds
freshly ground black pepper
½ teaspoon paprika
150 ml (¼ pint) soured cream
½ teaspoon caraway seeds, to garnish

Preparation time: 3 minutes
Cooking time: about 10 minutes

1. Bring 2.5 cm (1 inch) salted water to the boil in a large saucepan, add the cabbage, cover and cook over a moderate heat for 6–8 minutes, or until barely tender. Drain well.
2. Melt the butter in the rinsed pan, add the drained cabbage with the caraway seeds and stir well. Season to taste with salt and pepper, then stir in the paprika and soured cream. Cook over the lowest possible heat, without boiling, for 3 minutes until cooked through.
3. Transfer to a warmed serving dish, sprinkle with caraway seeds and serve.

CLOCKWISE FROM TOP LEFT: Cabbage with soured cream; Pork chops with juniper; French onion soup

TREACLE TART

225 g (8 oz) golden syrup
juice of ½ small lemon
50 g (2 oz) fresh white breadcrumbs

SHORTCRUST PASTRY:
175 g (6 oz) plain flour
pinch of salt
40 g (1½ oz) butter or hard
  margarine, cut into small pieces
40 g (1½ oz) lard, cut into pieces
2 tablespoons milk

Preparation time: 35 minutes, plus chilling
Cooking time: 35 minutes
Oven: 190°C, 375°F, Gas Mark 5

1. Make the shortcrust pastry. Sieve the flour and salt into a mixing bowl. Rub the butter and lard into the flour until the mixture resembles fine breadcrumbs. Avoid squeezing the fat into the flour, but rub it delicately between the thumbs and fingers.
2. Gradually stir in the milk until the mixture begins to bind. With the fingers mix the pastry to a smooth dough. Chill for 30 minutes.
3. Roll out the pastry on a lightly floured surface and use to line a 20 cm (8 inch) flan ring.
4. Trim the excess pastry and roll again. Cut into four 25 cm (10 inch) strips. Rest the flan case and strips for 30 minutes.

5. Gently warm the syrup and lemon juice in a pan and add the crumbs. Mix well and pour into the flan case.
6. Decorate with the strips of pastry and bake in a preheated oven for 35 minutes.
7. Allow to cool slightly and serve warm with custard or cream. If liked, sprinkle a little caster sugar over the top of the tart before you serve.

BELOW: Treacle tart

FRENCH BISTRO SUPPER FOR SIX

Goat's Cheese and Tomato Hors
d'Oeuvre

Provençal Beef Stew

French Beans in Garlic Sauce

Rice*

Lemon and Yogurt Ice Cream

Wine suggestion:
French country wine

COUNTDOWN

The day before
Prepare the ingredients for the Provençal beef stew and leave to marinate overnight.
Make the Lemon and yogurt ice cream.

2½ hours before the meal
Complete steps 2 to 6 of the Provençal beef stew.
Make the dressing for the Goat's cheese and tomato hors d'oeuvre.
Prepare the French beans.

½ hour before the meal
Complete steps 1 to 3 of the Goat's cheese and tomato hors d'oeuvre.
Complete steps 1 and 2 of the French beans in garlic sauce.
Cook the rice and keep it warm.
Whip the cream for the Lemon and yogurt ice cream.
Complete steps 7 and 8 of the Provençal beef stew.

Just before serving
Dress and garnish the Goat's cheese and tomato hors d'oeuvre.
Complete steps 3 and 4 of the French beans in garlic sauce.
Turn out the Lemon and yogurt ice cream and decorate.

GOAT'S CHEESE AND TOMATO HORS D'OEUVRE

250 g (12 oz) Ste Maure or other goat's cheese
½ cucumber, thinly sliced
5–6 large continental tomatoes, sliced
fresh chives or parsley

DRESSING:
6 tablespoons good flavoured oil, preferably olive oil
3 tablespoons wine vinegar
good pinch of dry mustard
salt
freshly ground black pepper

Preparation time: 10 minutes

1. Cut the cheese into 5 mm (¼ inch) slices. On individual plates, arrange the slices of cheese overlapping in a semi-circle round the top half of each plate.
2. Arrange the cucumber next to the cheese. Overlap the tomato slices around the bottom half of each plate.

3. To make the dressing, mix or shake the oil, vinegar, mustard, salt and pepper together.
4. Spoon a little dressing over the tomatoes and arrange the chives or parsley decoratively. Extra vinaigrette can be served separately if desired.

BELOW: Goat's cheese and tomato hors d'oeuvre

PROVENÇAL BEEF STEW

*1·5 kg (3 lb) lean chuck or blade-
  bone steak, trimmed and cut into
  4 cm (1½ inch) cubes*
3 onions, peeled and sliced
3 carrots, peeled and sliced
1 strip orange peel, without pith
1 bay leaf
4–5 peppercorns
300 ml (½ pint) red wine
4 tablespoons cognac
50 g (2 oz) dripping or vegetable fat
*2–3 garlic cloves, peeled and crushed
  with a little salt*
300 ml (½ pint) beef stock
salt
freshly ground black pepper
100 g (4 oz) black olives, pitted

TO GARNISH:
finely chopped fresh parsley

Preparation time: 20 minutes, plus
  marinating overnight
Cooking time: 2–2½ hours
Oven: 160°C, 325°F, Gas Mark 3

1. Place the meat in a deep dish with 1
sliced onion, the carrots, orange peel,
bay leaf and peppercorns. Pour on the
red wine and cognac, cover and leave
to marinate in the refrigerator
overnight.
2. Remove the meat and vegetables
from the liquid and drain well, reserving the marinade.
3. Heat the dripping in a flameproof
casserole, add the meat and brown on
all sides. Remove from the pan with a
slotted spoon.
4. Add the remaining onions and the
crushed garlic to the pan and cook
gently until golden brown.
5. Return the meat to the pan, together
with the liquid, vegetables, orange peel
and bay leaf used in the marinade.
Discard the peppercorns. Add the
stock, salt and pepper. Bring to the
boil.
6. Cover tightly, place in a preheated
oven and cook for 2–2½ hours until
tender.
7. Discard the bay leaf and skim any fat
from the surface of the sauce. Remove
the meat from the pan and boil the
sauce until reduced by half.
8. Return the meat to the casserole
with the black olives or place in another dish and pour the sauce over.
Sprinkle with finely chopped parsley.
9. Serve with rice.

FRENCH BEANS IN GARLIC SAUCE

*750 g (1½ lb) French beans or French
  butter beans, trimmed and cut in
  half*
salt
300 ml (½ pint) single cream
3 garlic cloves, peeled and crushed
white pepper
*chopped fresh chervil or parsley, to
  garnish*

Preparation time: 10 minutes
Cooking time: 20–25 minutes

1. Cook the beans in a pan of boiling,
salted water for 10–15 minutes until
just tender. Drain well.
2. Meanwhile, place the cream and
garlic in a pan and boil for about 7
minutes or until the cream thickens.
3. Add the beans, mix well together
and cook for a further 4–5 minutes.
Add salt and pepper.
4. Pour into a hot serving dish and
sprinkle with chopped chervil or
parsley.

LEMON AND YOGURT ICE CREAM

450 ml (¾ pint) plain unsweetened
yogurt
100 g (4 oz) caster sugar
finely grated rind of 1 lemon
4–5 tablespoons lemon juice

TO DECORATE:
6–8 tablespoons whipping cream,
stiffly whipped
strips of angelica
3–4 thin slices of lemon, cut in half
(optional)

Preparation time: 15 minutes, plus freezing

1. Beat the yogurt and sugar together until the sugar has dissolved. Add the lemon rind and juice. Taste and add a little more sugar if the mixture is too sharp, remembering that freezing dulls the sweetness of food.
2. Cover the bowl and place in the freezer or the frozen food compartment of the refrigerator and leave until the mixture is softly frozen. Beat the ice until it is quite smooth then place in a mould or bowl and freeze overnight until solid.

3. To serve, the ice cream can be turned out on to a serving dish and decorated with the whipped cream, angelica and sliced lemon (if liked).

CLOCKWISE FROM THE LEFT: Lemon and yogurt ice cream; French beans in garlic sauce; Provençal beef stew

FISHY SUPPER FOR SIX

Avocado Pâté with Crab Sticks

Monkfish and Scallop Casserole

Saffron Rice with Hazelnuts

Julienne of Courgettes and Leeks

Peach and Almond Tart

Wine suggestion:
Meursault, a white Burgundy

COUNTDOWN

In the morning
Make the Peach and almond tart, cover and chill.
Complete step 1 of the Julienne of courgettes and leeks.

1½ hours before the meal
Prepare all the ingredients for the Monkfish and scallop casserole.
Prepare step 1 of the Avocado pâté and make the Melba toast if required.

50 minutes before serving
Cook the Monkfish and scallop casserole.

20 minutes before serving
Cook the Saffron rice with hazelnuts.

15 minutes before serving
Complete steps 2 to 4 of the Avocado pâté with crab sticks and make the hot toast if required.

10 minutes before serving
Complete steps 2 and 3 of the Julienne of courgettes and leeks.

AVOCADO PATE WITH CRAB STICKS

50 g (2 oz) mature Cheddar cheese, finely grated
4 tablespoons thick set plain unsweetened yogurt
1 teaspoon finely grated raw onion
salt
freshly ground black pepper
12 crab or seafood sticks, thawed
few crisp cos or Little Gem lettuce leaves
2 ripe avocados
1 tablespoon lemon juice
6 parsley sprigs, to garnish

Preparation time: about 20 minutes

1. Combine the grated cheese, yogurt, onion and salt and pepper in a bowl, cover and chill.
2. Cut each crab or seafood stick in half lengthwise and arrange 4 pieces, together with a few spiky lettuce leaves, in a fan shape on each side plate.
3. Quarter, peel and mash or purée the avocados, adding lemon juice to the mixture as you mash. Beat in the cheese mixture and season to taste.
4. Put a spoonful of avocado pâté at the base of each 'fan' on the plates and top with a sprig of parsley. Serve almost immediately to prevent the avocado from discolouring. Accompany with Melba toast or fingers of hot toast and butter.

SAFFRON RICE WITH HAZELNUTS

few strands of saffron
350 g (12 oz) long grain rice
salt
25 g (1 oz) butter or margarine
50 g (2 oz) skinned hazelnuts, chopped
freshly ground black pepper
2 tablespoons chopped fresh parsley

Preparation time: 10 minutes
Cooking time: about 20 minutes

1. Put the saffron strands into a pan of boiling water and simmer until the colour emerges. Add the rice and salt to taste and boil for 13–14 minutes until the rice is just tender.
2. Drain the rice, rinse it under hot water, and drain it again thoroughly.

3. Meanwhile, melt the butter in a pan and fry the hazelnuts until they are lightly browned. Remove at once from the heat, season well and add the parsley. Stir the mixture through the rice and turn into a serving dish.

JULIENNE OF COURGETTES AND LEEKS

350 g (12 oz) courgettes
4 leeks, total weight about 450 g (1 lb), trimmed
50 g (2 oz) butter or margarine
salt
freshly ground black pepper
good pinch of ground coriander

Preparation time: about 20 minutes
Cooking time: 8–10 minutes

1. Top and tail the courgettes and cut them into julienne strips. Cut the leeks into julienne strips and wash them thoroughly. Drain and dry them on a clean tea towel.
2. Melt the fat in a pan and add the leeks. Cook over a low heat for 2–3

minutes, tossing them frequently, then add the courgettes and continue frying for 3–5 minutes until both vegetables are piping hot and just cooked, but still with a distinct 'bite' to them.
3. Season well with salt, pepper and coriander, drain and turn into a serving dish.

MONKFISH AND SCALLOP CASSEROLE

40 g (1½ oz) butter or margarine
1 onion, peeled and sliced
1 celery stick, sliced
1 large carrot, peeled and diced
1–2 garlic cloves, crushed
500 g (1¼ lb) monkfish
350 g (12 oz) prepared scallops
1 × 425 g (15 oz) can tomatoes
1 tablespoon tomato purée
½ teaspoon Worcestershire sauce
1 tablespoon lemon juice
150 ml (¼ pint) dry white wine
salt
freshly ground black pepper
good pinch of ground coriander
1 bay leaf
1 tablespoon cornflour

Preparation time: about 20 minutes
Cooking time: about 50 minutes
Oven: 160°C, 325°F, Gas Mark 3

1. Melt the fat in a flameproof casserole and fry the onion, celery, carrot and garlic gently until soft, stirring occasionally.
2. Skin the monkfish and cut it into 2 cm (¾ inch) cubes. Halve or quarter the scallops, depending on their size. Add the fish to the casserole and continue cooking for 2–3 minutes, stirring occasionally.
3. Add the can of tomatoes, tomato purée, Worcestershire sauce, lemon juice, wine, salt and pepper, coriander and the bay leaf and bring to the boil.
4. Cover the casserole tightly and cook in a preheated moderate oven for 40 minutes.
5. Blend the cornflour with a little cold water, add it to the casserole, and bring back to the boil for a minute or so. Taste and adjust the seasoning, discard the bay leaf and serve.

CLOCKWISE FROM TOP LEFT: Saffron rice with hazelnuts; Monkfish and scallop casserole; Avocado pâté with crab sticks; Julienne of courgettes and leeks

PEACH AND ALMOND TART

PATE SUCREE:
175 g (6 oz) plain flour
pinch of salt
75 g (3 oz) caster sugar
75 g (3 oz) butter, slightly softened
  and cut into cubes
3 egg yolks

FILLING:
25 g (1 oz) cornflour
450 ml (¾ pint) milk
150 ml (¼ pint) plain unsweetened
  yogurt
3 egg yolks
50 g (2 oz) caster sugar
75 g (3 oz) ground almonds
few drops of almond essence

TOPPING:
1 × 425 g (15 oz) can peach halves
3 tablespoons cranberry or
  redcurrant jelly
2 tablespoons sweet white wine
½ teaspoon arrowroot

Preparation time: about 1 hour, plus chilling and cooling
Cooking time: 45 minutes
Oven: 190°C, 375°F, Gas Mark 5

1. Make the pâte sucrée. Sift the flour and salt on to a work surface and make a well in the centre. Put the sugar, chopped butter and egg yolks into the centre and using the fingers of one hand, work them together until they form a paste, then gradually work in the flour from around the sides. Knead the pastry lightly until it is smooth, wrap it in polythene or foil and chill for at least 1 hour.
2. Roll out the pastry on a lightly floured surface and use to line a 25 cm (10 inch) fluted flan ring, tin or dish. Prick the base and bake blind in a preheated moderately hot oven for about 20 minutes. Remove the baking beans and paper and return the flan to the oven for 4–5 minutes to dry out, then cool on a wire tray.
3. Meanwhile, reroll the pastry trimmings and, using a 5 cm (2 inch) fluted round cutter, cut out 12 fluted crescent shapes. Stand the shapes on a greased baking sheet, prick and cook in the same oven for 12–15 minutes until lightly browned. Cool on a wire tray.
4. Make the filling. Blend the cornflour with a little of the milk, then heat the remainder to just below boiling point. Pour the milk on to the blended cornflour, return it to the pan and bring it slowly to the boil, stirring continuously. Add the yogurt, bring the mixture back to the boil and let it simmer for 1–2 minutes.
5. Stir in the egg yolks and return the pan to the heat for a minute or so, stirring vigorously. Remove the pan from the heat and beat in the sugar, almonds and almond essence. Leave the mixture to cool a little, then pour it into the cold flan case and leave it to set.
6. Make the topping. Drain the peaches and cut them into neat slices. Arrange the slices in circles attractively over the filling.
7. Heat the cranberry jelly with the wine until it has melted, then bring the mixture to the boil. Blend the arrowroot with a little cold water, add it to the melted mixture and bring back to the boil, stirring continuously, and cook until the mixture is clear. Allow to cool a little, then pour or brush over the peaches. Chill until required and decorate with the pastry crescents. Serve with whipped cream, if wished.

Variation: Use 4 or 5 fresh sliced peaches or about 450 g (1 lb) apricots, halved, stoned and arranged cut side downwards.

LEFT: Peach and almond tart

CREOLE SUPPER FOR SIX

Baked Avocados with Bacon and Prawns

Creole Spiced Beef

Creamed Yams

Sunshine Salad

Coconut Ice Cream

Stuffed Pineapple

Wine suggestion:
Californian Zinfandel

COUNTDOWN

Up to 1 week in advance
Make the Coconut ice cream.

1–2 days in advance
Prepare and marinate the Creole spiced beef.

In the morning
Fry the onion and bacon for the Baked avocados, cover and chill.
Prepare the oranges and grapefruit for the Sunshine salad, cover and chill.

2½ hours before the meal
Prepare and cook the Spiced beef.

1½ hours before the meal
Prepare and cook the Creamed yams.
Prepare the Stuffed pineapple.

1 hour before the meal
Transfer the Coconut ice cream from the freezer to the refrigerator.

45 minutes before the meal
Complete steps 2–5 of the Baked avocados.
Complete and garnish the Sunshine salad.

Just before serving
Discard the bay leaves and garnish the Creole spiced beef.

BAKED AVOCADOS WITH BACON AND PRAWNS

1 medium onion, peeled and finely chopped
50 g (2 oz) butter
225 g (8 oz) lean back bacon rashers, rinded and finely chopped
3 large ripe avocados
2 teaspoons lime juice
salt
freshly ground black pepper
175 g (6 oz) peeled prawns

TO GARNISH:
6 large unshelled prawns
6 wedges of lime

Preparation time: about 20 minutes
Cooking time: 20–25 minutes
Oven: 200°C, 400°F, Gas Mark 6

1. Fry the onion gently in the melted butter until it is soft. Add the bacon and continue frying gently until it softens, stirring frequently. Drain and cool.
2. Halve the avocados, remove the stones and scoop out the flesh. Mash it thoroughly, then beat in the lime juice, salt and pepper, and fold in the bacon and prawns.
3. Wrap the avocado shells in foil to prevent them blackening and stand them in a shallow ovenproof dish or tin. Spoon in the bacon and prawn mixture.
4. Cook in a preheated moderately hot oven for 15–20 minutes until well heated through.
5. Serve hot, garnished with a whole prawn and a wedge of lime.

CREOLE SPICED BEEF

1.25 kg (2½ lb) best braising steak
juice of 2 limes
4 garlic cloves, crushed
2 teaspoons ground cinnamon
¼ teaspoon ground cloves
2 teaspoons grated fresh ginger
1 green chilli, seeded and finely chopped
1½ teaspoons salt
3 tablespoons oil or dripping
3 bay leaves
½ teaspoon ground nutmeg
2 tablespoons dark rum
3 tablespoons water
2 teaspoons annatto liquid or orange liquid food colouring
freshly ground black pepper
fresh coriander leaves, to garnish

Preparation time: about 30 minutes, plus marinating
Cooking time: about 2 hours
Oven: 150°C, 300°F, Gas Mark 2

Annatto is the seed of a tree native to Central America and the West Indies. It is best known as a colouring agent, but the crushed seed is sometimes used as a spice. As the flavour is very delicate, orange food colouring can be used instead.

1. Cut the beef into 4 cm (1½ inch) cubes and place them in a shallow container.
2. Combine the juice of the limes, the garlic, cinnamon, ground cloves, ginger, chilli and salt. Pour over the beef, mix thoroughly, cover very securely and leave to marinate for 24–48 hours, turning the pieces of beef several times.
3. Heat the oil or dripping in a flame-proof casserole and add the beef and all the marinade. Fry gently for 10 minutes, stirring frequently. Add the bay leaves, nutmeg, rum, water and annatto, season with pepper and bring to the boil.
4. Cover the casserole tightly and cook in a preheated cool oven for 1 hour. Give the meat a good stir, replace the lid and return the casserole to the oven for 1 further hour or until the meat is tender.
5. Discard the bay leaves and serve garnished with fresh coriander leaves.

CREAMED YAMS

900 g (2 lb) yams
1 tablespoon lemon or lime juice
75 g (3 oz) butter or margarine
4 tablespoons single cream or top of
 the milk
salt
freshly ground black pepper
good pinch of ground nutmeg
chopped fresh coriander or parsley,
 to garnish (optional)

Preparation time: about 20 minutes
Cooking time: 45–50 minutes
Oven: 180°C, 350°F, Gas Mark 4

1. Peel the yams, cut them into cubes and put them into a saucepan with the lemon or lime juice.
2. Cover with cold water, bring to the boil, cover the pan and simmer for about 30 minutes or until the yams are tender. Drain thoroughly.
3. Put the yams into a food processor and purée, or mash them very thoroughly. Beat in the butter followed by the cream, and season to taste with salt, pepper and nutmeg.
4. Turn the purée into an ovenproof dish and cook in a preheated moderate oven for 15–20 minutes until lightly coloured. Serve hot sprinkled with chopped coriander or parsley, if liked.

SUNSHINE SALAD

1 small firm lettuce, shredded
2 oranges, peeled and all pith
 removed
2 pink grapefruit, peeled and all pith
 removed
2 firm bananas
little lemon or lime juice
½ cucumber, peeled, seeded and
 diced
2 tablespoons olive oil
1 teaspoon caster sugar
salt
freshly ground black pepper
bunch of watercress

Preparation time: about 25 minutes

1. Arrange the shredded lettuce in a salad bowl.
2. Remove the segments from the oranges and grapefruit, cutting carefully between the membranes, and put them into a bowl.
3. Peel and slice the bananas, dip them in the lemon or lime juice and add to the orange and grapefruit with the cucumber. Add the oil and sugar and season to taste with salt and pepper. Mix well and pile onto the lettuce.
4. Toss lightly and garnish with the sprigs of watercress.

COCONUT ICE CREAM

50 g (2 oz) packet coconut cream
 powder
300 ml (½ pint) milk
2 eggs
2 egg yolks
100 g (4 oz) caster sugar
few drops of vanilla essence
slithers of fresh coconut, to decorate
 (optional)

Preparation time: 30 minutes, plus chilling
Cooking time: about 15 minutes

1. Dissolve the coconut cream powder in 300 ml (½ pint) water as directed on the packet.
2. Heat together the coconut milk and the milk to just below boiling point.
3. Beat the eggs, egg yolks and sugar together. Pour onto the hot milk and strain into the top of a double saucepan or heatproof bowl.
4. Cook over a pan of gently simmering water, stirring occasionally, until the mixture has thickened. Add the vanilla essence, cover and leave until cold.
5. Pour into a fairly shallow freezer container, cover and freeze until the mixture is just solid, but not too firm. Whisk or beat until it is smooth and creamy and all the ice crystals have disappeared. Cover and freeze again until firm.
6. Whisk or beat the ice cream hard a second time until quite smooth. Cover and freeze until firm. ⑉
7. Transfer the ice cream to the refrigerator about 1 hour before serving, or leave it at room temperature for about 20 minutes so that it is not too hard. Serve decorated with slithers of fresh coconut, if available.

⑉ Freeze for up to 3 months.

STUFFED PINEAPPLE

1 large pineapple
2 tablespoons caster sugar
2 tablespoons Curaçao
2 tablespoons rum
juice of 1–2 passion fruits
1 ripe mango, peeled, stoned and
 cubed
1 ripe pawpaw or papaya, peeled,
 seeded and cubed
juice of 1 lime
lime quarters, to decorate

Preparation time: about 15 minutes

1. Cut the pineapple in half lengthways. Using a small knife, carefully remove the flesh and cut it into cubes, discarding the core.
2. Combine the sugar, Curaçao, rum and passion fruit juice in a bowl.
3. Add the mango, pawpaw and pineapple to the liqueur mixture and toss well together.
4. Spoon the fruit into the pineapple halves, piling it well up and pour the juice overall. Decorate with lime quarters and serve with the coconut ice cream.

CLOCKWISE FROM THE TOP: Stuffed pineapple; Sunshine salad; Baked avocados with bacon and prawns (page 133); Coconut ice cream; Creole spiced beef (page 133); Creamed yams

SEASONAL PARTIES

Easter Sunday, when suddenly spring is in the air; Midsummer, with its wealth of new, young vegetables, salads and soft fruits; Hallowe'en, a tradition children especially love to keep up, and the long, long festive season that stretches from Christmas Eve to New Year's Day – whatever the occasion, follow our step-by-step plans in detail. That way, with much of the preparation and cooking done in advance, you will be able to relax and enjoy all the parties.

FROM THE LEFT: Mocha Malakoff gâteau; Jerusalem artichoke salad; green peas (no recipe); Roast turkey; Cranberry sauce

EASTER LUNCH AND TEA FOR SIX

Lunch

Quail's Eggs in Vermouth Jelly

Stuffed Leg of Lamb with Kumquats

Scalloped Potatoes with Yogurt

Peas and Celeriac

Gingered Trifle

Wine suggestions:
Starter:
Fino sherry
Main course:
Pomerol or St. Emilion

Tea

Simnel Cake

Easter Spicy Biscuits

Easter Eggs

COUNTDOWN

Up to 4 days in advance

Make the Simnel cake and store in an airtight container.
Make the Easter spicy biscuits and store in an airtight container.
Make and decorate the Easter eggs and store in a cool place in an airtight container.

The day before

Make the Quail's eggs in vermouth jelly, cover and chill.
Complete the Gingered trifle up to the end of step 8, cover and chill.

In the morning

Complete steps 1 and 2 of the Stuffed leg of lamb with kumquats.
Decorate the trifle, cover and chill.
Make the Melba toast if serving with the Quail's eggs.

2¼ hours before the meal

Cook the lamb.

1 hour before the meal

Complete steps 1–4 of the Scalloped potatoes with yogurt.

30 minutes before the meal

Prepare and cook the Peas and celeriac.
Garnish the Quail's eggs in vermouth jelly.
Make the sauce for the Stuffed lamb with kumquats.
Finish cooking the Scalloped potatoes with yogurt.
Make the hot buttered toast if serving with the Quail's eggs.

QUAIL'S EGGS IN VERMOUTH JELLY

18 quail's eggs
500 ml (18 fl oz) beef consommé
2½ teaspoons powdered gelatine
4 tablespoons dry vermouth
1 tablespoon chopped fresh parsley (optional)
6 tablespoons soured cream or thick set plain unsweetened yogurt
6 teaspoons black lumpfish roe
sprigs of parsley, to garnish

Preparation time: about 30 minutes, plus chilling
Cooking time: about 5 minutes

The quail's eggs can either be served soft-boiled in which case they need only 45 seconds cooking or hard-boiled when they require 4 minutes – it is simply a matter of preference.

1. Boil the eggs for 45 seconds or for 4 minutes, if you prefer. Remove from the saucepan and cool under running cold water. Remove the shells carefully and put 3 eggs into each of 6 ramekin dishes.
2. Heat the consommé until liquid, if necessary. Put 2 tablespoons of the

vermouth into a small bowl and sprinkle over the gelatine. Place the bowl over a pan of gently simmering water until the gelatine dissolves, then stir to ensure that it is thoroughly blended. Stir the gelatine mixture into the consommé with the remaining 2 tablespoons of vermouth and the parsley, if using.
3. Cool and chill until the mixture begins to thicken, then pour over the

ABOVE: Quail's eggs in vermouth jelly

eggs to fill the dishes, making sure the parsley is evenly distributed. Chill until firmly set.

4. To serve, put a spoonful of soured cream or yogurt over each dish and spread it out a little. Top with a spoonful of lumpfish roe and a sprig of parsley. Serve with hot toast fingers or Melba toast and butter.

STUFFED LEG OF LAMB WITH KUMQUATS

1.75 kg (4 lb) leg of lamb, boned
salt
freshly ground black pepper
2–3 tablespoons oil or dripping

STUFFING:
225 g (8 oz) kumquats
2 rashers lean bacon, rinded and
 finely chopped
2 tablespoons chopped fresh parsley
50 g (2 oz) shelled walnuts, chopped

SAUCE:
200 ml (⅓ pint) red wine
200 ml (⅓ pint) beef stock
2–4 tablespoons brandy
2 tablespoons apricot jam
1 teaspoon tomato purée
2 tablespoons plain flour
sprigs of watercress, to garnish

Preparation time: about 25 minutes
Cooking time: about 2 hours
Oven: 220°C, 425°F, Gas Mark 7

1. Remove any excess fat from the lamb and season lightly.
2. To make the stuffing, chop 16–18 kumquats incorporating the peel, flesh, pips, etc. and mix with the bacon, parsley and walnuts and season with salt and pepper. Place the stuffing in the bone cavity of the lamb, cutting pockets in the flesh if necessary. Secure with skewers and string to enclose the stuffing completely.
3. Stand the lamb in a roasting tin and pour over the oil or dripping. Season, if liked, and cook in a preheated hot oven for 1¾–2 hours, basting 2 or 3 times. Allow 28–30 minutes per 450 g (1 lb) depending on the thickness of the joint.
4. To make the sauce, combine the wine, stock, brandy, apricot jam and tomato purée. When the joint is cooked, transfer it to a serving dish and keep it warm. Skim the fat from the roasting tin and whisk the flour into the pan juices. Cook for 1–2 minutes then gradually pour in the wine mixture and bring to the boil, stirring frequently. Simmer for 2 minutes.
5. Slice the remaining kumquats and put them into a saucepan. Strain the sauce over them and bring back to the boil. Simmer for 2 minutes, taste and adjust the seasoning and pour into a jug. Remove the string and skewers from the lamb and garnish with watercress. Carve into fairly thick slices.

SCALLOPED POTATOES WITH YOGURT

750 g (1½ lb) potatoes, scrubbed
salt
150 ml (¼ pint) plain unsweetened
 yogurt
2 tablespoons chopped fresh parsley
freshly ground black pepper
40 g (1½ oz) Cheddar cheese, grated
2 tablespoons fresh brown or white
 breadcrumbs

Preparation time: 15 minutes
Cooking time: about 30 minutes

1. Prick the potatoes and boil them in salted water until just tender. Drain.

2. Combine the yogurt and parsley and season with salt and pepper.

3. Slice the potatoes, but do not peel, and put them into a greased shallow oven-proof dish.

4. Pour the yogurt evenly over the potatoes and sprinkle with the cheese and breadcrumbs.

5. Cook under a moderate grill for about 5 minutes until well browned and crispy on top.

FROM THE LEFT: Stuffed leg of lamb with kumquats; Scalloped potatoes with yogurt; Peas and celeriac; Gingered trifle

PEAS AND CELERIAC

750 g (1½ lb) celeriac
salt
2 tablespoons lemon juice
175 g (6 oz) peas
25 g (1 oz) butter
freshly ground black pepper

Preparation time: 12–20 minutes
Cooking time: about 30 minutes

1. Peel the celeriac, removing all the tough skin and knobbles. Cut into even 1 cm (½ inch) dice.

2. Put the celeriac into a saucepan and cover with water. Season with salt, add 1 tablespoon of the lemon juice and bring to the boil. Cover and simmer for about 20 minutes or until almost tender.

3. Add the peas to the saucepan of celeriac and bring back to the boil. Simmer for about 3 minutes.

4. Melt the butter in a small saucepan, add the remaining lemon juice and season well, especially with pepper.

5. Drain the celeriac and peas, return to the pan, pour over the butter mixture and toss well. Drain, turn into a warmed dish and serve.

GINGERED TRIFLE

SPONGE:
100 g (4 oz) soft margarine
100 g (4 oz) caster sugar
2 eggs
grated rind of ½ orange
100 g (4 oz) self raising flour, sifted
1 teaspoon baking powder
225 g (8 oz) ginger preserve
150 ml (¼ pint) ginger wine
225 g (8 oz) raspberries, fresh or frozen and part-thawed
2 oranges, peeled and segments removed

CUSTARD:
450 ml (¾ pint) milk
3 egg yolks
1 egg
few drops vanilla essence
2 tablespoons caster sugar
1 teaspoon cornflour

TO DECORATE:
300 ml (½ pint) whipping cream
few pieces stem or crystallized ginger, sliced
silver dragées
strips of angelica

Preparation time: about 50 minutes, plus cooling and chilling
Cooking time: about 40 minutes
Oven: 180°C, 350°F, Gas Mark 4

1. To make the sponge, put the fat, sugar, eggs, orange rind, flour and baking powder into a bowl. Mix together, then beat hard for 2 minutes.

2. Grease and flour two 18 cm (7 inch) round sandwich tins and divide the mixture between them, levelling the tops. Cook in a preheated moderate oven for 20–25 minutes until well risen, golden brown and firm to the touch.

3. Turn out on to a wire tray and leave until cold.

4. When cold sandwich together with the ginger preserve. Cut the sponge into 4 cm (1½ inch) cubes and put into a glass serving bowl.

5. Pour the ginger wine over the sponge and then sprinkle first with the raspberries and then with the orange segments.

6. To make the custard, heat all but 2 tablespoons of the milk to just below boiling point. Blend the remaining milk with the egg yolks, whole egg, vanilla essence, sugar and cornflour.

7. Pour the hot milk on to the egg mixture and return to a heatproof bowl. Stand the bowl over a saucepan of very gently simmering water and cook gently, stirring frequently, until the custard thickens sufficiently to coat the back of a spoon quite thickly. Do not let it boil or it will curdle.

8. Cool the custard a little and pour it over the fruit and the sponge. Chill.

9. To decorate the trifle, whip the cream until stiff then pipe or spread it over the custard to cover completely. Arrange slices of ginger, silver dragées and strips of angelica over the top of the trifle. Chill until ready to serve.

SIMNEL CAKE

MAKES AN 18 cm (7 inch) SQUARE
 CAKE
175 g (6 oz) currants
175 g (6 oz) raisins
100 g (4 oz) sultanas
100 g (4 oz) cut mixed peel
grated rind of 1 orange
225 g (8 oz) plain flour
1 teaspoon ground cinnamon
1 teaspoon ground nutmeg
175 g (6 oz) butter or margarine
175 g (6 oz) light soft brown sugar
3 eggs
1 tablespoon lemon or orange juice
500 g (1¼ lb) marzipan
50 g (2 oz) apricot jam or
 redcurrant jelly
about 1 metre (1 yard) yellow satin
 ribbon, approx 3 cm (1¼ inches)
 wide

Preparation time: 40 minutes
Cooking time: about 2¾ hours
Oven: 160°C, 325°F, Gas Mark 3;
 then: 150°C, 300°F, Gas Mark 2

1. Grease and line an 18 cm (7 inch)
square cake tin with double greaseproof paper.
2. Combine the currants, raisins, sultanas, mixed peel and orange rind.
3. Sift together the flour and spices.
4. Cream together the butter and
sugar until very light and fluffy. Beat in
the eggs, one at a time, following each
one with a tablespoonful of flour.
5. Fold in the remaining flour, followed by the lemon juice to give a soft
dropping consistency. Add the fruit
and mix evenly.
6. Put half the cake mixture into the
cake tin and level the top.
7. Divide the marzipan into 3 equal
portions and roll out one piece to an
18 cm (7 inch) square to fit the cake tin;
lay on the remaining cake mixture and
level the top. Do not make a hollow.
8. Cook in a preheated moderate oven
for 1 hour, then reduce the oven temperature to cool and cook for a further
1¾ hours or until golden brown and
firm to the touch. You can test the cake
with a skewer, but remember that the
marzipan will be sticky while it is hot.
Leave in the tin until cold, then turn out
and remove the paper.
9. Roll out another portion of marzipan to fit the top of the cake. Brush
the top with the jam or jelly, then
position the marzipan carefully. Crimp
the edges.
10. Form the rest of the marzipan into
11 equal-sized balls and place them on
the top. If liked the marzipan may be
lightly browned under a fairly low grill,
but take care it does not burn.
11. Tie a yellow ribbon around the
side of the cake with a strip of greaseproof paper inside it to prevent grease
stains on the ribbon and complete
with a bow. If liked, fluffy rabbits,
chickens or flowers or tiny Easter eggs
may be put on top of the cake.

EASTER SPICY BISCUITS

MAKES ABOUT 18
75 g (3 oz) butter or margarine
65 g (2½ oz) light soft brown sugar
1 egg, separated
100 g (4 oz) self-raising flour
pinch of salt
½ teaspoon mixed spice
¼ teaspoon ground ginger
50 g (2 oz) wholemeal flour
50 g (2 oz) currants
25 g (1 oz) cut mixed peel
grated rind of ½ orange or lemon
1 tablespoon orange juice or milk
caster sugar, for sprinkling

Preparation time: 20 minutes
Cooking time: about 20 minutes
Oven: 200°C, 400°F, Gas Mark 6

1. Grease 2 baking sheets or cover
them with non-stick silicone paper.
2. Cream the fat and sugar together
until light and fluffy, then beat in the
egg yolk.
3. Sift the self-raising flour with the
salt, spice and ginger then mix in the
wholemeal flour. Add to the creamed
mixture with the currants, mixed peel,
orange rind and orange juice or milk
and mix to a pliable dough.
4. If the mixture is too soft, wrap it in
polythene and chill for 20 minutes.
5. Roll out the dough on a lightly
floured surface to about 5 mm (¼ inch)
thick. Using a fluted cutter, stamp it out
into 6 cm (2½ inch) rounds or squares
and place on the baking sheets.
6. Cook in a preheated moderately hot
oven for 10 minutes. Remove and
brush each biscuit with the lightly
whisked egg white and sprinkle with
caster sugar. Return to the oven for
about 8–10 minutes or until lightly
coloured with a crisp crust.
7. Cool on a wire rack and when cold
store in an airtight container.

MAKING AND DECORATING CHOCOLATE EASTER EGGS

If you are going to attempt to make
your Easter eggs then it is necessary to
buy or borrow Easter egg moulds.
They are available from specialist cake
decorating shops, sweet making shops
and occasionally on special offer from
chocolate manufacturers (see packs or
wrappers for details). Egg moulds are
available in a wide range of sizes and
can be made of metal, china or plastic.
Often the plastic ones are the easiest to
use as plastic separates most readily
from the chocolate egg.

Whatever you do, don't try to make
Easter eggs in a hurry. They need
several layers of chocolate and plenty
of time must be allowed for chilling
between each application to get an
even finish.

Easter eggs can be made with any type
of chocolate, but the higher the quality
of the chocolate, the easier it is to work
with and the better the flavour and look
of the finished egg. 225 g (8 oz) chocolate is sufficient to make a 15 cm (6
inch) egg.

Melt the chocolate in a bowl over a pan
of gently simmering water and then,
using a pastry brush, brush an even
layer all over the mould. Chill, then add
a second layer, melting the chocolate
again if neccessary. Chill again and add
a third coat. Chill very thoroughly, then
remove the egg carefully from the
mould. If to be filled, place the choco-
lates inside and stick the 2 halves
together with a little melted chocolate
and chill once more.

Write names and messages on Easter
eggs using milk chocolate on plain
chocolate or vice versa. White chocolate can be used for writing on both
milk and plain chocolate eggs.

Easter eggs can be enclosed in foil
wrappers which are available from the
same specialist shops as the moulds.

Alternatively, just tie a pretty ribbon
round the egg and tuck fluffy chickens
or rabbits into the bow. For the finishing touch, put the egg into a pretty box
in a nest of coloured tissue paper.

For a more elaborate presentation, decorate eggs with flowers made from royal icing, marzipan or fondant moulding paste, or even silk or artificial flowers. For a really special person, tie a ribbon round the egg and attach a real flower like an orchid, a rose or a spray of freesias.

CLOCKWISE FROM THE LEFT: Simnel cake; Chocolate Easter egg; Easter spicy biscuits

MIDSUMMER NIGHT'S DREAM DINNER FOR SIX

Asparagus with Herby Hollandaise

Nutty Scone Bars

Lobster Salad with Two Sauces

Minted New Potatoes*

Vegetable Salad Medley

Yogurt Mousse with Strawberries and Redcurrant Sauce

Wine suggestions:
Starter and main course:
Hermitage blanc
Dessert:
Premières Côtes de Bordeaux

COUNTDOWN

The day before
Prepare the Yogurt mousse up to the end of step 7.

In the morning
Make Redcurrant sauce for the Yogurt mousse, cover and chill.
Prepare the new potatoes.
Make the Nutty scone bars to serve with the asparagus.
Make the French dressing to go with the Vegetable salad medley.

In the afternoon
Chop the herbs and boil down and strain the vinegar mixture for the Herby hollandaise.
Prepare the Crab sauce for the lobsters, cover and chill.
Dress and prepare the lobsters, cover and chill.
Cook the French beans, mange touts and baby corn cobs for the Vegetable salad medley, cool and assemble on a large platter.

1½ hours before the meal
Complete the Herby hollandaise.
Prepare the asparagus.

1 hour before the meal
Turn out the Yogurt mousse and decorate with the strawberries and Redcurrant sauce.
Make the Watercress and avocado sauce for the lobsters.

20 minutes before the meal
Cook the asparagus.
Cook the new potatoes.

ASPARAGUS WITH HERBY HOLLANDAISE

750 g–1 kg (1½–2 lb) fresh asparagus
salt

HERBY HOLLANDAISE:
4 tablespoons white wine vinegar
2 tablespoons water
8 black peppercorns, crushed
4 egg yolks
175–225 g (6–8 oz) butter, slightly softened
white pepper
lemon juice, to taste
2 tablespoons chopped fresh mixed herbs

Preparation time: about 40 minutes
Cooking time: about 30 minutes

FROM THE LEFT: Nutty scone bars;
Asparagus with herby hollandaise

NUTTY SCONE BARS

MAKES 10
225 g (8 oz) self raising flour
pinch of salt
50 g (2 oz) butter or margarine
40 g (1½ oz) unsalted peanuts, finely
chopped
1 egg, beaten
about 5 tablespoons milk or sour
milk
sea salt crystals

Preparation time: about 15 minutes
Cooking time: about 15 minutes
Oven: 230°C, 450°F, Gas Mark 8

1. Sift the flour and salt into a bowl. Add the fat and rub in until the mixture resembles fine breadcrumbs. Add the peanuts and mix well.
2. Add the egg and sufficient milk to mix to a softish dough. Knead only very lightly.
3. Turn out onto a lightly floured surface and shape into a rectangle about 2.5 cm (1 inch) thick. Cut the rectangle into bars about 2.5 cm (1 inch) wide.
4. Transfer the bars to a well floured baking sheet, keeping them well apart.
5. Sprinkle these bars with sea salt crystals and cook in a preheated hot oven for 12–15 minutes until well risen, golden brown and just firm to the touch.
6. Place a clean tea towel on a wire rack, turn out the bars, wrap them in the cloth, and leave until cold. They may be served cold or just warm, but must be eaten on the day they are made.

1. To prepare the asparagus, cut off the woody ends of the stalks and scrape the white part lightly to remove any coarse spines. Tie the stalks loosely together in bundles with all the heads facing the same way.
2. Heat salted water in an oval flame-proof casserole or a large saucepan and carefully add the bundles of asparagus. Bring the water just to the boil and simmer very gently for about 10 minutes or until the asparagus is just tender. Keep the end of the pan containing the tips of asparagus off the heat to prevent the tips breaking up.
3. To make the Herby hollandaise, put the vinegar, water and peppercorns into a small saucepan and boil hard until the mixture is reduced to 3 tablespoons.
4. Strain the mixture into a heatproof bowl or the top of a double saucepan.

Gradually whisk in the egg yolks and stand the bowl over a pan of very gently simmering water.
5. Cook gently, stirring continuously, until the sauce thickens, taking care not to let it overheat or it may curdle.
6. Whisk in the slightly softened butter, a knob at a time, until a smooth coating consistency is obtained. Season to taste with salt, pepper and lemon juice. Keep the sauce warm while the asparagus is cooking.
7. To serve, drain the asparagus thoroughly, untie the bundles and arrange on 6 warmed plates. Stir the herbs into the sauce and pour it into a bowl. Serve slightly warm, dipping the spears into the sauce as you would with melted butter. Serve with the Nutty scone bars.

LOBSTER SALAD WITH TWO SAUCES

3 lobsters, about 450–750 g (1–1½ lb) each

WATERCRESS AND AVOCADO
  SAUCE:
½ bunch of watercress, trimmed
1 large ripe avocado
2 tablespoons double cream
2–3 teaspoons lemon juice
salt
freshly ground black pepper

CRAB SAUCE:
1 crab, weighing about 450 g (1 lb)
  or 1 frozen dressed crab, thawed
4 tablespoons thick mayonnaise
  (right)
1 tablespoon lemon juice

TO GARNISH:
crisp lettuce leaves
sprigs of watercress
¼ cucumber, sliced
3 lemons, quartered

Preparation time: about 1 hour

1. Split the lobsters in half and prepare following the instructions of page 18. Replace the meat in the shells, arrange the lobster halves on a large platter and garnish with lettuce leaves, watercress, slices of cucumber and wedges of lemon.
2. To make the watercress and avocado sauce, put the watercress into a food processor or liquidizer and blend until chopped. Quarter the avocado, remove the stone, peel and add the flesh to the watercress. Blend until smooth, then add the cream, lemon juice and salt and pepper to taste, and blend again. Turn into a bowl and cover with cling film.
3. To make the crab sauce, prepare the crab following the instructions on page 16 as far as step 10. Put the brown meat, pink coral, if present, mayonnaise and lemon juice into a food processor or blender and process until smooth. Add the chopped white crab meat, then taste and adjust the seasoning. Turn into a serving bowl with the large claws arranged around the edge and cover with cling film.
4. Serve the platter of lobsters with the two sauces and with a dish of tiny new potatoes, cooked in their skins, tossed in melted butter and a handful of freshly chopped mint.

MAYONNAISE

MAKES ABOUT 300 ml (½ pint)
2 egg yolks (at room temperature)
½ teaspoon made English mustard
300 ml (½ pint) olive oil
1 tablespoon lemon juice
1–2 tablespoons white wine or cider
  vinegar
1 teaspoon caster sugar
salt
white pepper

Preparation time: about 25 minutes

1. Put the egg yolks and mustard into a slightly warmed clean bowl.
2. Whisk in half the oil drop by drop, until thick, using a hand or electric hand-held whisk for preference. Do not be tempted to add the oil any quicker or it may curdle.
3. Whisk in the lemon juice, then continue to add the rest of the oil in the same way. The process may be speeded up a little towards the end.
4. Add the vinegar, sugar and salt and pepper to taste. Store in a screw-topped jar or plastic container for up to 3 weeks in the refrigerator.

VEGETABLE SALAD MEDLEY

350 g (12 oz) French beans
salt
350 g (12 oz) mange touts, trimmed
225–350 g (8–12 oz) baby corn cobs,
  fresh or frozen
150 ml (¼ pint) French dressing
  (page 121)

Preparation time: about 20 minutes
Cooking time: 15–20 minutes

1. Top and tail the French beans and cook them in boiling salted water for 4–5 minutes until they are barely tender and still have a good bite. Drain, rinse in cold water to prevent further cooking, and drain again.
2. Cook the mange touts in boiling salted water for 3–4 minutes until they are barely tender. Drain, rinse in cold water and drain again thoroughly.
3. Cook the baby corn cobs in the minimum of salted water for 5 minutes or according to the directions on the packet. Drain, rinse in cold water and drain again.
4. Take a fairly large flat platter and put

a small bowl in the centre. Arrange separate portions of the vegetables attractively fanning out from the centre to the edge. Fill the bowl with French dressing and cover the bowl and platter with cling film until required.

YOGURT MOUSSE WITH STRAWBERRIES AND REDCURRANT SAUCE

3 eggs
100 g (4 oz) caster sugar
200 ml (⅓ pint) milk
2 tablespoons white rum
1 tablespoon water
1 tablespoon powdered gelatine
150 ml (¼ pint) Greek yogurt

REDCURRANT SAUCE:
*225 g (8 oz) redcurrants, stalks
removed and thawed if frozen
4 tablespoons red wine
about 40 g (1½ oz) caster sugar
1 teaspoon arrowroot*

TO DECORATE:
*225 g (8 oz) strawberries
strawberry leaves
rose petals*

Preparation time: about 30 minutes,
plus chilling
Cooking time: about 25 minutes

1. Separate two of the eggs and put the yolks and the remaining whole egg into a heatproof bowl. Add 50 g (2 oz) of the sugar and beat until creamy.
2. Heat the milk to just below boiling point and pour it onto the eggs, whisking all the time.
3. Stand the bowl over a pan of very gently simmering water and cook until the custard thickens sufficiently to coat the back of a spoon quite thickly. Remove from the heat.
4. Put the rum and water in a small bowl over a pan of gently simmering water, sprinkle over the gelatine and leave to dissolve. Cool a little, then stir into the custard. Leave until cool.
5. Stir the yogurt until it is smooth and then stir it evenly through the custard. Chill until beginning to thicken.
6. Place the egg whites in a bowl and whisk until stiff, then whisk in the remaining sugar a little at a time and fold evenly through the custard mixture.
7. Turn into a lightly greased 900 ml (1½ pint) ring mould or other fancy mould. Chill until set.
8. To make the sauce, place the redcurrants and wine in a saucepan and stew gently until soft. Add sugar to taste. Mix the arrowroot with the minimum of cold water and stir into the sauce. Continue stirring over a low heat until the mixture is clear.
9. To serve, slice or halve the strawberries and arrange them around the outside of the mousse with the strawberry leaves and rose petals. Pour the redcurrant sauce into a jug and serve separately. This dish should not be served too cold.

*FROM THE LEFT: Vegetable salad
medley; Lobster salad with two sauces;
Yogurt mousse with strawberries and
Redcurrant sauce*

HALLOWE'EN PARTY FOR SIX

Minestrone alla Milanese

Leek, Potato and Coriander Bake

Hot Boston Beans

Coleslaw

Pumpkin Pie

Toffee Apples

Wine suggestion:
Valpolicella

COUNTDOWN

The day before
Soak the dried beans for the Minestrone alla Milanese and the Hot Boston beans.
Make the Toffee apples and store in the larder.
Make the Coleslaw and the dressing (but do not combine yet) and chill.
Make the pastry for the Pumpkin pie, cover and chill.

In the morning
Prepare all the ingredients for the Minestrone alla Milanese and complete steps 1 and 2.
Prepare the Hot Boston beans up to the end of step 5, cover and chill.

1½ hours before serving
Complete steps 1 to 6 of the Leek, potato and coriander bake.

1 hour before serving
Complete step 3 of the Minestrone alla Milanese.
Complete steps 2 to 4 of the Pumpkin pie.

½ hour before serving
Reheat the Hot Boston beans very slowly on the top of the cooker.
Pour the dressing over the Coleslaw and toss.
Complete step 4 of the Minestrone alla Milanese.
Whip the cream for the Pumpkin pie and place in a bowl.

Just before serving
Complete step 5 of the Minestrone alla Milanese.
Pour the soured cream over the Coleslaw, toss again and garnish.
Transfer the Leek, potato and coriander bake to a serving dish.

MINESTRONE ALLA MILANESE

100 g (4 oz) dried borlotti or red kidney beans, soaked in cold water overnight
2 tablespoons olive oil
100 g (4 oz) bacon, chopped
1 onion, peeled and chopped
1 garlic clove, peeled and chopped
225 g (8 oz) tomatoes, skinned and chopped
6 basil leaves, chopped
1 parsley sprig, chopped
2 litres (3½ pints) water
1 carrot, peeled and diced
1 celery stick, diced
275 g (10 oz) potatoes, peeled and diced
225 g (8 oz) courgettes, diced
225 g (8 oz) cabbage, shredded
100 g (4 oz) fresh peas, shelled
salt
freshly ground black pepper
200 g (7 oz) rice
50 g (2 oz) Parmesan cheese, grated

Preparation time: 30 minutes, plus soaking overnight.
Cooking time: about 3 hours.

1. Drain the beans and place in a saucepan of unsalted water. Bring to the boil and boil hard for 10 minutes. Drain.

2. Heat the oil in a large saucepan, add the bacon, onion and garlic and sauté for a few minutes. Add the tomatoes, beans, basil, parsley and water. Bring to the boil. Lower the heat, cover and simmer for about 1½ hours, stirring occasionally.

3. Add the diced carrot and celery and

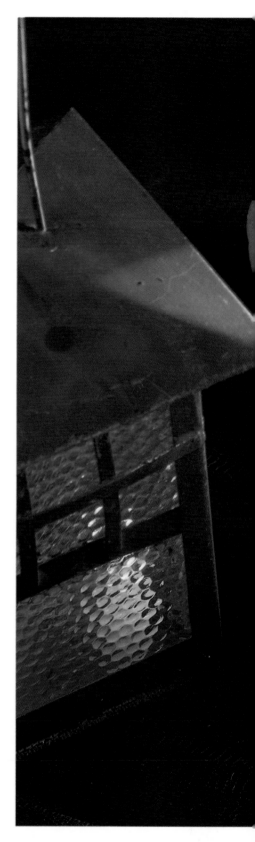

ABOVE: Minestrone alla Milanese

simmer for a further 30 minutes.

4. Add the remaining ingredients, except the cheese, with salt and pepper to taste. Simmer for 20 minutes or until all the vegetables are tender.

5. Taste and adjust the seasoning. Leave the soup to stand for 5 minutes, then add the Parmesan. Serve hot.

LEEK, POTATO AND CORIANDER BAKE

750 g (1½ lb) leeks, trimmed and washed
1.5 kg (3 lb) small potatoes, scrubbed and dried
1½ tablespoons oil
40 g (1½ oz) butter
1½ teaspoons black peppercorns
3 teaspoons coriander seeds
1½ teaspoons sea salt

Preparation time: 25 minutes
Cooking time: 1¼ hours
Oven: 200°C, 400°F, Gas Mark 6

Use a waxy type of potato like a Cyprus or a Jersey for this dish. It should be cooked in a large shallow roasting tin to make sure the potatoes and leeks are spread in one layer and become nicely browned. Serve it by itself or as an accompaniment to almost any dish.

1. Slice the leeks into 2 cm (¾ inch) rings and cut the potatoes into 1 cm (½ inch) slices.
2. Put the oil and butter into a large shallow roasting tin and place in the oven until the butter is just melted.
3. Add the leeks and potatoes, turning them over several times to coat them with the oil and butter.
4. Crush the peppercorns with the coriander seeds. If you have no pestle and mortar, put the seeds and peppercorns between two double sheets of kitchen paper or greaseproof paper and crush firmly with a rolling pin.
5. Put the crushed pepper and coriander into a small bowl, add the salt, sprinkle evenly over the potatoes and leeks and stir them through.
6. Cover the tin tightly with baking foil and place in the oven for 45 minutes. After this time remove the foil, turn the potatoes and leeks over and put back near the top of the oven for a further 30 minutes to become brown.
7. Transfer to a serving dish and serve hot.

HOT BOSTON BEANS

350 g (12 oz) haricot beans, soaked overnight in cold water
1½ tablespoons vegetable oil
3 medium onions, peeled and chopped
6 tablespoons clear honey
4½ tablespoons soy sauce
¾ teaspoon Tabasco sauce
4½ tablespoons wine vinegar
1 teaspoon English mustard powder
1 teaspoon ground chilli
1½ teaspoons paprika
6 tablespoons tomato purée
600 ml (1 pint) hot vegetable stock
6 tablespoons orange juice
1 tablespoon plain wholemeal flour
3 tablespoons water
3 red peppers, seeded and sliced
sprigs of parsley, to garnish

Preparation time: 30 minutes, plus soaking overnight
Cooking time: about 3 hours
Oven: 150°C, 300°F, Gas Mark 2

1. Rinse the beans and put into a pan with sufficient water to cover. Bring to the boil and simmer for 30 minutes. Drain and tip into a flameproof casserole.
2. Heat the oil in a large pan and gently fry the onions until golden. Stir in the honey, soy sauce, Tabasco sauce, vinegar, mustard, chilli, paprika and tomato purée.
3. Pour in the hot stock and orange juice and bring to the boil. Pour over the beans, cover and cook in the centre of the oven for 1½ hours.
4. Blend the flour with the water and stir into the beans. Add the red peppers.
5. Cover and return to the oven for 1 hour until the sauce is rich and thick and the beans tender.
6. Garnish and serve piping hot.

COLESLAW

225 g (8 oz) white cabbage, finely shredded
175 g (6 oz) red cabbage, finely shredded
1 small onion, peeled and thinly sliced
50 g (2 oz) walnuts, chopped, or canned chestnuts, drained and chopped
½ teaspoon caraway seeds, lightly crushed
1 tablespoon sultanas

DRESSING:
2 tablespoons cider vinegar or lemon juice
4 tablespoons olive oil
1 teaspoon clear honey
1 teaspoon Dijon mustard
¼ teaspoon salt
6 tablespoons soured cream
1 teaspoon paprika, to sprinkle

Preparation time: 10 minutes, plus standing

Pungent caraway seeds add flavour to this nutty and colourful salad.

1. Combine the cabbage, onion, walnuts, caraway seeds and the sultanas in a large salad bowl.
2. Combine all the dressing ingredients except the soured cream and the paprika in a jug, whisking with a fork until thoroughly blended. Pour over the salad and toss well. Leave to stand for 30 minutes.
3. Just before serving stir the soured cream briskly with a fork until smooth, then pour over the dressed salad and toss again. Sprinkle the salad with the paprika.

CLOCKWISE FROM THE LEFT: Coleslaw, Hot Boston beans; Leek, potato and coriander bake

PUMPKIN PIE

225 g (8 oz) plain flour
pinch of salt
50 g (2 oz) lard
50 g (2 oz) butter or margarine,
  diced
2 tablespoons cold water
whipped cream, to serve

FILLING:
1 × 400 g (14 oz) can pumpkin
  purée
175 g (6 oz) caster sugar
1 tablespoon cornflour
1 tablespoon black treacle
2 teaspoons mixed spice
150 ml (¼ pint) single cream
3 eggs, size 3, well-beaten

Preparation time: 20 minutes
Cooking time: 45 minutes, plus
  resting
Oven: 200°C, 400°F, Gas Mark 6

This pie is traditionally quite sweet, so
serve it in small portions.

1. Place the flour and salt in a bowl.
Add the fat and rub in until the mixture
resembles fine breadcrumbs. Add the
water and mix to form a fairly firm
dough. Knead lightly. Wrap in cling film
and chill in the refrigerator for at least
15 minutes before using.
2. Roll out the pastry fairly thinly on a
floured board or work surface and use
to line the base and sides of a 23 cm
(9 inch), lightly greased, fluted flan
dish.
3. To make the filling, put all the ingredients into a mixing bowl and beat
with a wooden spoon until thoroughly
combined. Pour the mixture into the
pastry case.
4. Bake in a preheated oven for 45
minutes, then open the oven door,
switch off the heat and leave the pie in
the oven for a further 15 minutes.
5. Serve the pie warm, cut into
wedges, with whipped cream.

*FROM THE TOP: Toffee apples; Pumpkin
pie*

TOFFEE APPLES

6 eating apples, washed, dried and
  stalks removed
6 wooden sticks
175 g (6 oz) sugar
25 g (1 oz) butter
50 g (2 oz) golden syrup
½ teaspoon lemon juice
6 tablespoons water

Preparation time: 15 minutes
Cooking time: 20 minutes

1. Push a wooden stick into each
apple.
2. Place the sugar, butter, golden
syrup, lemon juice and water in a
heavy-based pan. Stir gently over a low
heat until the sugar has dissolved, then
increase the heat and boil rapidly until
the toffee registers 145°C (290°F) on
the sugar thermometer, or, if the syrup
is dropped into cold water, it will form
brittle threads which snap easily.
3. Dip the apples into the pan one at a
time, twisting the pan to coat evenly.
4. Immediately plunge each apple into
a bowl of cold water to set the toffee,
then stand them on a piece of oiled
greaseproof paper until cold.

THREE DAYS OF CHRISTMAS FOR SIX

CHRISTMAS EVE SUPPER

Fish Pie

Green Salad*

Mince Pies

CHRISTMAS LUNCH OR DINNER

Gravad Lax

Roast Turkey with Chestnut and Sausagemeat Stuffing and Cranberry Sauce

Roast Potatoes and Brussels Sprouts*

Christmas Pudding with Brandy Butter

French Christmas Pudding

TEA

Christmas Star Cake

Christmas Tree Biscuits

BOXING DAY LUNCH

Brussels Soup

Four ways with leftover turkey:

Turkey Salad

Instant Turkey Hollandaise

Deep Dish Turkey Pie

Exotic Turkey Marinade

Tangerines, Stilton and Nuts*

COUNTDOWN

Many of these Christmas dishes can be made well ahead of time and frozen. These have been indicated with an F in the recipe and brief freezing and thawing instructions appear at the end. The countdown is planned for the more difficult task of preparing for Christmas without a freezer.

Up to 2 months in advance

Make the Mincemeat for the Mince pies. Cover and store in a cool, dry place.
Make the Christmas pudding, cover and store in a cool, dry place.

3 days in advance

Complete steps 1 and 2 of the Gravad lax.
Make and decorate the Christmas star cake. Store in an airtight container.
Make the Christmas tree biscuits and decorate with chocolate, if wished.

CHRISTMAS EVE

In the morning

Cover the Christmas tree biscuits with marzipan and decorate, if wished.
Make the Shortcrust pastry and fill the Mince pies.
Make the stuffing for the turkey, cover and chill.
Make the Brandy butter, cover and chill.
Make the dressing to serve with the Gravad lax.
Complete step 1 of the Fish pie.
Prepare the Green salad and the dressing to serve with the Fish pie. Cover and chill.

1 hour before serving

Complete steps 2 and 3 of the Fish pie.

½ hour before serving

Complete steps 4 and 5 of the Fish pie.
Bake the Mince pies.

Just before serving

Dress the Green salad.

CHRISTMAS DAY

At least 5 hours before the meal

Stuff and start roasting the turkey. (Be guided by the weight to allow sufficient cooking and standing time.)
Slice the Gravad lax, arrange on a platter and garnish. Cover with cling film.
Prepare the Brussels sprouts.
Peel the potatoes.

3½ hours before the meal

Start to reheat the Christmas pudding.

2½ hours before the meal

Make and bake the French Christmas pudding.
Make the Chocolate sauce to serve with the French Christmas pudding.
Parboil the potatoes.

1½ hours before the meal

Arrange the parboiled potatoes round the turkey for the last 1½ hours of cooking time, or cook in hot dripping in a separate tin.
Make the Cranberry sauce.

½ hour before the meal

Boil the Brussels sprouts and keep warm.
Remove the turkey from oven, transfer to a serving dish and cover with foil.
Turn out the French Christmas pudding and decorate.
Turn out the Christmas pudding, decorate and keep warm.

Just before serving

Reheat the Chocolate sauce.
Pour the warmed brandy over the Christmas pudding and light.

CHRISTMAS EVE

CHRISTMAS EVE SUPPER

Fish Pie

Green Salad*

Mince Pies

Wine suggestion:
Tokay d'Alsace, a dry white

FISH PIE

6 eggs
1 kg (2 lb) potatoes, unpeeled
300 ml (½ pint) milk
75 g (3 oz) butter
salt
freshly ground black pepper
2 tablespoons chopped fresh dill
2 tablespoons chopped fresh chervil
1 kg (2 lb) haddock fillets, skinned
chopped fresh dill, to garnish

Preparation time: 35 minutes
Cooking time: 50–60 minutes

1. Bring a saucepan of lightly salted water to the boil, then reduce the heat slightly, lower in the eggs and cook for 5 minutes. Plunge the eggs into a bowl of cold water, and shell them as soon as they are cool enough to handle. Slice and set aside.
2. Boil the potatoes in their skins for about 20 minutes or until tender, then drain. As soon as the potatoes are cool enough to handle, remove the skins. Pass the potatoes through a medium food mill until smooth. Transfer to a clean saucepan and stir over a gentle heat for 2–3 minutes to dry them out, taking care that they do not catch on the bottom of the saucepan and burn.
3. Heat the milk in a small saucepan with the butter and plenty of salt and pepper. When the butter has melted, gradually stir the mixture into the potato, beating vigorously with a wooden spoon. Stir in the chopped herbs, cover and keep warm.
4. Put the haddock fillets into a large

shallow saucepan and pour in enough cold water to just cover. Remove the haddock with a fish slice. Add ½ teaspoon salt to the water and bring to the boil. Return the haddock to the pan and simmer over a very gentle heat for about 8 minutes, until the fish flakes away from the bone easily.
5. Remove the haddock from the pan and when it is cool enough to handle flake it into a heated lightly greased ovenproof dish. Cover with the potato purée, smooth the surface, and arrange the sliced eggs on top. Garnish with dill and serve immediately. The pie should be eaten with a crisp green salad of lettuce and cress.

MINCE PIES

MAKES 16–18
450 g (1 lb) mincemeat (right)
1 egg white, beaten, to glaze
caster sugar, to dredge

SPECIAL SHORTCRUST PASTRY:
225 g (8 oz) self-raising flour
pinch of salt
50 g (2 oz) butter
50 g (2 oz) block margarine
25 g (1 oz) lard
1 egg yolk
milk, to mix

Preparation time: 40 minutes
Cooking time: 20 minutes
Oven: 200°C, 400°F, Gas Mark 6

1. To make the pastry, sift the flour and salt into a mixing bowl. Rub in the butter, margarine and lard with the fingertips until the mixture resembles fine breadcrumbs. Add the egg yolk and enough milk to mix a pliable dough, using a round-bladed knife. Turn the dough on to a lightly floured board or work surface and knead lightly until smooth and even.

2. Roll out the pastry and with a fluted 7.5 cm (3 inch) pastry cutter cut out 16–18 rounds. Cut out 16–18 slightly smaller rounds for the lids.

3. Fit the large rounds into greased patty tins and spoon about 2 teaspoons mincemeat into each one. Dampen the edges of the lids and press down lightly to seal. ⊞

4. Brush the tops of the mince pies with egg white and dredge lightly with sugar. Make a small hole in the top of each mince pie and bake in a preheated fairly hot oven for about 20 minutes. Leave to cool slightly in the tins, then carefully transfer to a wire tray to cool completely.

⊞ Open-freeze in patty tins then remove and pack in rigid containers. Freeze for up to 2 months. To serve, replace in patty tins and bake from frozen as directed.

MINCEMEAT

TO MAKE ABOUT 1.75 kg (4 lb)
350 g (12 oz) cooking apples
  peeled, cored and finely chopped
225 g (8 oz) currants, chopped
225 g (8 oz) sultanas, chopped
225 g (8 oz) seedless raisins, chopped
225 g (8 oz) cut mixed peel
75 g (3 oz) blanched almonds,
  chopped
450 g (1 lb) dark soft brown sugar
100 g (4 oz) shredded suet, chopped
1 teaspoon ground nutmeg
1 teaspoon ground cinnamon
grated rind of 1 orange
grated rind and juice of 1 lemon
2 tablespoons rum or brandy

Preparation time: about 30 minutes
Cooking time: about 5 minutes

1. Blanch the apples in boiling water for 30 seconds, then drain very thoroughly in a colander and cool.

2. Combine the currants, sultanas and raisins with the mixed peel in a large mixing bowl. Stir in the almonds, sugar, suet and spices. Add the drained apple, orange and lemon rind, lemon juice, rum or brandy and stir thoroughly to mix. ⊞

⊞ Freeze in plastic containers or small freezer polythene bags in 225 g (8 oz) quantities, for up to 2 months. Thaw overnight in the refrigerator before using.

FROM THE LEFT: Mince pies; Fish pie

CHRISTMAS DAY

CHRISTMAS LUNCH OR DINNER

Gravad Lax

*Roast Turkey with Chestnut and
Sausagemeat Stuffing and
Cranberry Sauce*

*Roast Potatoes and Brussels
Sprouts**

*Christmas Pudding with Brandy
Butter*

French Christmas Pudding

Wine suggestions:
Starter:
White Burgundy
Main course:
Château-bottled St Emilion
Dessert:
Barsac or *Malmsey*

CHRISTMAS TEA

Christmas Star Cake

Christmas Tree Biscuits

GRAVAD LAX

2 tablespoons sea salt
1½ tablespoons light soft brown sugar
*1 teaspoon crushed black
 peppercorns*
1 tablespoon gin or brandy
*2 tablespoons finely chopped fresh dill
 or 2 teaspoons dried dill*
*750 g (1¾ lb) fresh salmon, middle
 cut or tailpiece, cut into 2 fillets but
 unskinned*
fresh dill or fennel leaves, to garnish

DRESSING:
4 tablespoons olive oil
1 tablespoon white wine vinegar
1 tablespoon German mustard
salt
freshly ground black pepper

Preparation time: 10 minutes, plus
 marinating

This method of preparing salmon is
popular in Scandinavia, where it is
often preferred to smoked salmon.
The raw fish is marinated in a light,
spicy pickle and then served sliced,
with a dressing passed separately.

1. Combine the salt, sugar, peppercorns, gin or brandy and dill in a bowl
and stir well to mix. Spread a quarter of
the mixture over a large plate and lay
one salmon fillet on top, skin side
down. Spread half the remaining mixture over the cut side. Place the other
salmon fillet, skin side up, on top and
spread with the remaining mixture,
rubbing it in well. Cover the salmon
with foil, then lay a plate on top and
weight down with a couple of cans.
2. Chill the salmon in the bottom of
the refrigerator for between 36 hours
and 5 days, turning it once a day.
3. Slice the salmon thinly and arrange
the slices overlapping on a board or
serving dish. If wished, remove the
skin. Garnish with fresh dill.
4. Combine all the dressing ingredients in a jug, whisk with a fork to
blend thoroughly, then leave to stand
for 10 minutes. Whisk again and serve.

ROAST TURKEY

*1 oven ready turkey, about 5–6 kg
 (11–12 lb) plus giblets*
*1 small onion, peeled and stuck with
 4 cloves*
1 bay leaf
softened butter
salt
freshly ground black pepper

CHESTNUT AND SAUSAGEMEAT
 STUFFING:
butter for frying
*1 large onion, peeled and finely
 chopped*
*2 large cooking apples, peeled, cored
 and chopped*
225 g (8 oz) pork sausagemeat
100 g (4 oz) fresh white breadcrumbs
*1 × 425 g (15 oz) can unsweetened
 chestnut purée*
salt
freshly ground black pepper

Preparation time: about 30 minutes
Cooking time: about 4½ hours
Oven: 180°C, 350°F, Gas Mark 4

1. Remove the giblets from the turkey
and place them in a saucepan with the
onion, bay leaf and sufficient water to
cover. Bring to the boil, cover and
simmer for 1 hour.
2. Meanwhile make the stuffing. Melt a
knob of butter in a saucepan. Add the
onion and fry until golden. Transfer to
a mixing bowl and add the remaining
ingredients and salt and pepper to
taste. Stir well to combine
thoroughly. F
3. Wipe the turkey inside and out with
paper towels. Push the stuffing into the
neck end of the bird and truss. (If there
is any stuffing leftover it can be cooked
in a separate dish in the oven with the
turkey for 30 minutes.) Place the turkey in a greased roasting tin. Rub all
over with softened butter, season lightly and cover with foil.
4. Cook in a preheated moderate oven
for 4–4½ hours, basting several times
during cooking. Remove the foil for the
last 15–20 minutes of cooking to
brown the turkey.
5. Check the turkey is cooked by in-
serting a skewer in the deepest part of
the thigh and then remove to a serving
dish and allow to 'set' for about 10
minutes. If the turkey was taken
straight from the refrigerator allow an
extra 15 minutes cooking time. Pour
off the fat from the pan juices and use
the juices with the giblet stock to make
gravy.
6. Serve the turkey with gravy, Cranberry sauce, roast potatoes and Brussels sprouts, and garnish with a few
sprigs of holly and fresh cranberries.

F Pack the stuffing into a polythene
bag and freeze for up to 1 month.
Thaw overnight in the refrigerator.

CRANBERRY SAUCE

For an orange cranberry sauce, use orange juice in place of all or part of the water and add the grated rind of ½ orange.

175 g (6 oz) sugar
150 ml (¼ pint) water
225 g (8 oz) cranberries, fresh or
* frozen*
1–2 tablespoons port (optional)

Preparation time: about 5 minutes
Cooking time: about 15 minutes

1. Dissolve the sugar in the water in a saucepan, and bring up to the boil. Stir occasionally and boil for about 5 minutes.
2. Add the cranberries, cover the pan and simmer gently until they have all popped. Remove the lid from the pan and continue simmering for about 5 minutes, until they are quite tender.
3. If liked, add 1–2 tablespoons port, and leave to cool.

CLOCKWISE FROM TOP LEFT: Roast turkey; Cranberry sauce; Gravad lax

CHRISTMAS PUDDING

75 g (3 oz) self raising flour
pinch of salt
1 teaspoon mixed spice
1 teaspoon grated nutmeg
1 teaspoon ground cinnamon
150 g (5 oz) stoned raisins
100 g (4 oz) sultanas
75 g (3 oz) currants
75 g (3 oz) candied peel
50 g (2 oz) dates, chopped
50 g (2 oz) candied pineapple
50 g (2 oz) candied papaya
25 g (1 oz) glacé cherries
1 dessert apple, peeled and grated
1 carrot, peeled and grated
50 g (2 oz) almonds, blanched and
  chopped
200 g (7 oz) shredded suet
175 g (6 oz) fresh white breadcrumbs
100 g (4 oz) dark soft brown sugar
3 eggs, beaten
3 tablespoons brandy
85 ml (3 fl oz) brown ale
juice and grated rind of 1 orange
butter, for greasing
sprigs of holly, to decorate
1 tablespoon brandy, to serve

Preparation time: 1 hour
Cooking time: 6 hours, plus 3 hours,
  on the day

This unusually light Christmas pudding is just what one wants after a traditionally filling main course. Candied pineapple and papaya are available from health food shops. The pudding can be made in advance and left to mature in the same way as heavier puddings.

1. Sift the flour, salt and spices into a large bowl. Add the dried and candied fruits, the apple, carrot, almonds, suet, breadcrumbs and sugar and mix well. Stir in the eggs, brandy, beer and the orange juice and rind.
2. Grease a 1.5 litre (2½ pint) pudding basin with butter. Line the base with a circle of greaseproof paper, buttered on both sides. Spoon the mixture into the basin, packing it in tightly, and level the top.
3. Cover with greased greaseproof paper and a piece of aluminium foil, pleated to allow for expansion, and tie on with string.
4. Place the basin in a large saucepan. Pour in boiling water to come two-thirds up the side of the basin.

5. Cover the saucepan and steam steadily for 6 hours, topping up with hot water when necessary.
6. At the end of the cooking time, remove the basin from the saucepan and leave to cool. Take off the string, paper and foil and replace them with a fresh cover. Store in a cool, dry place.
7. On the day of serving, steam the pudding again for 3 hours.
8. Remove the string, paper and foil and turn the pudding out on to a warmed dish.
9. Decorate the pudding with a sprig of holly.
10. Just before serving, remove the holly, pour a tablespoon of warmed brandy over the pudding and light with a match.

BRANDY BUTTER

75 g (3 oz) unsalted butter, softened
75 g (3 oz) icing sugar, sifted
finely grated rind and juice of ½
  orange
2 tablespoons brandy

Preparation time: 10 minutes, plus chilling

1. Place the butter in a bowl and cream until light and fluffy. Gradually beat in the icing sugar and then the orange rind and juice and the brandy.
2. Pile into a serving bowl and chill in the refrigerator until quite firm. [F]

[F] Pack in a rigid container and freeze for up to 2 months. Thaw for 2 hours at room temperature.

FRENCH CHRISTMAS PUDDING

1 × 425 g (15 oz) can unsweetened
  chestnut purée
100 g (4 oz) unsalted butter, softened
4 eggs, separated
175 g (6 oz) caster sugar
2 tablespoons brandy (optional)

CHOCOLATE SAUCE:
150 ml (¼ pint) double cream
225 g (8 oz) plain dark chocolate,
  broken into pieces
2 tablespoons brandy
4 marrons glacés, sliced, to decorate
  (optional)

Preparation time: 30 minutes
Cooking time: 2 hours
Oven: 180°C, 350°F, Gas Mark 4

1. Cream the chestnut purée and the butter together in a bowl.
2. Beat in the egg yolks and the sugar.
3. Whisk the egg whites until stiff and fold them into the chestnut purée mixture.
4. Grease a 1.2 litre (2 pint) non-stick or enamel loaf tin and line the bottom with a piece of greaseproof paper. Pour the mixture into the tin.
5. Place the tin in a bain-marie and bake in a preheated oven for 2 hours until set. If the top of the pudding looks as if it is browning too quickly, cover with a piece of buttered foil.
6. Meanwhile, prepare the sauce. Heat the cream in a small heavy saucepan over a gentle heat. Do not let it boil. Add the broken chocolate and brandy. Stir over a very gentle heat until the chocolate has melted and the sauce is smooth.
7. Remove the pudding from the oven and let it cool in the tin for about 5–10 minutes. Run a knife around the edge to loosen it and turn out on to a warmed dish.
8. Coat the pudding with a little Chocolate sauce and decorate with the sliced marrons glacés. Hand the remaining sauce separately.

CLOCKWISE FROM THE TOP: Christmas pudding; Brandy butter; French Christmas pudding

CHRISTMAS STAR CAKE

175 g (6 oz) butter or margarine
175 g (6 oz) light soft brown sugar
3 eggs
175 g (6 oz) self raising flour
75 g (3 oz) plain flour
grated rind of 1 orange
grated rind of 1 lemon
4 teaspoons lemon juice
50 g (2 oz) glacé pineapple or
  crystallized ginger, chopped
50 g (2 oz) glacé cherries, chopped
25 g (1 oz) angelica, chopped
75 g (3 oz) no-need-to-soak prunes,
  chopped
40 g (1½ oz) shelled pecan nuts or
  blanched almonds, chopped
750 g (1½ lb) white marzipan
little apricot jam, sieved
1 straight gold candle, about 10 cm
  (4 inches) tall
green and red liquid food colouring

ICING:
225 g (8 oz) unsalted butter
450 g (1 lb) icing sugar, sifted
2 tablespoons lemon juice

Preparation time: about 1¼ hours,
  plus cooling and setting
Cooking time: about 1½ hours
Oven: 160°C, 325°F, Gas Mark 3

If you cannot buy or hire a star-shaped cake tin you can make the cake in a 20 cm (8 inch) round tin, increasing the cooking time by about 15 minutes. Pipe a star shape on top of the cake and decorate it in the same way as the star-shaped cake.

1. To make the cake, grease and line a 5 or 6 point star cake tin, about 25 cm (10 inches) in diameter, with greased greaseproof or non-stick silicone paper.
2. In a large bowl cream the butter and sugar until light and fluffy, then beat in the eggs, one at a time, following each one with a spoonful of flour.
3. Sift the remaining flours together and fold them into the cake mixture, followed by the orange and lemon rinds and lemon juice. Fold in the pineapple or ginger, cherries, angelica, prunes and nuts and turn the mixture into the tin, making sure there is plenty in the points.
4. Cook in a preheated moderate oven for about 1½ hours until well risen and firm to the touch. To test if the cake is done, insert a skewer in the centre: it should come out clean. Let the cake cool in the tin for 5 minutes, then turn it out onto a wire rack and leave until cold.
5. Roll out 500 g (1¼ lb) of the marzipan and cut out a star shape to fit the top of the cake, and long strips to fit the sides so that the cake is completely covered. Brush the cake all over with jam and position the marzipan, pressing it to fit evenly.

6. To make the icing, cream the butter until soft, then slowly beat in the icing sugar, adding the lemon juice as you go until the mixture has a spreading consistency.

7. Use about three-quarters of the icing to mask the whole cake, marking it attractively with a small palette knife. Position the candle in the centre of the cake.

8. Put the remaining icing into a piping bag fitted with a star nozzle and pipe a series of stars around the candle. Next, pipe a row of shells running from the top to the base of each point, then pipe a shell border around the top of the cake and another around the base.

9. Colour a tiny piece of marzipan red by kneading in the food colouring and shape it into about 25 tiny holly berries.

10. Colour the rest of the marzipan a deep green, roll it out and cut out 30–36 holly leaves.

11. Arrange some of the leaves and berries around the candle and place the rest around the base of the cake. Leave to set.

CHRISTMAS TREE BISCUITS

MAKES 12–14
90 g (3½ oz) self raising flour
15 g (½ oz) cornflour
1½ teaspoons cocoa
½ teaspoon ground cinnamon
50 g (2 oz) butter or margarine
50 g (2 oz) caster sugar
1 egg yolk
1 teaspoon milk or coffee essence

TO DECORATE:
175 g (6 oz) white marzipan
green and blue liquid food colouring
little sieved apricot jam
coloured or silver balls or 150 g
 (5 oz) plain chocolate, melted
icing sugar for dredging (optional)

Preparation time: about 45 minutes
Cooking time: 10–12 minutes
Oven: 200°C, 400°F, Gas Mark 6

These biscuits can be finished in three ways. Either cover them with a layer of green marzipan and decorate the 'branches' with silver or coloured balls or part dip them in chocolate and dredge with icing sugar. Alternatively leave them plain and dredge with icing sugar 'snow'.

1. Sift the flour, cornflour, cocoa and cinnamon into a bowl. Rub in the fat until the mixture resembles fine breadcrumbs, then stir in the sugar.

2. Add the egg yolk and milk or coffee essence and mix to a pliable dough.

3. Cover 2 baking sheets with non-stick silicone paper. Roll out the dough thinly and, using a special Christmas tree cutter, cut out Christmas trees about 10 cm (4 inches) high. Alternatively make your own pattern by drawing a tree on a piece of thick card and cutting it out. Place the tree shape on the dough and cut round the outside with a knife.

4. Carefully transfer the biscuits to the baking sheets and cook them in a

FROM THE LEFT: Christmas star cake; Christmas tree biscuits

preheated moderately hot oven for 10–12 minutes until they are just firm. Leave on the baking sheets until they are completely firm, then transfer carefully to a wire rack and leave until cold.

5. To make 'green' trees, colour the marzipan a deep green by kneading in the green and blue liquid food colourings until suitably dark. Roll out the marzipan thinly and, using the same cutters as for the biscuits, cut it into tree shapes. Spread the biscuits lightly with the apricot jam and position the marzipan on top. Decorate each 'branch' with a coloured or silver ball and, if liked, dredge lightly with sifted icing sugar.

6. To make chocolate trees, melt the chocolate in a basin over a pan of gently simmering water. Dip half of each tree into the chocolate and leave to set, then dredge lightly all over with sifted icing sugar.

BOXING DAY LUNCH

Brussels Soup

Turkey Salad or

Instant Turkey Hollandaise or

Deep Dish Turkey Pie or

Exotic Turkey Marinade

Tangerines, Stilton and Nuts*

Wine suggestions:
Chianti classico or Soave

COUNTDOWN

This is a simple meal giving four alternative recipes for using up the remains of the turkey. The Brussels sprouts for the soup can be prepared at the same time as the ones for the Christmas Dinner, covered and chilled overnight.

The soup can then be made 1 hour before lunch and the Deep dish turkey pie could be prepared and cooked at the same time. The Exotic turkey marinade needs to marinate for at least 4 hours, so it could be made after the Christmas Dinner or early on Boxing Day morning.

The Instant turkey hollandaise could be prepared and cooked while the soup is simmering, while the Special turkey salad can be assembled 20 minutes before it is required. Follow with tangerines, nuts and Stilton.

BRUSSELS SOUP

50 g (2 oz) butter or margarine
2 large leeks, total weight about
  400 g (14 oz), trimmed and sliced
350 g (12 oz) Brussels sprouts,
  trimmed and shredded
1 litre (1¾ pints) chicken stock
1 tablespoon lemon juice
1 teaspoon Worcestershire sauce
pinch of ground mace
salt
freshly ground black pepper
300 ml (½ pint) milk or half milk and
  half single cream
fried onion rings, to garnish

Preparation time: 20 minutes
Cooking time: about 45 minutes

1. Melt the fat in a saucepan, add the leeks and fry over a gentle heat for 5 minutes, stirring occasionally.
2. Add the Brussels sprouts, stir well, then add the stock, lemon juice, Worcestershire sauce, mace and salt and pepper and bring to the boil.
3. Cover the pan and simmer for 20–25 minutes or until the vegetables are very tender. Cool slightly, then purée in a food processor or blender, or pass through a sieve.
4. Return the soup to the rinsed out

ABOVE: Brussels soup

pan with the milk. Return to the boil, taste and adjust the seasoning. Serve the soup in warmed individual soup bowls, garnished with fried onion rings and accompanied by toasted slices of French bread.

TURKEY SALAD

75 g (3 oz) hazelnuts
75 g (3 oz) grapes, quartered and
  seeded
175 g (6 oz) canned water chestnuts,
  drained
350 g (12 oz) Chinese leaves, finely
  shredded
750 g (1½ lb) cooked turkey meat, cut
  into bite-size pieces

DRESSING:
3 teaspoons grated Parmesan cheese
1 egg
2 teaspoons olive, sunflower or
  walnut oil
2 teaspoons lemon or orange juice
pinch of English mustard powder
1 clove garlic, peeled and crushed
  (optional)
pinch of freshly ground black pepper
pinch of sea salt
few drops of Worcestershire sauce
150 ml (¼ pint) plain unsweetened
  yogurt

Preparation time: 15 minutes
Cooking time: 2–3 minutes

1. Place the hazelnuts in an ungreased heavy-based pan over a low heat for 2–3 minutes, stirring until lightly browned.
2. Combine the hazelnuts with all the other salad ingredients and arrange in a large bowl.
3. Blend all the dressing ingredients except the yogurt in a liquidizer. Transfer to a jug.
4. Mix the yogurt into the dressing by hand and stir the dressing into the salad. Mix well then serve.

INSTANT TURKEY HOLLANDAISE

350 g (12 oz) frozen broccoli spears
salt
about 350 g (12 oz) cooked turkey,
  sliced
275 g (10 oz) can condensed cream
  of chicken soup
2 tablespoons lemon juice
2–3 tablespoons dry white wine
4 tablespoons thick mayonnaise
freshly ground black pepper
25–40 g (1–1½ oz) fresh white
  breadcrumbs
25–40 g (1–1½ oz) mature Cheddar
  cheese, grated

Preparation time: 5–10 minutes
Cooking time: 30 minutes
Oven: 220°C, 425°F, Gas Mark 7

1. Cook the broccoli in a saucepan of boiling salted water for 2–3 minutes, then drain and arrange in a greased shallow ovenproof dish.
2. Arrange the turkey slices over the broccoli.
3. Combine the chicken soup, lemon juice, wine and mayonnaise and season well with salt and pepper. Pour evenly over the turkey.
4. Mix the breadcrumbs with the cheese and sprinkle evenly over the surface of the dish.
5. Cook towards the top of a preheated hot oven for 25–30 minutes until bubbling and golden brown. Serve at once.

DEEP DISH TURKEY PIE

6 medium potatoes, peeled and
  quartered
6 medium carrots, scraped and
  quartered
25 g (1 oz) butter or margarine
1 small onion, peeled and coarsely
  chopped
1 small green pepper, cored, seeded
  and coarsely chopped
1 × 275 g (10 oz) can condensed
  cream of chicken soup
350–450 g (12–16 oz) cooked turkey,
  coarsely diced

BISCUIT TOPPING:
200 g (7 oz) plain flour
2 teaspoons baking powder
½ teaspoon salt
50 g (2 oz) hard margarine or
  butter
120 ml (4 fl oz) milk

Preparation time: about 10 minutes
Cooking time: about 45–50 minutes
Oven: 220°C, 425°F, Gas Mark 7

1. Cook the potatoes and carrots in boiling salted water until just tender. Strain and measure out 250 ml (8 fl oz) of the liquid and set aside.
2. Meanwhile, heat the fat and gently cook the onion and green pepper until soft.
3. Mix the chicken soup (undiluted) with the reserved vegetable stock. Put the turkey and the vegetables into a casserole, add the sauce, and cook, uncovered, in the preheated hot oven for 15 minutes.
4. To make the biscuit top, sift the dry ingredients together and cut in the fat until it feels like coarse breadcrumbs. Stir in the milk – do not beat – until the mixture is just moist.
5. Knead gently on a lightly floured board for about 2 minutes. Pat out – do not roll – into a circle to fit the top of the casserole. Place on top of the turkey mixture and mark out wedges. Bake for 15 minutes longer.

CLOCKWISE FROM BOTTOM LEFT: Deep dish turkey pie; Exotic turkey marinade; Turkey salad; Instant turkey hollandaise

EXOTIC TURKEY MARINADE

1 fresh green chilli, with the seeds
  discarded (see method)
100 g (4 oz) firm white cabbage,
  finely shredded
½ small green pepper, finely
  shredded
¼ cucumber, cut into thin matchstick
  strips
2.5 cm (1 inch) fresh root ginger,
  peeled and finely sliced
1 large carrot, peeled and grated
225–275 g (8–10 oz) cooked turkey,
  sliced into thin pieces
2 teaspoons sesame seeds
4 tablespoons clear honey
4 tablespoons dry sherry
2 tablespoons soy sauce
150 ml (¼ pint) water
salt
freshly ground black pepper

Preparation time: 30 minutes, plus
marinating
Cooking time: 5 minutes

1. The seeds are the hottest part of
chillies. Remove them before using the
chilli or include a few as you prefer,
according to taste.
2. Mix the vegetables together in a
shallow serving dish. Arrange the turkey on top of the vegetables in an
attractive pattern. Set aside.
3. Dry-fry the sesame seeds in a heavy-
based saucepan. Mix together the
honey, sherry, soy sauce and water and
pour into the pan. Bring to the boil,
stirring, then pour over the turkey and
vegetables. Add salt and pepper to
taste. Leave to cool, then cover the dish
and marinate in the refrigerator for at
least 4 hours, or overnight if you prefer. Spoon the marinade over the meat
occasionally during this time. Allow the
dish to come to room temperature for

30 minutes before serving.
4. Serve with deep-fried prawn
crackers and chilled dry white wine.

NEW YEAR'S EVE SUPPER PARTY FOR SIX

Jerusalem Artichoke Salad

Tournedos with Mustard, Anchovy and Herb Dressing

Lyonnaise Potatoes

Baked Courgettes

Mocha Malakoff Gâteau

Wine suggestions:
Starter:
Mosel
Main course:
Châteauneuf-du-Pape
Dessert:
Medium-sweet Champagne

COUNTDOWN

The day before

Make the Mocha Malakoff gâteau, cover and chill.

4–5 hours before the meal

Cook and marinate the artichokes for the Jerusalem artichoke salad.
Prepare all the ingredients for the Baked courgettes, except for adding the hot stock.

1½ hours before the meal

Turn out the Mocha Malakoff gâteau and decorate.

1¼ hours before the meal

Prepare the potatoes and onions for the Lyonnaise potatoes.
Add the hot stock and cook the Baked courgettes.

45 minutes before the meal

Prepare the Tournedos and make the dressing.

30 minutes before the meal

Complete the Jerusalem artichoke salad.
Cook the Lyonnaise potatoes.

About 10 minutes before the meal

Cook the Tournedos. Spoon over the dressing and garnish.

JERUSALEM ARTICHOKE SALAD

750 g (1½ lb) Jerusalem artichokes
salt
1 tablespoon lemon juice
150 ml (¼ pint) French dressing (page 121)
2 tablespoons capers
2 carrots, peeled and cut into julienne strips
2 green celery sticks, thinly sliced
12 black olives, halved and stoned

TO GARNISH:
40 g (1½ oz) split blanched almonds, toasted
sprigs of watercress

Preparation time: about 35 minutes, plus marinating
Cooking time: 25 minutes

1. Peel the artichokes carefully and put them into a bowl of salted water to prevent discoloration.
2. Drain the artichokes and put them into a saucepan with the lemon juice and a pinch of salt. Cover them with water, bring to the boil, cover and simmer for 15–20 minutes until they are just tender.
3. Drain the artichokes and put them into a bowl, cutting all the pieces to an even size. Add the dressing and toss well. Cover and leave in a cool place for 3–4 hours, stirring occasionally.
4. Just before serving, add the capers, carrots, celery and olives and toss well. Divide the salad among 6 small plates, leaving behind any excess dressing. Sprinkle each portion with toasted almonds and garnish with sprigs of watercress.

RIGHT: Jerusalem artichoke salad

TOURNEDOS WITH MUSTARD, ANCHOVY AND HERB DRESSING

6 tournedos steaks about 2.5 cm (1 inch) thick
1 garlic clove, crushed
salt
freshly ground black pepper
25 g (1 oz) butter
2 tablespoons oil

DRESSING:
50 g (2 oz) butter
3 tablespoons finely chopped onion
1 × 50 g (2 oz) can anchovy fillets, drained and finely chopped
4 teaspoons coarse grain mustard
1½ tablespoons chopped fresh parsley
1 tablespoon chopped fresh mixed herbs or 1½ teaspoons dried mixed herbs
2 tablespoons lemon juice

TO GARNISH:
fresh herbs
raw onion rings

Preparation time: about 20 minutes
Cooking time: about 15 minutes

1. Trim the tournedos, if necessary, and rub them all over with the crushed garlic. Season with salt and black pepper.
2. To make the dressing, melt the butter in a pan and fry the onion very gently until it is soft. Add the anchovies, mustard and herbs and cook gently for a minute or so. Add the lemon juice, season with salt and pepper and heat through. Keep warm.
3. When you are ready to serve, heat the butter and oil in a large frying pan. Add the steaks and fry them for about 3 minutes on each side for rare steak, 4 minutes on each side for medium steak and 6–7 minutes on each side for well cooked steak. Alternatively cook the steaks for the same length of time under a preheated grill.
4. Place the tournedos on individual plates and spoon the dressing partly over each one. Garnish with sprigs of fresh herbs and onion rings.

LYONNAISE POTATOES

750 g (1½ lb) potatoes
salt
3 tablespoons oil or dripping
225 g (8 oz) onions, peeled and thinly sliced
chopped fresh parsley or chives, to garnish

Preparation time: about 20 minutes
Cooking time: about 25 minutes

1. Peel the potatoes and parboil for 5 minutes in boiling salted water, then drain and dice or slice.
2. Heat 2 tablespoons of the oil in a frying pan and fry the onions gently until they are soft and golden brown. Remove the onions from the pan and keep warm.
3. Add the remaining oil to the pan and, when hot, add the potatoes. Fry until they are golden brown, turning them over from time to time.
4. Return the onions to the pan and mix well with the potatoes, then drain on absorbent paper towels. Turn into a warmed serving dish and serve hot, sprinkled with parsley or chives.

BAKED COURGETTES

450 g (1 lb) courgettes, trimmed
salt
freshly ground black pepper
3–4 tomatoes, peeled and sliced
4 tablespoons hot beef, chicken or
vegetable stock
2 tablespoons fresh breadcrumbs
1 tablespoon grated Parmesan
cheese

Preparation time: about 10 minutes
Cooking time: about 55 minutes
Oven: 180°C, 350°F, Gas Mark 4

1. Cut the courgettes into sticks about 5 cm (2 inches) long, lay them in a lightly greased shallow ovenproof dish, and season lightly.
2. Place the sliced tomatoes over the courgettes, then add the hot stock to the dish. Cover with foil or a lid and cook in a preheated moderate oven for 30 minutes.
3. Remove the foil, sprinkle first with the breadcrumbs and then the cheese, and return the dish to the oven for 20–25 minutes, until the courgettes are just tender and the topping lightly browned.

MOCHA MALAKOFF GATEAU

SERVES 8–10
100 g (4 oz) caster sugar
150 g (5 oz) blanched almonds,
  roughly chopped
175 g (6 oz) butter
2 egg yolks
6 tablespoons dark rum or brandy
75 g (3 oz) plain chocolate, melted
1 tablespoon coffee essence
5 tablespoons milk
1½–2 packets boudoir or sponge
  finger biscuits

TO DECORATE:
300 ml (½ pint) double cream
1 tablespoon coffee essence
chocolate mini curls (see right)
8 crystallized or sugared violets
  (purchased)

Preparation time: 1 hour, plus chilling
Cooking time: 5 minutes

1. Line a 23 × 13 cm (9 × 5) inch loaf tin with non-stick silicone paper or greased greaseproof paper.
2. Put 50 g (2 oz) of the sugar into a heavy-based saucepan with the almonds, and heat gently until the sugar melts and turns a light caramel colour, shaking the pan so that all the nuts are coated. Turn out the nuts onto a greased baking sheet in a single layer and leave until cold, then crush them in a food processor or blender, or with a rolling pin.

CLOCKWISE FROM THE TOP: Mocha Malakoff gâteau; Tournedos with mustard, anchovy and herb dressing; Lyonnaise potatoes; Baked courgettes

3. Cream the butter until light and fluffy, then beat in the remaining sugar followed by the egg yolks, 3 tablespoons of the rum or brandy and the melted, but cooled, chocolate. When the mixture is smooth, beat in the crushed nuts.
4. Combine the remaining rum or brandy, coffee essence and milk.
5. Put a layer of boudoir biscuits into the base of the lined tin and sprinkle them with 3 tablespoons of the rum milk mixture. Cover with half the chocolate nut mixture.
6. Add a second layer of biscuits, sprinkle them with another 3 tablespoons of the rum milk mixture and top with the remaining chocolate mixture. Cover with another layer of biscuits and the rest of the rum milk mixture. Press down evenly and cover with a piece of non-stick or greased greaseproof paper and then a layer of foil.
7. Chill for at least 12, and preferably 24, hours with a light weight on the top if possible.
8. To serve, turn out the gâteau onto a serving dish and peel off the paper. Whip the cream and coffee essence together until stiff and use some of it to mask the whole cake. Put the remainder into a piping bag fitted with a large star nozzle and pipe two or three wavy lines along the length of the top of the gâteau. Fill the spaces with chocolate mini curls and complete the decoration with the crystallized violets. Serve cut into slices.

CHOCOLATE MINI CURLS: Using a block of plain chocolate which is not too cold and firm, pare off small curls with a potato peeler. Once made the curls will store for several weeks in an airtight container.

AL FRESCO PARTIES

Step into the garden, wander down to the beach, drive into the countryside – and enjoy our inspirational food for the great outdoors. You won't be able to resist, for example, Ratty's picnic, which finishes with a flourish of summer fruits in wine; a high-spirited menu for a Wild West barbecue; and a refreshingly original selection of finger foods for Guy Fawkes' night.

CLOCKWISE FROM TOP LEFT: Salamagundy; Raised turkey and pickled walnut pie; Banana salad with limes; Carrot, peanut and cabbage slaw; Belgian apricot flan

WINTER PICNIC HAMPER FOR FOUR

Crab Bisque with Whisky

Raised Turkey and Pickled Walnut Pie

Carrot, Peanut and Cabbage Slaw

Cheese and Herb Rolls

Individual Dried Fruit Brûlées

Stilton, Celery and Black Grapes*

Wine suggestion:
Beaujolais nouveau

COUNTDOWN

Two days before
Complete step 1 of the Dried fruit brûlées.

The day before
Complete the Dried fruit brûlées, cover and chill.
Make the Raised turkey and pickled walnut pie.
Make the Cheese and herb rolls.

Early in the morning before the picnic
Make the Crab bisque and pour into a warmed vaccum flask.
Make the Carrot, peanut and cabbage slaw, cover and chill.
Pack all the picnic food into a hamper, along with the plates, cutlery, salt and pepper, wine, glasses and a corkscrew and coffee.

CRAB BISQUE WITH WHISKY

1 crab weighing about 450 g (1 lb)
1 onion, peeled and chopped
2 carrots, peeled and chopped
2 celery sticks, sliced
1 bouquet garni
1.5 litres (2½ pints) water
40 g (1½ oz) butter or margarine
40 g (1½ oz) plain flour
1 tablespoon lemon juice
150 ml (¼ pint) white wine
25 g (1 oz) long grain rice
4 tablespoons double cream
salt
freshly ground black pepper
1–2 tablespoons chopped fresh parsley (optional)
2–3 tablespoons whisky

Preparation time: about 45 minutes
Cooking time: 1½ hours

A bisque is a shellfish purée soup, traditionally always highly spiced or flavoured. Whisky seems an unusual flavouring, but in this case it provides a good contrast to the rich creaminess of the bisque. Crabs are generally available all year round, but if you have trouble finding one, frozen dressed crab is widely available in supermarkets. If the frozen crab comes unshelled, use a fish stock cube instead of the crab stock.

1. Remove both the brown and the white crab meat from the cleaned shell and chop (page 16). Chill until required. Break up the shell and put it into a saucepan with the onion, carrots, celery, bouquet garni and water.

ABOVE: Crab bisque with whisky

Bring to the boil, cover and simmer for 45 minutes. Strain the liquid and reserve 1 litre (1¾ pints).

2. Melt the fat in a pan, stir in the flour and cook for 1–2 minutes. Gradually add the crab stock and bring to the boil. Add the lemon juice, wine and rice and simmer for 10 minutes, stirring occasionally.

3. Add the crab meat and simmer for a further 10 minutes. Add the cream and season to taste. Reheat gently and stir in the parsley, if using, and the whisky.

4. Pour into a heated vacuum flask to transport.

RAISED TURKEY AND PICKLED WALNUT PIE

PASTRY:
350 g (12 oz) plain flour
1 teaspoon salt
75 g (3 oz) lard
6 tablespoons water
3 tablespoons milk

FILLING:
350 g (12 oz) raw turkey fillets,
  diced
225 g (8 oz) cooked ham, coarsely
  minced or very finely chopped
1 small onion, peeled and minced
good pinch of ground coriander
salt
freshly ground black pepper
6 pickled walnuts, well drained
beaten egg, to glaze
150 ml (¼ pint) chicken stock
1 teaspoon powdered gelatine
parsley, to garnish (optional)

Preparation time: about 40 minutes
Cooking time: 1½ hours
Oven: 200°C, 400°F, Gas Mark 6;
  then: 180°C, 350°F, Gas Mark 4

1. Prepare the filling for the pie. Put the turkey, ham, onion and coriander into a bowl, season with salt and pepper and mix well.
2. To make the pastry, sift the flour and salt into a bowl and make a well in the centre. Put the lard, water and milk into a saucepan and heat gently until the lard melts, then bring gradually to the boil.
3. Pour immediately onto the flour and mix to an even dough, using a flat whisk or a wooden spoon.
4. Take almost three-quarters of the pastry, keeping the remainder warm in the bowl covered with a hot damp cloth, and roll out the larger piece and use to line a lightly greased 15 cm (6 inch) round cake tin, preferably one with a loose base.

5. Put half the turkey mixture into the tin and arrange the walnuts evenly over it. Cover with the remaining turkey mixture and level the top.
6. Roll out the reserved pastry to make a lid, damp the edges and place in position. Trim off the excess, press the edges together and crimp. Make a hole in the centre of the pie for the steam to escape. Brush the pastry with beaten egg. Roll out the pastry trimmings and cut out leaves. Arrange them on the top of the pie, around the hole, and glaze again.
7. Stand the tin on a baking sheet and cook in a preheated moderately hot oven for 30 minutes. Reduce the temperature to moderate, glaze the pie again and cook for a further 1 hour. Lay a sheet of greaseproof paper over the pie when it is sufficiently browned.
8. Heat the stock, sprinkle over the gelatine, and heat gently to dissolve. Season well and allow to cool a little.
9. Remove the pie from the oven, leave

CLOCKWISE FROM TOP LEFT: Cheese
and herb rolls; Raised turkey and pickled
walnut pie; Carrot, peanut and cabbage
slaw

it to cool for 10 minutes, then, using a
small funnel, pour in the stock through
the central hole. Add as much stock as
you can, then leave the pie to cool.
When it is cold, chill it thoroughly –
preferably for at least 12 hours or
longer if you can.
10. To transport, unmould the pie and
wrap it in foil. Serve cut into wedges.
Garnish with parsley if wished.

CARROT, PEANUT
AND CABBAGE SLAW

*1 large carrot, peeled and coarsely
  grated*
3 celery sticks, sliced
75 g (3 oz) salted peanuts
50 g (2 oz) raisins
*175 g (6 oz) white cabbage, finely
  shredded*

DRESSING:
3 tablespoons thick mayonnaise
*1 tablespoon French dressing
  (page 121)*
salt
freshly ground black pepper

Preparation time: about 25 minutes

1. Combine the carrot, celery, peanuts, raisins and cabbage in a bowl.
2. In another bowl, combine the
dressing ingredients, adding salt and
pepper to taste. Pour the dressing over
the salad and toss thoroughly.
3. Turn into a polythene container or
serving dish and cover tightly, then
chill until ready to transport. This salad
is best if it is made 3–6 hours before
serving.

CHEESE AND HERB
ROLLS

MAKES ABOUT 12
450 g (1 lb) strong white flour
2 teaspoons salt
1 teaspoon dry mustard
pinch of black pepper
1 tablespoon dried mixed herbs
*100–175 g (4–6 oz) mature Cheddar
  cheese, finely grated, or 2–3
  tablespoons grated Parmesan
  cheese*
*15 g ($\frac{1}{2}$ oz) fresh yeast or 1$\frac{1}{2}$
  teaspoons dried yeast plus 1
  teaspoon caster sugar*
300 ml ($\frac{1}{2}$ pint) warm water

Preparation time: about 40 minutes,
  plus rising
Cooking time: about 20 minutes
Oven: 190°C, 375°F, Gas Mark 5

As making yeast dough takes a fair
amount of time it is better to make
more rolls than you require and freeze
the surplus to use another day. They
will freeze for up to 2 months.

1. Sift the flour, salt, mustard and pepper into a bowl and mix in the herbs
and most of the cheese.
2. Blend the fresh yeast with the warm
water or, if using dried yeast, dissolve
the sugar in the water, sprinkle the
yeast on top and leave in a warm place
for about 10 minutes until frothy.
3. Add the yeast liquid to the dry
ingredients and mix to form a firm
dough, adding extra flour if necessary,
to leave the sides of the bowl clean.
4. Turn the mixture onto a floured
surface and knead until smooth and
elastic and no longer sticky. This takes
about 10 minutes by hand or 3–4
minutes in an electric mixer fitted with
a dough hook. Shape the dough into a
ball, place it in an oiled polythene bag
and put it in a warm place to rise for
about 1 hour or until it has doubled in
size.
5. Remove the dough from the bag,
knock it back and knead until smooth,
then divide it into 50 g (2 oz) pieces
and shape into rolls. Either form into
long finger rolls, round bun shapes or
divide each piece in half and roll into
sausages of about 20 cm (8 inches)
and twist the two pieces together for
twisted rolls.
6. Stand the rolls on greased baking
sheets and lay a sheet of oiled polythene loosely over them. Put in a warm
place to rise until doubled in size.
7. Remove the polythene, sprinkle
with the remaining cheese and cook in
a preheated moderately hot oven for
15–20 minutes until well risen,
browned and firm. Take care and
watch carefully for cheese bread tends
to overbrown easily and quickly.
8. Cool the rolls on a wire tray. Transport in a rigid container or a polythene
bag.

DRIED FRUIT BRULEES

225 g (8 oz) mixed dried fruits (e.g.
 apricots, prunes, peaches, pears or
 apple rings
750 ml (1¼ pints) boiling milkless tea
2–4 tablespoons brandy
2 tablespoons granulated sugar
250 ml (8 fl oz) soured cream
about 6 tablespoons demerara sugar

Preparation time: about 30 minutes,
 plus soaking overnight and chilling
Cooking time: about 25 minutes

1. Put the dried fruit into a bowl and pour the boiling tea over it. Add the brandy, cover and leave to soak for at least 12, and preferably 24, hours.
2. Transfer the fruit and juice to a pan and bring slowly to the boil. Cover and simmer for 10–15 minutes until tender. Drain the fruit reserving the juices, chop it roughly and divide between 4 individual flameproof dishes.
3. Put the cooking juices and the granulated sugar into a pan and heat gently until the sugar has dissolved, then boil until about 4 tablespoons remain. Cool and pour over the fruit, then chill.

ABOVE: Dried fruit brûlées

4. Spread the soured cream over the dried fruit and cover each one with a layer of about 1½ tablespoons demerara sugar.
5. Stand the dishes in a grill pan and place under a moderately hot grill until the sugar melts and caramelizes. Remove quickly, cool and chill thoroughly.
6. To transport, cover each dish securely with foil.

RATTY'S PICNIC FOR EIGHT

Samosas with Curry Mayonnaise Dip

Chicken and Grape Stuffed Loaf

Seafood and Fennel Salad

New Potato, Cheshire Cheese and Cashew Nut Salad

Mushroom and Tomato Salad

Wedges of Crisp Lettuce*

Belgian Apricot Flan

Peaches and Strawberries in Wine

Wine suggestion:
Muscadet

COUNTDOWN

The day before
Make the Chicken and grape stuffed loaf, wrap in foil and chill.
Make the Belgian apricot flan, cool, then wrap in foil.
Make the Curry mayonnaise dip, cover and chill.
Prepare the Samosas up to the end of step 4.

Early in the morning of the picnic
Cook the Samosas. Leave to cool, then pack into a rigid airtight container.
Make the Seafood and fennel salad.
Make the New potato, Cheshire cheese and cashew nut salad, cover and chill.
Prepare the Mushroom and tomato salad, cover and chill.
Prepare the lettuce wedges and pack.
Make the Peaches and strawberries in wine, cover and chill.

About 1 hour before leaving
Pack everything into cold boxes and baskets. Do not forget the plates, knives, forks, spoons, napkins, salt and pepper, wine glasses and corkscrew and the coffee.

SAMOSAS WITH CURRY MAYONNAISE DIP

MAKES 16
FILLING:
2 tablespoons oil
1 medium onion, peeled and finely chopped
1 garlic clove, crushed
1–2 teaspoons freshly grated raw root ginger (optional)
1 large carrot, peeled and coarsely grated
1½–2 teaspoons garam masala
4 tablespoons water
salt
freshly ground black pepper
225 g (8 oz) cooked peas
225 g (8 oz) boiled potatoes, cut into small dice

DOUGH:
225 g (8 oz) plain flour
½ teaspoon salt
25 g (1 oz) butter
about 100 ml (3½ fl oz) cold water
oil or fat for deep frying

CURRY DIP:
150 ml (¼ pint) thick mayonnaise (page 146)
3 tablespoons soured cream
1½ teaspoons curry powder
¼ teaspoon ground coriander
1 teaspoon tomato purée
1 tablespoon mango chutney, chopped

Preparation time: about 40 minutes, plus cooling
Cooking time: about 25 minutes

These samosas can be prepared up to 12 hours before they are required provided the raw dough is covered with a damp cloth and kept in a cool place to prevent it drying out. If you are going to serve the samosas hot, fry them when you want them; but if you are going to take them to the picnic to eat cold, then fry them a couple of hours before you set out.

1. To make the filling, heat the oil in a pan and fry the onion, garlic and ginger, if using, until soft. Add the carrot and continue frying for 2–3 minutes. Stir in the garam masala, add the water, season with salt and pepper and simmer gently until the liquid is almost absorbed. Remove the pan from the heat, stir in the peas and potatoes and leave until cold.
2. To make the dough, sift the flour and salt into a bowl and rub in the butter finely. Add sufficient water to mix to a smooth, elastic dough, kneading continually.
3. Cut the dough into 16 even-sized pieces and keep them covered. Remove one piece at a time, dip it into a little oil or coat lightly with flour and roll out to a 13 cm (5 inch) circle.
4. Put 1–2 tablespoons of the filling on one side of the circle, damp the edge, fold over and seal firmly. Once made, keep the samosas covered with a damp cloth to prevent them from drying out.
5. Heat the oil to 180°–190°C/ 350°–375°F or until a cube of bread browns in 30 seconds; then fry the samosas, a few at a time, for 3–4 minutes until they are golden brown, turning them once or twice. Drain on absorbent paper towels and fry the remaining ones in the same way. Leave to cool.
6. To make the dip, combine all the ingredients and put them into an airtight plastic container. Pack the samosas into a rigid airtight container to transport.

CHICKEN AND GRAPE STUFFED LOAF

1 small bloomer loaf, or another small, deep fancy loaf

FILLING:
40 g (1½ oz) butter or margarine
1 onion, peeled and finely chopped
25 g (1 oz) plain flour
300 ml (½ pint) milk
salt
freshly ground black pepper
1 tablespoon aspic jelly powder
200 ml (⅓ pint) boiling water
2 tablespoons chopped fresh parsley (optional)
175 g (6 oz) green grapes, halved and pips removed
350 g (12 oz) cooked chicken, diced
2 hard-boiled eggs, chopped

Preparation time: about 40 minutes, plus cooling and chilling
Cooking time: 10 minutes

1. Melt the fat in a pan and fry the onion until it is soft but not coloured. Stir in the flour and cook for 1 minute. Gradually add the milk, bring it to the boil and simmer for 2 minutes, stirring all the time. Remove from the heat and season well with salt and pepper.
2. Dissolve the aspic jelly powder in the boiling water, heating gently if necessary. Allow to cool slightly before stirring the aspic mixture evenly through the white sauce with the parsley, if using. Cover with cling film and leave until it is cool but not set.
3. Stir the grapes, chicken and chopped eggs into the sauce, then taste and adjust the seasoning. Leave until on the point of setting.
4. Cut off the top of the loaf along the whole length and scoop out all the crumb. (Reserve to make breadcrumbs for another dish.)
5. Spoon the chicken filling into the loaf, replace the top and wrap the whole loaf securely in foil. Chill until set, preferably overnight.
6. Transport to the picnic in a cold box, still wrapped in foil. Serve cut into slices, using a serrated knife for easy slicing.

SEAFOOD AND FENNEL SALAD

100 g (4 oz) long grain rice
salt
2 salmon steaks, about 175–225 g (6–8 oz) each
1 tablespoon lemon juice
freshly ground black pepper
350 g (12 oz) prawns
1 × 150 g (5 oz) jar mussels in brine, drained
4 spring onions, trimmed and sliced
1 fennel bulb
4 tablespoons French dressing (page 121)
2 tablespoons single or soured cream

Preparation time: about 40 minutes
Cooking time: about 30 minutes

To make this dish more economical replace the salmon steaks with 2 large cod steaks.

1. Cook the rice for 13–14 minutes in boiling salted water until it is just tender. Drain, rinse in boiling water, drain again thoroughly and turn into a bowl.
2. Poach the salmon steaks in the minimum of water seasoned with the lemon juice, salt and pepper, for 7–8 minutes until tender. Leave in the water until cold, then remove and flake the salmon, discarding the skin and bones. Add the flaked salmon to the rice.
3. Add the prawns to the rice with the drained mussels and the spring onions.
4. Remove any feathery fronds from the fennel and reserve for a garnish if available. Chop the rest of the fennel bulb, add it to the salad and mix well.
5. Combine the French dressing and the cream, season well with salt and pepper and add to the salad. Toss thoroughly and turn into a polythene container. Arrange the pieces of fennel on top as a garnish, and cover. Chill until ready to transport.

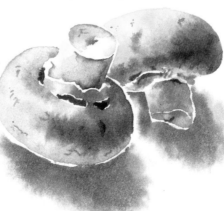

NEW POTATO, CHESHIRE CHEESE AND CASHEW NUT SALAD

750 g (1½ lb) new potatoes, scrubbed
salt
6 tablespoons French dressing (page 121)
4 spring onions, trimmed and sliced or 2 tablespoons snipped chives
100 g (4 oz) Cheshire cheese, finely diced
75 g (3 oz) salted cashew nuts
12–16 black olives, stoned and halved
freshly ground black pepper

Preparation time: about 20 minutes, plus cooling
Cooking time: about 10–15 minutes

1. Cook the potatoes in boiling salted water for about 10–15 minutes until they are just tender. Drain and roughly dice.
2. Put them into a bowl and while they are still hot, add the dressing. Mix well, add the spring onions or chives, then cover and leave to cool.
3. Add the cheese, cashews and olives, season well with salt and pepper and mix lightly. Turn the salad into a polythene container, cover tightly and chill until ready to transport.

MUSHROOM AND TOMATO SALAD

225 g (8 oz) tiny button mushrooms
100 g (4 oz) oyster mushrooms
150 ml (¼ pint) French dressing
  (page 121)
2 tablespoons chopped fresh mint
225 g (8 oz) tiny cherry tomatoes,
  wiped

Preparation time: about 15 minutes, plus marinating

If the really tiny button mushrooms are not available, use larger ones and cut them into halves or quarters depending on their size.

CLOCKWISE FROM TOP RIGHT: Chicken and grape stuffed loaf; Samosas with Curry mayonnaise dip (page 177); New potato, Cheshire cheese and cashew nut salad; Seafood and fennel salad; Mushroom and tomato salad

1. Trim and wipe the mushrooms and put them into a dish.
2. Combine the dressing and the mint and pour it over the mushrooms. Cover tightly and leave to marinate for at least 3–4 hours, turning occasionally.
3. Drain the excess dressing (but not the mint) and arrange the mushrooms in a serving bowl or polythene container. Add the tomatoes and cover tightly ready to transport.

BELGIAN APRICOT FLAN

*175 g (6 oz) no-need-to-soak dried
  apricots*
3 tablespoons brandy
3 tablespoons apricot jam
*1 cooking apple, peeled, cored and
  finely chopped*
225 g (8 oz) butter
75 g (3 oz) light soft brown sugar
2 tablespoons vegetable oil
1 egg
450 g (1 lb) plain flour
2 teaspoons baking powder
1 teaspoon ground cinnamon
icing sugar, sifted, to decorate

Preparation time: about 40 minutes
Cooking time: 1¼–1½ hours
Oven: 150°C, 300°F, Gas Mark 2

1. Chop the apricots finely and mix them with the brandy, jam and apple. Cover and leave to stand for 20 minutes or while making the pastry.
2. Cream the butter until soft in a large bowl, then beat in the sugar and oil until light and fluffy. Beat in the egg.
3. Sift the flour, baking powder and cinnamon together and gradually work into the creamed mixture to give a shortbread-like dough.
4. Line a shallow rectangular tin, approx 28 × 18 × 4 cm (11 × 7 × 1½ inches) with non-stick silicone paper or greased greaseproof paper.
5. Take two-thirds of the dough and press over the base and sides of the tin to line it evenly. Spread the apricot mixture over the dough.
6. Using the coarse side of a grater, grate the remaining dough so it covers the filling evenly.
7. Cook in a preheated cool oven for 1¼–1½ hours until lightly browned. Leave in the tin until cold.
8. Before serving, dredge the flan heavily with the sifted icing sugar and serve it cut into fingers or squares. Take the flan to the picnic still in the tin, overwrapped in foil.

PEACHES AND STRAWBERRIES IN WINE

3 ripe peaches
3 tablespoons caster sugar
300 ml (½ pint) white dessert wine
450 g (1 lb) strawberries, hulled
*wild strawberries to decorate
  (optional)*

Preparation time: about 15 minutes,
  plus standing and chilling

1. Halve the peaches, remove the stones and slice the fruit into a bowl. Sprinkle with the sugar and leave to stand for 5 minutes.
2. Pour the wine over the peaches and leave to stand for 15 minutes.
3. Add the strawberries, mix them lightly with the peaches and, if you can find them, a few wild strawberries, then cover and chill for 2 hours.
4. Transport to the picnic in an airtight plastic container.

Variation: Nectarines may be used in place of peaches. If you prefer the peaches to be peeled, dip each one into boiling water for 30 seconds and then into cold water. This loosens the skins and makes it easy to peel them.

*FROM THE TOP: Belgian apricot flan;
Peaches and strawberries in wine*

FINGER FOOD FOR GUY FAWKES NIGHT FOR TEN

Curried Vegetable Soup

Porky Meatballs with Mango Dip

Granary Roquefort and Courgette Lattice Pie

Krisprolls with Cheese and Salami Cones

Date and Apple Cake

Mocha Brownies

Drink suggestion:
Glühwein

COUNTDOWN

2 days before
Make the Date and apple cake and wrap in foil.

1–2 days before
Make the Mocha brownies and store in an airtight container.

The day before or on the day
Make the Curried vegetable soup, cover and chill.
Make the Granary Roquefort and courgette lattice pie, cover and chill.

In the morning
Make the Mango dip.
Prepare the mixture and cook the Porky meatballs.

Before the party
Make the Glühwein.
Make the Krisprolls with cheese and salami cones.
Cut up the Date and apple cake and the Mocha brownies, arrange on a platter and cover with foil.

Just before the party
Reheat the Porky meatballs.
Reheat the Curried vegetable soup.
Reheat the Glühwein.
Reheat the Granary Roquefort and cheese lattice pie for 15 minutes.

CURRIED VEGETABLE SOUP

100 g (4 oz) butter or margarine
225 g (8 oz) carrots, peeled and diced
225 g (8 oz) onions, peeled and diced
225 g (8 oz) celery, sliced
225 g (8 oz) parsnips, peeled and chopped
1 large or 2 small leeks, trimmed, washed and chopped
1 tablespoon medium curry powder
50 g (2 oz) plain flour
2 litres (3½ pints) beef, chicken or vegetable stock
1½ tablespoons tomato purée
2 bay leaves
good pinch of ground nutmeg
salt
freshly ground black pepper
450–600 ml (¾–1 pint) milk

Preparation time: about 30 minutes
Cooking time: about 40 minutes

If you prefer a clear soup with small pieces of vegetables in it to a thicker one, chop all the raw vegetables very finely either by hand or in a food processor, then there will be no need to purée the soup later.

1. Melt the fat in a large saucepan and add all the vegetables. Fry them gently for 10 minutes, stirring occasionally, until they are soft but not coloured.
2. Stir in the curry powder and the flour and cook for 1–2 minutes, then gradually add the stock and bring the soup to the boil, stirring occasionally. Add the tomato purée and the bay leaves then cover and simmer gently for about 25 minutes or until the vegetables are tender.
3. Discard the bay leaves, and liquidize, purée or sieve the soup.
4. Return the soup to a clean pan, add the milk and bring back to the boil. Taste and adjust the seasoning, simmer for 2–3 minutes and serve. The soup may be reheated on a barbecue near the bonfire and is best served in mugs.

PORKY MEATBALLS WITH MANGO DIP

MAKES 40
1 kg (2 lb) finely minced pork
2 onions, peeled and minced
½ teaspoon dried marjoram
½ teaspoon ground coriander
3 tablespoons plain flour
2 eggs, beaten
salt
freshly ground black pepper
oil or fat for deep frying

MANGO DIP:
6 tablespoons French dressing (page 121)
8 tablespoons mango chutney
2 teaspoons lemon juice
2 tablespoons soured cream

Preparation time: about 30 minutes
Cooking time: about 25 minutes

1. Combine the pork, onions, herbs, coriander, flour and eggs, season with salt and pepper, and beat until smooth. Form into 40 balls about the size of a small walnut.
2. Heat the oil to 180°C/350°F or until a cube of bread will brown in about 1 minute.
3. Fry the meatballs, a few at a time, for about 4 minutes until golden brown. Drain on absorbent paper towels and keep warm.
4. To make the mango dip, put all the ingredients into a food processor or mixer and blend until thoroughly emulsified and almost smooth.
5. Turn the dip into a bowl and stand the bowl on a large plate. When you are ready to serve, arrange the meatballs around the bowl, spearing each one with a cocktail stick ready for guests to help themselves.

GRANARY ROQUEFORT AND COURGETTE LATTICE PIE

PASTRY:
225 g (8 oz) granary flour
100 g (4 oz) plain flour
pinch of salt
75 g (3 oz) lard
75 g (3 oz) margarine
about 5 tablespoons cold water, to mix

FILLING:
450 g (1 lb) courgettes, trimmed
50 g (2 oz) butter
1 onion, peeled and finely chopped
3 eggs
100 g (4 oz) Roquefort cheese, crumbled or mashed
150 ml (¼ pint) milk or single cream
salt
freshly ground black pepper

Preparation time: about 30 minutes
Cooking time: about 45 minutes
Oven: 200°C, 400°F, Gas Mark 6;
    then: 180°C, 350°F, Gas Mark 4

1. To make the pastry, mix together the granary and plain flours, add the salt and rub in the fats until the mixture resembles fine breadcrumbs. Add sufficient water to mix to a pliable dough. Wrap the dough in polythene or foil and chill while preparing the filling.
2. Dice the courgettes. Melt the butter in a pan and add the onion. Fry gently until soft, then add the courgettes and fry until they are lightly browned. Drain and cool.
3. Whisk the eggs and Roquefort cheese together, using a food processor if you want it really smooth, then add the milk or cream and plenty of salt and pepper.
4. Roll out three-quarters of the pastry and use it to line a 28 cm (11 inch) fluted flan ring, tin or dish.
5. Spoon in the courgette mixture then pour the cheese custard over.
6. Roll out the reserved pastry and cut it into strips about 1.5 cm (½ inch) wide. Lay the strips over the filling in a lattice pattern, trimming off the ends and attaching them to the sides of the flan.

7. Cook in a preheated moderately hot oven for 25 minutes, then reduce the temperature to moderate and cook for a further 20–25 minutes until the pie is well risen, golden brown and the pastry is cooked. Leave to cool.

KRISPROLLS WITH CHEESE AND SALAMI CONES

10 krisprolls
butter, for spreading
10 slices salami
175 g (6 oz) full fat cream cheese
1 tablespoon thick mayonnaise (page 146)
1 teaspoon lemon juice
good pinch of celery salt
freshly ground black pepper
10 small leafy celery sticks

Preparation time: about 20 minutes

1. Spread each krisproll with butter and stand it on a platter.
2. Roll each slice of salami into a cone.
3. Cream the cheese with the mayonnaise, lemon juice, celery salt and add pepper to taste. Put the mixture into a piping bag fitted with a large star nozzle and pipe a large whirl into each salami cone.
4. Push a small leafy stick of celery into each salami cone and lay one on each krisproll, attaching it to the butter. Cover with cling film until you are ready to serve.

CLOCKWISE FROM TOP LEFT: Curried vegetable soup (page 181); Porky meatballs with Mango dip; Krisprolls with cheese and salami cones; Granary Roquefort and courgette lattice pie

DATE AND APPLE CAKE

225 g (8 oz) plain flour
½ teaspoon bicarbonate of soda
1 teaspoon mixed spice
½ teaspoon ground cinnamon or
  ginger
100 g (4 oz) butter or margarine
175 g (6 oz) light soft brown sugar
2 eggs
175 g (6 oz) sultanas
100 g (4 oz) stoned dates, chopped
grated rind of 1 orange
50 g (2 oz) cut mixed peel
225 g (8 oz) cooking apples, peeled,
  cored and coarsely grated

Preparation time: about 30 minutes
Cooking time: about 1½ hours
Oven: 180°C, 350°F, Gas Mark 4

1. Grease and line a 20 cm (8 inch) round cake tin with greased grease-proof paper.
2. Sift the flour into a bowl with the bicarbonate of soda, mixed spice and cinnamon or ginger.
3. Cream together the fat and sugar until very light and fluffy. Beat in the eggs, one at a time, adding a table-spoonful of flour after each one, then fold in the remaining flour.
4. Add the sultanas, dates, orange rind and peel and mix in lightly. Finally mix in the grated apple.
5. Turn the mixture into the tin, level and top and cook in a preheated moderate oven for 1¼–1½ hours until well risen, golden brown and firm to the touch. Cool in the tin for 5 minutes before turning out onto a wire tray. Leave until cold. [F]

[F] Overwrap in foil and freeze for up to 3 months.

MOCHA BROWNIES

MAKES 10–12
50 g (2 oz) plain chocolate
65 g (2½ oz) butter or margarine
175 g (6 oz) caster sugar
1½ teaspoons coffee essence
2 eggs, beaten
65 g (2½ oz) self raising flour
50 g (2 oz) shelled walnuts, chopped

COFFEE ICING:
100 g (4 oz) icing sugar, sifted
1½ teaspoons coffee essence
1½–2 teaspoons warm water

Preparation time: about 25 minutes,
  plus cooling
Cooking time: 35–40 minutes
Oven: 180°C, 350°F, Gas Mark 4

1. Grease and line a shallow square 20 cm (8 inch) sandwich tin with greased greaseproof paper.
2. Melt the chocolate and fat in a heatproof bowl over a pan of gently simmering water.
3. Beat in the sugar until melted then beat in the coffee essence, followed by the eggs.
4. Add the flour and walnuts to the mixture and beat until smooth. Pour it into the prepared tin and cook in a preheated moderate oven for 35–40 minutes until it is well risen and just beginning to shrink from the edges of the tin. Leave to cool in the tin.
5. When it is cold, make the glacé icing. Sift the icing sugar into a bowl and beat in the coffee essence with sufficient water to give a thick spreading consistency. Spread the icing over the brownies and leave to set. When cold, cut into 10–12 slices.

GLUHWEIN

MAKES APPROX 20 GLASSES
1 × 3 litre box red wine or 4 bottles
  red wine
225 g (8 oz) light soft brown sugar
4 cinnamon sticks, halved
2 lemons, each stuck with 14 whole
  cloves
150 ml (¼ pint) brandy (optional)

Preparation time: about 10 minutes
Cooking time: about 15 minutes

1. Put all the ingredients except the brandy into a large heavy-based sauce-pan and heat very gently until the sugar has dissolved, stirring occasionally.
2. Bring slowly to the boil, then cover the pan and simmer gently for 3–5 minutes. Remove from the heat and add the brandy, if using.
3. Serve at once, or cool and reheat very gently without boiling.

CLOCKWISE FROM TOP LEFT: Date and apple cake; Glühwein, Mocha brownies

WILD WEST BARBECUE FOR TEN

Chilli Chicken Drumsticks

Steak Rolls with Mustard Sauce

Corn Kebabs

Three Bean Salad

Frankfurter and Rice Salad

Walnut Flan

Banana Salad with Limes

Drink suggestion:
Craz-y-cider cup

ABOVE: Craz-y-cider cup

COUNTDOWN

The day before
Put the beans to soak for the Three bean salad.

In the morning
Complete steps 1 and 2 of the Craz-y-cider cup.
Make the French dressing for the Three bean salad, cover and chill.
Complete steps 1 and 2 of the Three bean salad.
Complete steps 1–3 of the Frankfurter and rice salad, cover and chill.
Make the Walnut flan.
Make the Banana salad with limes

In the afternoon
Prepare the Chilli chicken drumsticks up to the end of step 3.
Prepare the Steak rolls with mustard sauce up to the end of step 4.
Boil the corn cobs and thread onto skewers.
Complete the Three bean salad.

1 hour before the barbecue
Complete the Frankfurter and rice salad.

30 minutes before the barbecue
Light the barbecue.
Complete the Craz-y-cider cup.

When the guests arrive
Start cooking the Steak rolls with mustard sauce, the Chilli chicken drumsticks and the Corn kebabs.

CRAZ-Y-CIDER CUP

MAKES 20 GLASSES
900 ml (1½ pints) tea
100 g (4 oz) white sugar
200 ml (⅓ pint) brandy
600 ml (1 pint) unsweetened orange juice
2 oranges, thinly sliced
1 lemon, thinly sliced
2.25 litres (4 pints) cider

Preparation time: about 15 minutes, plus chilling

1. Make the tea freshly and strain it onto the sugar. Stir until dissolved, then leave until cool.
2. Add the brandy and orange juice and the slices of fruit. Cover and chill for at least 1 hour.
3. Just before serving, add the cider and mix well. Serve in wine glasses.

CHILLI CHICKEN DRUMSTICKS

2 tablespoons oil
1 onion, peeled and finely chopped
1 garlic clove, crushed
150 ml ($\frac{1}{4}$ pint) tomato ketchup
3 tablespoons Worcestershire sauce
2–3 teaspoons chilli seasoning
150 ml ($\frac{1}{4}$ pint) red wine vinegar
2 tablespoons apricot jam
1 teaspoon dry mustard
20 chicken drumsticks
sprigs of parsley, to garnish

Preparation time: about 20 minutes,
 plus marinating
Cooking time: about 20 minutes

If the weather is bad, either cook the drumsticks under a preheated moderately hot grill for 10 minutes each side, or put them into a preheated hot oven (220°C, 425°F, Gas Mark 7) for about 40 minutes, turning once, until browned and cooked through.

1. Heat the oil in a pan and fry the onion and garlic until soft, then continue frying until lightly coloured.
2. Add the ketchup, Worcestershire sauce, chilli seasoning, vinegar, jam and mustard and bring slowly to the boil. Simmer gently for 2 minutes, then remove from the heat and leave to cool.
3. Arrange the drumsticks in a roasting tin or on a large platter in a single layer and pour the sauce over them. Leave to marinate in a cool place for at least 3 hours, turning the chicken occasionally.
4. When you are ready to cook, drain the marinade from the drumsticks and reserve, and put the drumsticks onto a moderately heated barbecue. Cook for 5–8 minutes on each side until they are cooked right through and well browned. Put on to a platter, garnish, and keep warm.
5. Heat the reserved marinade in a saucepan and serve with the drumsticks.

STEAK ROLLS WITH MUSTARD SAUCE

10 thin sirloin steaks, or thin buttock
 or quick-fry steaks weighing about
 150–175 g (5–6 oz) each and 5 mm
 ($\frac{1}{4}$ inch) thick
about 5 tablespoons coarse-grain
 tarragon mustard
salt
freshly ground black pepper

MUSTARD SAUCE:
150 ml ($\frac{1}{4}$ pint) thick mayonnaise
150 ml ($\frac{1}{4}$ pint) soured cream
1 tablespoon coarse-grain tarragon
 mustard
1 teaspoon Dijon mustard
1 tablespoon wine vinegar
1 teaspoon caster sugar
1 tablespoon chopped fresh tarragon
 or parsley

Preparation time: 20 minutes, plus
 marinating
Cooking time: about 20 minutes

CLOCKWISE FROM TOP LEFT: Chilli chicken drumsticks; Frankfurter and rice salad; Three bean salad; Steak rolls with mustard sauce; Corn kebabs

for medium-rare steak, turning once during cooking.

6. Serve the steak rolls from the barbecue with the sauce.

CORN KEBABS

10 corn cobs, husks and silky threads
  removed
salt
little melted butter
freshly ground black pepper

Preparation time: about 10 minutes
Cooking time: about 10 minutes

1. Place the corn cobs in a large saucepan of boiling salted water and cook for 4–5 minutes. Drain.
2. Cut each corn cob into 3 or 4 slices and thread on to skewers.
3. Brush each one with melted butter, sprinkle lightly with pepper and cook on the barbecue for 5–10 minutes, turning several times to brown lightly and pick up the smoky flavour.

THREE BEAN SALAD

225 g (8 oz) red kidney beans,
  soaked overnight
225 g (8 oz) black eye beans, soaked
  overnight
225 g (8 oz) mung beans
150 ml ($\frac{1}{4}$ pint) French dressing
  (page 121)
salt
freshly ground black pepper
$\frac{1}{2}$ bunch spring onions, trimmed and
  thinly sliced
2 tablespoons chopped fresh mixed
  herbs or parsley

Preparation time: about 30 minutes,
  plus soaking overnight and chilling
Cooking time: about 1 hour

Should the weather not be good enough to cook on a barbecue, these steak rolls can be cooked under a preheated moderate grill, allowing 8–10 minutes for rare steak or longer if you like it well cooked.

1. If the steaks seem a little thick put them between two sheets of cling film or greaseproof paper and beat them with a rolling pin until they are a little thinner.
2. Spread each steak with mustard and season lightly with salt and pepper. Roll up loosely with the mustard inside. Thread the rolls on skewers leaving plenty of space between each one; or put each one on its own skewer.
3. Cover and chill for at least 1 hour and up to 3 hours.
4. To make the sauce, combine all the ingredients and place them in a bowl. Cover with cling film and chill until required.
5. Make sure the barbecue is moderately hot, then cook for 8–10 minutes

1. Drain the red and the black eye beans and place each type in a separate saucepan of unsalted water. Wash the mung beans and put them in another pan and cover them with unsalted water. (Mung beans do not need soaking). Bring all the pans to the boil and boil hard for 10 minutes, then turn them all down, cover and simmer gently for about 20 minutes for the mung beans, and 40–50 for the other two.
2. Drain all the beans, rinse and mix together in a large bowl. While still warm, add the dressing and season with salt and pepper and toss well. Cover and leave until cold.
3. Just before serving, add the onions and herbs, mix well and turn into a serving bowl. Cover with cling film until required.

FRANKFURTER AND RICE SALAD

225 g (8 oz) long grain rice
salt
3 tablespoons oil
1 large onion, peeled and sliced
1 red pepper, seeded and chopped
1 green pepper, seeded and chopped
$\frac{1}{4}$ cucumber, diced
50 g (2 oz) raisins
2 carrots, peeled and cut into
  julienne strips
8–10 frankfurters, thinly sliced
freshly ground black pepper
crisp lettuce leaves or spinach leaves,
  to serve

Preparation time: about 25 minutes
Cooking time: about 25 minutes

1. Cook the rice in boiling salted water for about 14 minutes until just tender. Drain, rinse with boiling water and drain again very thoroughly. Put into a bowl.
2. Meanwhile heat the oil in a pan and fry the onion until it is soft. Add the peppers and continue frying gently for 2–3 minutes, stirring frequently. Cool a little, then stir through the rice.
3. Add the cucumber, raisins, carrots and frankfurters to the rice and season with plenty of salt and pepper. Mix thoroughly.
4. Line a bowl with crisp lettuce leaves or spinach leaves with the stalks removed, and spoon the salad on top. Cover with cling film until the salad is required.

WALNUT FLAN

PASTRY:
225 g (8 oz) plain flour
pinch of salt
50 g (2 oz) butter or margarine
50 g (2 oz) lard or white fat
cold water, to mix

FILLING:
25 g (1 oz) butter or margarine
175 g (6 oz) light soft brown sugar
3 eggs
175 ml (6 fl oz) maple syrup
1 teaspoon vanilla essence
grated rind of 1 lemon
grated rind of ½ orange
175 g (6 oz) walnut halves

Preparation time: about 30 minutes
Cooking time: about 1 hour
Oven: 220°C, 425°F, Gas Mark 7;
  then: 190°C, 375°F, Gas Mark 5

This is a very rich flan so only serve it in small slices. The filling rises rather alarmingly during cooking but sinks back as it cools. It is particularly good served with vanilla ice cream.

1. To make the pastry, sift the flour and salt into a bowl and rub in the fats until the mixture resembles fine bread-crumbs. Add sufficient water to mix to a pliable dough, then knead lightly.
2. Roll out the pastry on a lightly floured surface and use to line a 23 cm (9 inch) fluted flan ring, dish or tin.
3. Prick the base and bake blind in a preheated hot oven for 15 minutes, then remove the paper and beans. Reduce the oven temperature.
4. To make the filling, combine the fat, sugar and eggs in a bowl and beat well; then beat in the maple syrup, vanilla essence and lemon and orange rinds.
5. Arrange the walnut halves in the pastry case, flat side downwards, and pour the syrup mixture over them.
6. Bake in the oven for 35–40 minutes. Allow the flan to cool, when the filling will sink back to normal. Serve cold with cream or ice cream.

BANANA SALAD WITH LIMES

2 limes
8–10 bananas
100 g (4 oz) granulated sugar
6 tablespoons water
*150 ml (¼ pint) fresh unsweetened
  orange juice*

FROM THE LEFT: Walnut flan; Banana salad with limes

Preparation time: about 20 minutes, plus chilling
Cooking time: about 5 minutes

1. Grate the rind from the limes onto a plate and squeeze the juice into a saucer.
2. Peel the bananas and cut each one into three pieces. Coat them in the lime juice and place in a bowl. Cover with cling film.
3. Put the sugar and water into a small saucepan, heat gently, stirring all the time, until the sugar dissolves and then boil, without stirring, until the syrup is caramel coloured. Remove quickly from the heat and add the orange juice and the remaining lime juice. If necessary reheat gently to melt the caramel, then pour over the bananas. Sprinkle with the grated lime rind and mix lightly.
4. Cover the bowl, cool and then chill for at least 6 hours before serving.

PATIO PARTY FOR SIX

Individual Salmon and
Cucumber Mousses

Salamagundy

New Potatoes with Fennel and
Mint

Baked Alaska

Wine suggestion:
Vinho verde

COUNTDOWN

The day before
Make the Individual salmon and
cucumber mousses, cover and chill.
Make the sponge cake for the Baked
alaska, cool and store in an airtight tin.

2 hours before the party
Prepare the new potatoes and the
fennel, and chop the mint.
Complete steps 1 to 4 of the Salamagundy and arrange all the salad items.

½ hour before the party
Complete steps 6 and 7 of the Baked
alaska.
Complete steps 1 and 2 of the New
potatoes with fennel and mint.

**Just before serving each
course**
Complete steps 3 and 4 of the New
potatoes with fennel and mint.
Dress and garnish the Salamagundy.
Complete steps 8 and 9 of the Baked
alaska.

*RIGHT: Individual salmon and
cucumber mousses*

INDIVIDUAL SALMON AND CUCUMBER MOUSSES

3 eggs, separated
3 teaspoons lemon juice
few drops of anchovy essence
salt
freshly ground white pepper
15 g (½ oz) powdered gelatine
200 ml (⅓ pint) fish stock
350 g (12 oz) fresh or canned
salmon, skin and bones removed

TO GARNISH:
thin cucumber slices
sprigs of dill
12 tablespoons liquid aspic

Preparation time: 15 minutes, plus
cooling and chilling

1. Beat the egg yolks with the lemon
juice, essence and salt and pepper over
hot water until they thicken slightly.
Allow to cool, beating lightly.
2. Place the fish stock in a small heatproof bowl, sprinkle over the gelatine
and leave for 5 minutes until spongy.
Stand the bowl in a pan of hot water
and stir gently with a metal spoon for
about 5 minutes until clear. Add to the
egg mixture, blending well.
3. Flake the salmon and fold into the
egg mixture.
4. Whisk the egg whites until they
stand in stiff peaks and fold into the
salmon mixture with a metal spoon.
Pour into 6 10 cm (4 inch) ring moulds
and chill until set, about 30 minutes.
5. Turn out the mousses and garnish
with the cucumber slices and dill and
spoon over the aspic. Chill until set. If
wished, fill with radishes.

SALAMAGUNDY

1 cold roast chicken
16 button onions, skinned
275 g (10 oz) green beans
1 × 50 g (2 oz) can anchovy fillets
4 hard-boiled eggs, shelled and
quartered or 16 quails' eggs, hard-
boiled and shelled
1 large lettuce, washed
175 g (6 oz) black grapes, seeded
1 large orange, cut into segments
(optional)
50 g (2 oz) flaked slithered almonds
50 g (2 oz) raisins
fresh herbs, to garnish

VINAIGRETTE:
½ teaspoon finely chopped fresh
chervil
1 teaspoon finely chopped fresh chives
1 tablespoon finely chopped fresh
parsley
1 teaspoon prepared French mustard
½ teaspoon salt
large pinch freshly ground black
pepper
1 garlic clove, crushed
175 ml (6 fl oz) olive oil
4 tablespoons wine vinegar
2 teaspoons lemon juice

Preparation time: about 1 hour
Cooking time: about 15 minutes

This old English recipe, dates back to the 16th century, or possibly even earlier. Mrs. Hannah Glasse, author of *The Art of Cookery Made Plain and Easy*, first published in 1747, gives several versions in different editions of her book, saying "You may always make Salamagundy of such things as you have according to your fancy."

1. Carve the chicken into slices.
2. Place the onions in a pan of boiling salted water and cook for 10–15 minutes until tender. Drain and leave to cool.
3. Place the green beans in boiling salted water for 3 minutes until tender. Drain and leave to cool.
4. Put all the ingredients for the vinaigrette into a screw-topped jar and shake vigorously until well blended.
5. Set out all the salad items attractively on a large platter. Scatter fresh herbs over them and pour on the vinaigrette dressing.

FROM THE TOP: New potatoes with fennel and mint; Salamagundy; Baked alaska

NEW POTATOES WITH FENNEL AND MINT

salt
1 kg (2 lb) tiny new potatoes
15 g (½ oz) butter
1 small fennel bulb, trimmed and
freshly chopped
freshly ground black pepper
2 tablespoons chopped fresh mint,
plus sprigs of mint to garnish

Preparation time: 10 minutes
Cooking time: 15–20 minutes

1. Bring a pan of salted water to the boil, and add the potatoes. Simmer for about 15 minutes until tender, then drain.
2. Put the butter into the warm pan and heat gently. Add the fennel and fry for about 5 minutes until just beginning to brown, then season well with pepper.
3. Tip the cooked potatoes into the pan, add the mint and toss the potatoes so that they are coated with butter, mint and fennel.
4. Serve hot, garnished with sprigs of mint.

BAKED ALASKA

SPONGE:
2 eggs
50 g (2 oz) caster sugar
50 g (2 oz) plain flour

FILLING AND TOPPING:
3 tablespoons raspberry jam,
1 × 400 g (14 oz) can raspberries,
drained with juice reserved
3 egg whites
175 g (6 oz) caster sugar
15 g (½ oz) toasted flaked almonds,
chopped (optional)
1 × 483 ml (17 fl oz) packet vanilla
or Neapolitan ice cream

Preparation time: 10 minutes
Cooking time: 18–20 minutes
Oven: 190°C, 375°F, Gas Mark 5;
then: 230°C, 450°F, Gas Mark 8

This popular dessert always looks impressive and is so easy to make. To be certain of success every time, pile the meringue topping over the filling to enclose it completely bringing it right down to the serving dish all round and making sure there are no gaps.

1. Grease an 18 cm (7 inch) round sandwich cake tin and line the base with greased greaseproof paper.
2. To make the sponge, place the eggs and sugar in a large heatproof bowl set over a saucepan of gently simmering water. Whisk the mixture with an electric hand whisk for about 3 minutes until light, creamy and thick and the whisk leaves a trail when lifted for a few seconds.
3. Remove the bowl from the heat and whisk until the mixture is cold.
4. Sift the flour over the mixture and fold in very gently, using a large metal spoon.
5. Pour the mixture into the prepared tin and level the surface. Bake in a preheated moderately hot oven for 15 minutes, until the sponge is well risen and cooked through. Turn out on to a wire rack, remove the lining paper and leave to cool completely.
6. Split the cake into 2 thin layers. Spread the bottom layer with jam and cover with the top layer. Place the cake on an ovenproof serving plate. Spoon 3 tablespoons of the reserved raspberry juice over the cake.
7. Whisk the egg whites until stiff. Whisk in 75 g (3 oz) of the sugar until the mixture is stiff and glossy. Gently fold in the remaining sugar and almonds, if using, using a large metal spoon.
8. Spoon the raspberries over the cake, and place the ice cream block on top. Pile the meringue mixture over, spreading it out to cover the cake, ice cream and fruit completely, making sure there are no gaps.
9. Bake the alaska in a preheated hot oven for 3–5 minutes, until the meringue is light golden. Serve at once.

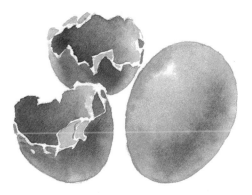

STYLISH PICNIC FOR FOUR

Chilled Cream of Lettuce Soup or Asparagus Mousse

Italian Fish and Pasta Salad

Provençal Tomato Salad

Mushrooms à la Grecque

Chicory, Orange and Olive Salad

French Bread*

Beaumes de Venise Jellies

Cheese*

Wine suggestions:
Starter and main course:
Sancerre
Dessert:
Muscat de Beaumes de Venise

COUNTDOWN

The day before
Complete steps 1 and 2 of the Chilled cream of lettuce soup, cover and chill. Prepare the Asparagus mousse up to the end of step 5, cover and chill. Prepare the Italian fish and pasta salad up to the end of step 7, cover and chill. Make the Beaumes de Venise jellies. Make the dressing for the Chicory, orange and olive salad and the Provençal tomato salad and pour into a screw-top jar.
Prepare the Mushrooms à la Grecque up to the end of step 4.
Assemble all the non-perishable items remembering to pack a corkscrew, a damp sponge in a plastic bag, salt and pepper and a dustbin liner bag for rubbish.

On the day
Complete steps 1 and 2 of the Chicory, orange and olive salad.
Make the Provençal tomato salad.
Put all the food into lidded plastic containers and pack into insulated coldbags. Don't forget the garnishes or the dressings.

Just before serving
Dress and garnish the dishes.

CHILLED CREAM OF LETTUCE SOUP

25 g (1 oz) butter
1 lettuce
1 bunch spring onions, chopped
2 potatoes, peeled and diced
600 ml (1 pint) chicken stock
salt
freshly ground black pepper

TO SERVE:
1 × 150 ml (¼ pint) carton single cream
1 tablespoon snipped chives (optional)

Preparation time: 10 minutes
Cooking time: 30 minutes

1. Melt the butter in a pan, add the lettuce, reserving a little of the heart for garnish, spring onions and potatoes. Cover the pan and cook gently for 10 minutes, stirring frequently to prevent sticking.
2. Add the stock, salt and pepper. Bring to the boil and simmer for 20 minutes. Cool, then blend until smooth.
3. Chill well, then add the cream. Pour into a chilled flask to transport. Garnish with snipped chives and lettuce heart.

FROM THE LEFT: Asparagus mousse; Chilled cream of lettuce soup

ASPARAGUS MOUSSE

450 g (1 lb) fresh asparagus
300 ml (½ pint) water or milk
25 g (1 oz) butter or margarine
25 g (1 oz) plain flour
30 g (1 oz) powdered gelatine, dissolved in 4 tablespoons hot water
150 ml (¼ pint) soured cream or plain unsweetened yogurt
grated rind of ½ lemon
1 tablespoon lemon juice
1 hard-boiled egg, shelled and finely chopped
salt
freshly ground black pepper
1 lettuce, to serve (optional)

Preparation time: 30 minutes, plus setting

Cooking time: 25–40 minutes

If fresh asparagus is not available, substitute 450 g (1 lb) frozen asparagus. Simmer the tips for 5 minutes, and the stems for 6–8 minutes, then use according to the recipe instructions.

1. Wash the asparagus and trim off any tough woody parts at the bottom of the stalks. Cut off the tips with about 5 cm (2 inches) of the stem and simmer in the salted water for about 5–10 minutes until tender but not limp. Remove the tips with a slotted spoon and leave on one side to cool.

2. Chop the remaining parts of the asparagus stems into small pieces and add to the simmering water. Cover and simmer for 15–30 minutes until soft. Drain, reserving the cooking water.

3. Make up the cooking water to 300 ml ($\frac{1}{2}$ pint) with water or milk. Melt the butter or margarine in a pan and stir in the flour. When smooth, gradually stir in the cooking liquid and bring to the boil, stirring until thickened. Add the drained chopped asparagus stems and simmer for 3 minutes, stirring from time to time.

4. Pour the sauce into a bowl. Dip a few of the asparagus tips into the dissolved gelatine and place at the bottom of the mould. Drizzle over a very little gelatine and leave to set in the refrigerator. Stir the remaining gelatine into the sauce mixture and allow to cool.

5. Stir in the soured cream or yogurt, lemon rind and juice and chopped hard-boiled egg. Add salt and pepper to taste. Pour into the mould and chill until set. Cover the reserved asparagus tips and chill until required.

6. To transport, cover the mould tightly with foil and pack the reserved asparagus tips and the lettuce leaves, if using, into lidded plastic containers.

7. To serve, turn out the mould onto a plate and garnish.

ITALIAN FISH AND PASTA SALAD

225 g (8 oz) pasta shells, penne or
  other small shapes
450 g (1 lb) squid, cleaned
5 tablespoons olive oil
2 garlic cloves, peeled and crushed
1 kg (2 lb) fresh mussels, shells
  scraped and beards removed
100 g (4 oz) peeled prawns
salt
freshly ground black pepper
6 celery sticks, sliced, tops reserved
1 green pepper, cored, seeded and
  cut into strips

DRESSING:
1 garlic clove, peeled and crushed
8 tablespoons olive oil
2 tablespoons lemon juice
1 teaspoon sugar (optional)
2 teaspoons finely chopped parsley

TO SERVE:
½ Webbs lettuce (optional)

Preparation time: 45 minutes
Cooking time: 25 minutes

1. Cook the pasta shapes in salted
boiling water for 12–15 minutes until
just tender. Drain. Rinse with cold
water and drain thoroughly.
2. Cut the squid body into rings. Reserve the tentacles. Rinse and dry on
paper towels.
3. Put a large frying pan over high heat.
Put in the squid rings and cook, stirring, for 3–4 minutes – a pink liquid will
collect which can be discarded. Remove the squid and reserve.
4. Wipe the pan with paper towels,
heat 1 tablespoon of the oil and fry one
crushed garlic clove, without browning. Return the squid and reserved
tentacles to the pan and cook for 3
minutes, then transfer to a bowl.
5. Place the frying pan over high heat
again, then add the mussels with another crushed garlic clove. Cover and
cook over high heat, shaking the pan
from time to time for 5 minutes or until
the mussel shells have opened. Discard

any which do not open. Remove the
mussels from their shells, reserving a
few in their shells for garnish, if liked.
6. Mix the squid, shelled mussels and
peeled prawns together and season
lightly with salt and pepper.
7. To make the dressing, mix together
the garlic clove, olive oil, lemon juice,
sugar, parsley and seasoning and pour
over the fish. Add the celery, pepper
and pasta shapes, toss well and chill
until required.
8. To transport, pack the salad into a
rigid plastic container. Pack the reserved unshelled mussels, and the
celery tops into another container and
put the lettuce into a polythene bag.
9. To serve, line a bowl or platter with
the lettuce leaves, spoon in the salad
and garnish.

CLOCKWISE FROM THE LEFT:
Mushrooms à la Grecque; Beaumes de
Venise jellies; Provençal tomato salad;
Chicory, orange and olive salad; Italian
fish and pasta salad

PROVENÇAL TOMATO SALAD

3 continental tomatoes, skinned and
* sliced*
1 medium onion, peeled and cut
* into rings*
1 tablespoon chopped fresh basil

DRESSING:
2 tablespoons olive oil
1 tablespoon white wine vinegar
1 tablespoon French mustard
1 garlic clove, peeled and crushed
2 teaspoons lemon juice
salt
freshly ground black pepper

Preparation time: 30 minutes plus
  standing

1. Arrange the tomato and onion
slices in layers in a shallow dish or
plastic container, sprinkling with a little
basil between each layer. Finish with a
layer of onion. Chill until required.
2. To make the dressing, mix all the
ingredients together and place them in
a blender or food processor. If you do
not possess either of these machines,
place all the ingredients in a screw-top
jar and shake really well.
3. Pour the dressing over the salad at
least 30 minutes before serving.

MUSHROOMS A LA GRECQUE

4–5 tablespoons olive oil
200 ml ($\frac{1}{3}$ pint) water
3 tablespoons lemon juice
6 black peppercorns
6 fennel seeds
6 coriander seeds
1 shallot or tiny onion, peeled and
* chopped*
1 celery stick, finely chopped
225 g (8 oz) button mushrooms
1 tablespoon chopped parsley,
* tarragon or herbs of your choice*

TO SERVE:
French bread
sprig of tarragon

Preparation time: 15 minutes, plus
  cooling
Cooking time: 20 minutes

1. Put the oil, water, lemon juice, peppercorns, fennel and coriander seeds
into a pan with the chopped shallot
and celery.
2. Bring to the boil, then simmer for
about 8–10 minutes.
3. Add the mushrooms and the herbs
and simmer again for 5–8 minutes.
4. Transfer the mushrooms to a serving dish or plastic container. Reduce
the cooking liquid to half by fast boiling. Strain over the mushrooms and
leave to cool, then chill until required.
5. Garnish with a sprig of tarragon and
serve with French bread.

CHICORY, ORANGE AND OLIVE SALAD

3 large or 4 small heads chicory
3 medium oranges
2 small onions, peeled and cut into
* rings*
8 large black olives, stoned
4 tablespoons French dressing (page
* 121)*

Preparation time: 15 minutes

1. Separate the chicory leaves and
place in a salad bowl or a rigid plastic
container.
2. Remove the peel and pith from the
oranges. Cut the flesh into segments
and arrange in the bowl squeezing in
any juice as well. Add the onions and

black olives. Chill until required.
3. Just before serving, pour the French
dressing over and toss well.

BEAUMES DE VENISE JELLIES

90 g (3$\frac{1}{2}$ oz) sugar
300 ml ($\frac{1}{2}$ pint) water
150 ml ($\frac{1}{4}$ pint) lemon juice
grated rind of 2 limes
25 g (1 oz) powdered gelatine
400 ml (14 fl oz) Muscat de Beaumes
* de Venise*
lemon-scented geranium leaves, to
* decorate (optional)*

Preparation time: 10 minutes, plus
  setting
Cooking time: 15 minutes

Muscat de Beaumes de Venise is a
delicious, sweet white dessert wine
made from the Muscat grape in the
Rhône area of France. It is now readily
available from supermarkets and good
wine merchants.

1. Put the sugar into a large saucepan
with the water, lemon juice and grated
rind of the limes. Bring to the boil, then
simmer for about 10 minutes until the
sugar has dissolved. Leave to cool.
2. Put 2 tablespoons cold water into a
small bowl, sprinkle over the gelatine,
then place the bowl in a pan of barely
simmering water until the gelatine has
dissolved. Take off the heat and leave
for a few minutes.
3. Stir the wine into the sugar syrup,
then add the cooled gelatine, stirring
thoroughly. Reserve 150 ml ($\frac{1}{4}$ pint) of
the liquid.
4. Pour the rest of the wine liquid into
ramekins or wine glasses and place a
lemon-scented geranium leaf, stalk removed (if using), on top of the liquid
in each one without letting it sink. Chill
for 2 hours.
5. Gently heat the reserved wine until
just liquid, then pour a little over each
geranium leaf to just cover, and return
the dishes to the refrigerator for a
further 2–3 hours.
6. To transport, pack the jellies into an
insulated coldbag.

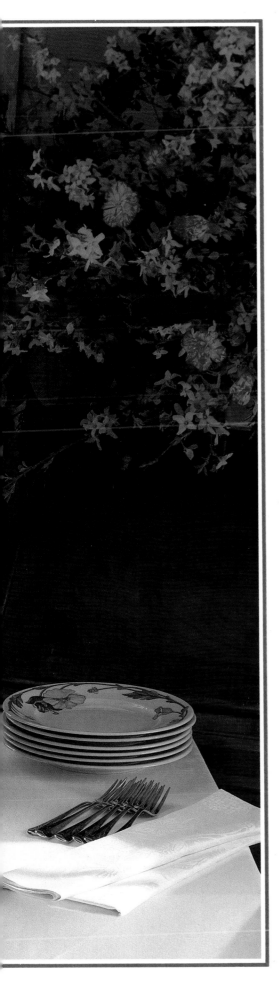

BUFFET PARTIES

As the numbers on your guest list mount, take a cool look at the menu and at the shopping, preparation and cooking involved – and rise to the exciting challenge calmly and methodically. Our buffet menus include a three-course wedding reception for forty – ideal for any autumn or winter celebration; a lunchtime drinks party to cut a dash on a hot summer's day, and an American-style brunch to start Sunday with a sparkle.

CLOCKWISE FROM THE TOP: Pink flamingo; Raymond's gâteau; Cheese and anchovy aigrettes with whisky mayonnaise; Italian salad; Fish and prawn terrine

SUNDAY BRUNCH FOR TEN

Exotic Melon Cocktail

Herby Pork Sausages

Potato Fritters

American Pancakes with Bacon

Kedgeree

Drink suggestions:
Coffee*
Buck's Fizz

COUNTDOWN

With the exception of the Exotic melon cocktail, all the quantities in these recipes have been worked out on the assumption that all the guests will take a little of each. If you are not going to make all the dishes, then make larger quantities.

The day before

Prepare the onions for the Potato fritters, put in a plastic bag and chill.
Make the Herby pork sausages, cover and chill.
Hardboil the eggs and poach the fish for the Kedgeree, cover and chill.
Make the batter for the American pancakes, cover and chill.

Early in the morning

Make the Exotic melon cocktail, cover and chill.
Prepare the potatoes for the fritters, cover and chill.

1 hour before the guests arrive

Cook the Kedgeree and keep it warm.
Make the American pancakes (thinning the batter a little, if necessary) and keep warm.

½ hour before the guests arrive

Cook the Potato fritters.
Cook the bacon to serve with the American pancakes and keep it warm.

When the guests arrive

Make the coffee.
Reheat the Herby pork sausages.
Make the Buck's fizz.

EXOTIC MELON COCKTAIL

SERVES 10
1 large Ogen melon
1 large honeydew melon
450 g (1 lb) raspberries, hulled
juice of 3 limes
juice of 1 orange
2–3 tablespoons caster sugar (optional)
1–2 tablespoons finely chopped fresh mint

Preparation time: 20 minutes

1. Slice the melons in half, remove the seeds and scoop out the flesh with a melon baller and place it in a serving bowl. Add the raspberries, pour over the fruit juices and stir well to mix. Sweeten with a little sugar, if liked.
2. Stir in the mint, cover with cling film and chill for 1–2 hours before serving.

BELOW: Exotic melon cocktail

HERBY PORK SAUSAGES

MAKES ABOUT 15–16 SAUSAGES
1.5 kg (3 lb) lean belly of pork,
* trimmed, boned and skinned*
50 g (2 oz) fresh white breadcrumbs
2 tablespoons milk
½ teaspoon ground mace
2 teaspoons dried sage
salt
freshly ground black pepper
seasoned flour
lard, for frying

Preparation time: 20 minutes
Cooking time: 10–15 minutes per
  batch

1. Finely mince the pork twice or
grind in a food processor. (You may be
able to buy pork ready-minced in some
supermarkets or your butcher may
mince it for you.)
2. Put the minced pork into a bowl,
add the breadcrumbs, milk, mace,
dried sage, salt and pepper. Mix well.
3. Form into 16 sausage shapes. Roll in
seasoned flour, heat the lard and fry the
sausages gently until brown on all sides.

POTATO FRITTERS

MAKES 10–12
50 g (2 oz) plain flour
½ teaspoon salt
freshly ground black pepper
1 egg, beaten
3 tablespoons milk
750 g (1½ lb) potatoes, peeled and
* coarsely grated*
1 tablespoon chopped fresh parsley
6 tablespoons vegetable oil

Preparation time: 10–15 minutes
Cooking time: 5–6 minutes

CLOCKWISE FROM THE TOP: Herby pork sausages; Kedgeree; Potato fritters; American pancakes; Buck's fizz

1. Sift the flour with the salt and pepper into a mixing bowl and make a well in the centre. Pour in the egg and milk. Using a wooden spoon, gradually draw the flour into the liquid, stirring vigorously, until thoroughly mixed.
2. Wash and drain the grated potatoes, then stir into the flour mixture with the parsley and mix well. Heat half the oil in a large frying pan and when it sizzles add 6 rounded tablespoons of the potato mixture, slightly apart. Flatten the potato fritters slightly with a fish slice and fry for 2–3 minutes until golden brown on the underside.
3. Carefully turn the fritters with a fish slice and cook for a further 2–3 minutes, turning once or twice, until golden brown all over. Drain on absorbent paper and keep hot while frying the remaining potato mixture in the same way. Sprinkle with salt and keep hot.

AMERICAN PANCAKES

MAKES ABOUT 15 PANCAKES
225 g (8 oz) plain flour
2¼ teaspoons baking powder
½ teaspoon salt
1 egg, well beaten
about 350 ml (12 fl oz) milk
50 g (2 oz) butter or margarine,
  melted, or vegetable oil

TO SERVE:
maple syrup, warmed
butter
crisp bacon rashers

Preparation time: about 8 minutes
Cooking time: 2–3 minutes for each
  pancake

These pancakes, which are also known as griddle cakes, hot cakes, wheat cakes and 'stack o' wheats' are thicker than the English variety.

1. Sift the dry ingredients together. Beat the egg into the milk and add the melted butter or oil.
2. Stir the liquid into the flour mixture just until the large lumps disappear –

do not beat as this makes the pancakes tough.
3. Heat a griddle or heavy frying pan until a few drops of cold water flicked on to the surface dance around like quicksilver. If they merely splutter, the pan is not hot enough; if they disappear instantly, it is too hot. Lightly grease the surface with a piece of crumpled paper towel dipped in oil.
4. Stir the batter: it should be about the thickness of double cream. Pour on to the griddle in well-spaced pools, preferably from a lipped jug – the pancakes should be about 13–15 cm (5–6 inches) in diameter.
5. Cook until the pancakes look dry around the edges, and bubbles on the surface begin to break. Turn and cook for about half as much time on the second side. Serve at once or keep warm wrapped in a folded teatowel in a very cool oven (110°C, 225°F, Gas Mark ¼). The pancakes should be well buttered just before serving with crisp bacon rashers and a liberal helping of maple syrup.

KEDGEREE

750 g (1½ lb) smoked haddock fillets
300 ml (½ pint) milk
6 eggs
450 g (1 lb) long-grain rice
salt
2.25 litres (4 pints) water
100 g (4 oz) butter
freshly ground white pepper
4 tablespoons chopped fresh parsley

TO GARNISH:
parsley sprigs

Preparation time: 7–10 minutes
Cooking time: 20 minutes

1. Place the fish and the milk in a large shallow pan and poach for 5–6 minutes or until the fish flakes when pierced with a sharp knife.
2. Meanwhile, hardboil the eggs, then cook the rice in a large saucepan of boiling, salted water for 12–15 minutes or until just tender. Drain well and stir in the butter.
3. Strain the cooking liquid from the fish into the rice. Flake the fish, discarding any bones or skin. Heat the rice through over a very gentle heat and season with plenty of pepper and a little salt if required. Lightly fork the fish into the rice and reheat, stirring gently

to avoid breaking up the fish.
4. Shell the eggs. Finely chop 2 of them and stir into the kedgeree with the chopped parsley. Pile the kedgeree into a warmed serving dish. Cut the remaining eggs into quarters and use to garnish the kedgeree with the parsley sprigs.

BUCK'S FIZZ

1 part fresh orange juice, chilled
1 part chilled champagne

Any size of glass can be used – a 300 ml (½ pint) is a good size – but remember when calculating amounts, the glass cannot be filled to the top as room has to be left for the bubbling of the champagne. Buck's Fizz can also be made in a jug.

Preparation time: 5 minutes

1. Pour some orange juice into a chilled glass or a jug. Top up with an equal amount of champagne.

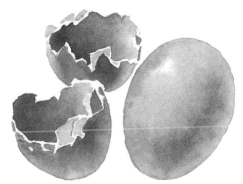

SUMMER LUNCHTIME DRINKS PARTY FOR TWENTY

Monkfish Bites with Mint Dip

Smoked Salmon and Cress Pinwheels

Marinated Stuffed Mushrooms

Cheese and Anchovy Aigrettes with Whisky Mayonnaise

Courgette and Oregano Mini Quiches

Parma Ham Nibbles

Demon Dates

Drink suggestions:
Calypso Cup
Pink Flamingo

COUNTDOWN

The night before
Prepare the Smoked salmon and cress pinwheels up to the end of step 4.
Make the Mint dip for the Monkfish bites, cover and chill.
Make the Whisky mayonnaise for the Cheese and anchovy aigrettes.
Prepare the filling for the mushrooms, cover and chill.
Make the pastry for the Courgette and oregano quiches, cover and chill.

Early in the morning
Complete steps 1–3 of the Monkfish bites.
Complete steps 2 and 3 of the aigrette mixture. Cover and chill until ready to cook.
Prepare and marinate the mushrooms.
Make the Parma ham nibbles.
Prepare the Demon dates up to the end of step 2.

2 hours before the party
Make and bake the Courgette and oregano mini quiches.

1½ hours before the party
Complete step 1 of the Calypso cup.
Complete step 1 of the Pink flamingo.
Stuff and garnish the Marinated stuffed mushrooms.
Cut up the Smoked salmon and cress pinwheels.

1 hour before the party
Cook the Cheese and anchovy aigrettes and keep them warm.

30 minutes before the party
Grill the Demon dates and spear with cocktail sticks.
Complete step 5 of the Monkfish bites.

10 minutes before the party
Complete the Calypso cup and the Pink flamingo.

MONKFISH BITES WITH MINT DIP

4 tablespoons lemon juice
4 tablespoons oil
2 teaspoons white wine vinegar
salt
freshly ground black pepper
1 onion, peeled and very finely chopped
1 tablespoon chopped fresh mint
1 kg (2 lb) monkfish

MINT DIP:
3 tablespoons thick mayonnaise (page 146)
3 tablespoons thick set plain unsweetened yogurt
1 teaspoon lemon juice
2 tablespoons chopped fresh mint
½ teaspoon caster sugar
sprig of mint, to garnish

Preparation time: about 25 minutes, plus marinating
Cooking time: about 10 minutes

1. In a bowl combine the lemon juice, oil, vinegar, salt, pepper, onion and mint.
2. Cut the pieces of monkfish into 2.5 cm (1 inch) cubes, making sure all the skin and bone is removed.
3. Add the fish to the marinade, cover, and leave to stand in a cool place for about 2 hours.
4. To make the dip, mix together all the ingredients and season to taste with salt and pepper. Spoon the dip into a small bowl, cover with cling film and chill.
5. To serve, drain the pieces of fish and thread them onto long skewers. Cook under a preheated moderate grill for about 5 minutes on each side until they are cooked through. Stand the dip in the centre of a plate, garnish with a sprig of mint, and arrange the pieces of monkfish around it, spearing each one with a cocktail stick.

FROM THE TOP: Calypso cup (page 207); Monkfish bites with mint dip

SMOKED SALMON AND CRESS PINWHEELS

MAKES 8 ROLLS
150 ml ($\frac{1}{4}$ pint) thick mayonnaise
salt
freshly ground black pepper
grated rind of $\frac{1}{4}$ lemon
1 teaspoon lemon juice
2 cartons mustard and cress,
  chopped
8 thinly cut slices of very fresh brown
  bread
100 g (4 oz) thinly sliced smoked
  salmon
sprigs of parsley, to garnish
lemon quarters, to garnish

Preparation time: about 25 minutes,
  plus chilling

1. Combine the mayonnaise, salt, pepper, lemon rind, lemon juice and
chopped mustard and cress.

2. Cut the crusts off the bread and
spread each slice evenly with the cress
mayonnaise.
3. Cut pieces of smoked salmon to fit
each slice of bread leaving 1 cm ($\frac{1}{2}$
inch) uncovered at one end of each
slice.
4. Carefully roll up the slices of bread,
beginning at the plain end. Wrap each
roll tightly in cling film and chill for at
least 1 hour and up to 12 hours before
serving.
5. To serve, uwrap the rolls and cut
each one into 6 slices. Arrange them on
a plate, garnish, and cover with cling
film until you are ready to serve.

MARINATED STUFFED MUSHROOMS

40 button mushrooms, total weight
  about 450 g (1 lb)
5 tablespoons safflower or sunflower
  oil
4 tablespoons dry white wine
salt
freshly ground black pepper
1 garlic clove, crushed

FILLING:
175 g (6 oz) chicken liver or other
  soft pâté
75 g (3 oz) butter, softened
75 g (3 oz) full fat soft cream cheese
3 tablespoons chopped fresh parsley
  or chervil

TO GARNISH:
sliced stuffed olives or small pieces of
  pickled walnut
tiny sprigs of parsley (optional)

FROM THE LEFT: Smoked salmon and cress pinwheels; Marinated stuffed mushrooms; Cheese and anchovy aigrettes

Preparation time: about 30 minutes, plus marinating

1. Carefully remove the stems from the mushrooms and wipe them.
2. Whisk the oil, wine, salt, pepper and garlic together in a bowl. Add the mushrooms and mix to coat them evenly with the dressing.
3. Cover and leave to marinate for 1–2 hours, giving the mushrooms an occasional stir.
4. To make the filling, cream together the pâté, butter and cream cheese until evenly blended, then beat in the parsley and add salt and papper to taste.
5. Put the filling into a piping bag fitted with a large star vegetable nozzle.
6. Drain the mushrooms, turning them upside-down on absorbent paper towels, then pipe a whirl of the pâté and cheese mixture into each cup. Top each mushroom with a slice of stuffed olive or a piece of pickled walnut and a tiny sprig of parsley, if wished.

CHEESE AND ANCHOVY AIGRETTES

MAKES ABOUT 50
50 g (2 oz) butter
150 ml ($\frac{1}{4}$ pint) water
65 g (2$\frac{1}{2}$ oz) plain flour, sifted
pinch of salt
2 eggs (size 3), beaten
2 tablespoons grated Parmesan
50 g (2 oz) mature Cheddar, grated
1 × 50 g (2 oz) can anchovy fillets, well drained and chopped
deep fat or oil for frying
sprig of parsley, to garnish

WHISKY MAYONNAISE:
1 egg yolk
$\frac{1}{2}$ teaspoon dry mustard
150 ml ($\frac{1}{4}$ pint) sunflower oil
1 teaspoon lemon juice
1 tablespoon whisky
salt
white pepper
$\frac{1}{2}$ teaspoon caster sugar

Preparation time: about 30 minutes
Cooking time: about 30 minutes

1. To make the whisky mayonnaise, whisk together the egg yolk and mustard in a clean, grease-free bowl, then whisk in the oil, drop by drop, until half of it has been incorporated. Beat in the lemon juice, then gradually add the rest of the oil in the same way. Add the whisky, salt, pepper and sugar and beat until smooth. Cover with cling film and chill until required.
2. Melt the butter in the water in a saucepan then bring to the boil. Add the flour and salt all at once and beat until the mixture is smooth and forms a paste which leaves the sides of the pan clean. Leave to cool a little.
3. Gradually beat in the egg, a little at a time, incorporating as much air as possible until the mixture is smooth and glossy; then beat in the two cheeses and the anchovies.
4. Place the oil in a deep fryer or a deep saucepan and heat to 180°C/350°F or until a cube of bread browns in 30 seconds. Put the aigrette mixture into a piping bag fitted with a plain 2 cm ($\frac{3}{4}$ inch) vegetable nozzle. Pipe out lengths about 2–2.5 cm ($\frac{3}{4}$–1 inch) long and drop them carefully into the hot fat. Cook about 12 at a time for 4–5 minutes, until they are golden brown and crisp, turning them over, if necessary.
5. Drain the aigrettes on absorbent paper towels and keep them warm while frying the remainder. Garnish and serve warm or cold using cocktail sticks to dip into the mayonnaise.

COURGETTE AND OREGANO MINI QUICHES

MAKES 24
PASTRY:
175 g (6 oz) plain flour
pinch of salt
40 g (1½ oz) butter or block
margarine
40 g (1½ oz) lard or white fat
cold water, to mix

FILLING:
350 g (12 oz) courgettes, trimmed
2 tablespoons oil
2 eggs
3 tablespoons grated Parmesan
cheese
1 garlic clove, crushed, or a little
powdered garlic
6 tablespoons milk
salt
freshly ground black pepper
dried oregano

Preparation time: about 30 minutes
Cooking time: about 30 minutes
Oven: 200°C, 400°F, Gas Mark 6

1. To make the pastry, sift the flour and salt into a bowl and rub in the fats until the mixture resembles fine breadcrumbs. Add sufficient water to mix to a pliable dough. Cover and leave to rest while making the filling.
2. To make the filling, coarsely grate the courgettes and sauté them lightly in the oil for a few minutes; then cool and drain off any surplus liquid.
3. Beat the eggs with the Parmesan, garlic and milk and add salt and pepper to taste.
4. Roll out the pastry thinly, cut it into fluted circles about 7.5 cm (3 inches) in diameter and use it to line 24 patty tins.
5. Divide the grated courgettes between the pastry cases and sprinkle each one with a pinch of dried oregano. Spoon some of the egg mixture into each quiche so that the courgette mixture is covered.
6. Cook in a preheated moderately hot oven for about 25–30 minutes until the quiches are well risen and golden brown and the pastry is crispy. Remove the quiches to a wire rack to cool. They may be served cold, or can be reheated for a few minutes in a moderate oven and served hot.

PARMA HAM NIBBLES

about 15 thin slices of Parma ham,
total weight about 225 g (8 oz)
3 kiwi fruit
⅓ Ogen or honeydew melon
½ fresh pineapple
½ white cabbage, to serve (optional)

Preparation time: about 20 minutes

1. Cut each slice of Parma ham into long strips about 2.5 cm (1 inch) wide. You should get 4 strips from each slice.
2. Peel the kiwi fruit and cut each one in half lengthways, then cut each half into 3 long wedges, giving 18 pieces altogether.
3. Remove the seeds from the melon and cut it into 10 thin slices about 1–2 cm (½–¾ inch) thick. Remove the skin and cut each slice in half.
4. Cut the pineapple into 7 slices and remove the skin. Cut each slice into 3 wedges giving 21 pieces in all.
5. Wrap a piece of Parma ham around each piece of fruit and spear it with a cocktail stick. Arrange the nibbles in rows on a fairly large plate or tray or stick them into half a cabbage positioned on a plate. Cover with cling film until required.

DEMON DATES

MAKES 40
40 fresh dates, total weight about
750 g (1½ lb) or 2 × 225 g (8 oz)
boxes dates
40 hickory smoked whole almonds or
toasted whole almonds
40 short streaky bacon rashers,
rinded
sprig of parsley, to garnish

Preparation time: about 40 minutes
Cooking time: about 10 minutes

1. Remove the stones from the dates and replace them with the almonds.
2. Stretch the bacon a little with the back of a knife and then wrap 1 rasher around each date and thread them onto a long skewer, placing about 10 dates on each skewer.
3. When you are ready to serve, put the skewers under a preheated moderate grill and cook them for 4–5 minutes on each side until the bacon is well browned. Remove them from the skewers and serve warm. Garnish with a sprig of parsley.

CLOCKWISE FROM THE TOP: Calypso cup; Pink flamingo; Demon dates; Parma ham nibbles; Courgette and oregano mini quiches

CALYPSO CUP

MAKES 40 GLASSES
1.75 litres (3 pints) tropical fruit
  juice, chilled
300 ml (½ pint) brandy
crushed ice
2 oranges, sliced
2 limes, sliced
4 bottles dry sparkling white wine,
  well chilled

Preparation time: about 15 minutes

1. Pour the tropical fruit juice and brandy into a large bowl or jugs. Chill.
2. Just before serving, add the crushed ice, sliced oranges and limes and then gradually add the sparkling wine. Mix well and serve in wine glasses.

PINK FLAMINGO

MAKES 35–40 GLASSES
300 ml (½ pint) crème de cassis
4 bottles rosé wine, well chilled
1.75 litres (3 pints) tonic water, well
  chilled
crushed ice
fresh mint, to garnish

Preparation time: about 15 minutes

1. Pour the crème de cassis and wine into a large bowl or jugs and chill.
2. Just before serving, add the tonic water and crushed ice and garnish with fresh mint. Serve in wine glasses.

WINTER WEDDING RECEPTION FOR FORTY

Fish and Prawn Terrine

Globe Artichokes and Asparagus with Walnut Dressing

Turkey and Pheasant Galantine

Planked Beef with Rosy Béarnaise Sauce

Cheese, Onion and Anchovy Flan

Potato, Broad Bean and Olive Salad

Italian Salad

Tomatoes with Tarragon Cream Dressing

Tabbouleh with Peppers

Raymond's Gâteau

Lime Mousse with Frosted Mint Leaves

Almond Cream Charlotte

Three-tier Wedding Cake

Suggested drinks:
Mulled Red Wine
Champagne

COUNTDOWN

Probably none of your guests will want to sample every dish on the menu, so servings have been suggested assuming that they will all want some of each of the main courses and salads, but only one of the starters and maybe a little of one or two of the desserts. All the starters and desserts should feed 12 people, so make double or triple quantities if you think they will be particularly popular.

Catering for a reception of this size needs more space than most people have in their kitchens, so ask friends and relatives if you can store some of the dishes in their freezers and refrigerators.

Needless to say, you will need lots of help in the kitchen. If possible, ask a friend to make one or two of the dishes, just to reduce the work load. The most complicated dishes to make are the galantines. If you have never boned a bird before, this is perhaps not the best time to learn! Find a friendly butcher who will do it for you (be sure to explain that he must leave the skin whole and undamaged).

2–3 months in advance
Make the three tiers for the Wedding cake. Cover and store in cake tins in a cool, dry place.

2–3 weeks in advance
Cover the Wedding cakes with marzipan. Cover and store in a cool, dry place.

1 week in advance
Ice and decorate the Wedding cake. Cover and store in a cool, dry place.
Make and freeze the Lime mousses.
Make and freeze the Cheese, onion and anchovy flans.

4 days in advance
Make the Walnut dressing for the globe artichokes and asparagus. Cover and chill.

3 days in advance
Marinate the Planked beef.
Make sufficient French dressing for all the salads.

2 days in advance
Prepare and cook the Turkey and pheasant galantines up to the end of step 10. Cover and chill.
Cook the Planked beef.

The day before
Make the Fish and prawn terrines. Cover and chill.
Cook the globe artichokes and asparagus. Cover and chill.
Complete the Turkey and pheasant galantines. Cover and chill.
Complete steps 1–9 of the Almond cream charlottes.
Complete steps 1–7 of Raymond's gâteau. Store the choux buns in an airtight container.
Prepare all the ingredients for the Italian salad and chill in separate containers.
Make the Tarragon cream dressing. Cover and chill.
Make the Potato, broad bean and olive salad. Cover and chill.
Make the Rosy béarnaise sauce.
Make the Tabbouleh with peppers. Cover and chill.
Thaw the Lime mousses and Cheese, onion and anchovy flans in the refrigerator overnight.

On the day
Complete Raymond's gâteau.
Prepare the frosted mint leaves and decorate the Lime mousses.
Decorate the Almond cream charlottes. Garnish the Cheese, onion and anchovy flans.
Turn out and garnish the Fish and prawn terrines. Make the melba toast.
Complete the Globe artichokes and asparagus.
Prepare the tomatoes to serve with the Tarragon cream dressing.
Set out the Turkey and pheasant galantines.
Garnish the Planked beef and set out the Rosy béarnaise sauce.
Dress the Italian salad.
Complete the Tomatoes with tarragon cream dressing.
Set out the Tabbouleh with peppers and the Potato, broad bean and olive salad.
Make the Mulled red wine.
Set out the Wedding cake.

FISH AND PRAWN TERRINE

SERVES 12 – MAKE 2

225 g (8 oz) fresh salmon fillet or
pink trout fillets
3 tablespoons lemon juice
salt
freshly ground black pepper
300 ml (½ pint) water
1 kg (2 lb) cod fillets, skinned
4 egg whites
300 ml (½ pint) double cream
150 ml (¼ pint) soured cream
225 g (8 oz) peeled prawns
2 tablespoons chopped fresh dill

TO GARNISH:
thick mayonnaise (page 146)
black lumpfish roe
fresh prawns in shells (optional)
sprigs of dill

Preparation time: about 45 minutes
Cooking time: 1 hour
Oven: 180°C, 350°F, Gas Mark 4

1. Place the salmon fillet or trout fillets in a small frying pan. Add 2 tablespoons of the lemon juice, salt, pepper and water and bring to the boil. Simmer gently for 4 minutes, then remove the fish and let it cool.
2. Purée the cod fillet in a food processor until smooth, then add the egg whites followed by the double cream, soured cream, the remaining lemon juice and plenty of salt and pepper. Process until smooth. If you do not have a food processor, mince the fish twice, then beat in all the other ingredients, one by one, until the mixture is smooth.
3. Line a 1 kg (2 lb) loaf tin with non-stick silicone paper or greased greaseproof paper and spread about a quarter of the fish mixture evenly over the base.
4. Cover the fish purée with 100 g (4 oz) of the prawns and sprinkle over 1 tablespoon of the dill. Cover with another quarter of the white fish mixture.
5. Remove the skin from the salmon

ABOVE: Fish and prawn terrine

or trout fillets and lay them on top. Cover with another quarter of the white fish mixture, top with the remaining prawns and dill and finally spoon over the rest of the white fish mixture.
6. Cover the terrine with a piece of non-stick silicone paper or greased foil and stand the loaf tin in a roasting tin with hot water coming half-way up the sides of the tin.
7. Cook in a preheated moderate oven for 1 hour. Remove the terrine from the oven and take off the covering. Leave until cold, then chill in the refrigerator overnight.
8. To serve, carefully turn out the terrine on to a serving dish and peel off the paper. Pipe or spread a thick line of mayonnaise down the centre, and garnish with small spoons of lumpfish roe, whole prawns, if wished, and sprigs of dill. Serve in slices with melba toast.

GLOBE ARTICHOKES AND ASPARAGUS WITH WALNUT DRESSING

SERVES 24
12 globe artichokes
about 72 asparagus spears
1 small endive
1 large head radicchio
2 cos lettuces

DRESSING:
300 ml (½ pint) walnut oil, or 150 ml
  (¼ pint) walnut oil and 150 ml
  (¼ pint) olive oil)
3 tablespoons wine vinegar
finely grated rind of ½ orange
3 tablespoons orange juice
salt
freshly ground black pepper
1½ teaspoons caster sugar

Preparation time: about 1 hour
Cooking time: about 50 minutes

1. Put all the ingredients for the dressing into a screw-topped jar and shake until thoroughly emulsified.
2. Wash the artichokes. Cut off the stalks and neatly trim the leaves with a pair of scissors. Place in boiling salted water and cook for 30–40 minutes. Drain, then leave to cool. Cut the artichokes in half, discard the hairy chokes and reserve the hearts.
3. Prepare and cook the asparagus (page 145). Drain, cool and place on a plate. Cover with cling film and chill.
4. Tear up the endive, shred the radicchio and tear or shred the lettuces. Arrange the pieces on a large oval platter and place the artichoke halves in the centre and the asparagus spears at each end. Cover with cling film and chill until required.
5. To serve, put the salad dish on the table, or arrange half an artichoke, 3 asparagus spears and a little of the salad on each of 24 side plates. Put the dressing into bowls for guests to help themselves.

FROM THE LEFT: Globe artichokes and asparagus with Walnut dressing; Turkey and pheasant galantine

TURKEY AND PHEASANT GALANTINE

SERVES 20 (MAKE 2)
3.5 kg (8 lb) oven-ready turkey
1 oven-ready pheasant
150 ml (¼ pint) dry white wine
4 tablespoons water

STUFFING:
1 large onion, peeled and finely
  chopped
1 garlic clove, crushed
2 tablespoons oil
225 g (8 oz) chicken livers, roughly
  chopped
100 g (4 oz) fresh white breadcrumbs
2 tablespoons chopped fresh parsley
1 teaspoon dried thyme
750 g (1½ lb) pork sausage meat
1 egg, beaten
salt
freshly ground black pepper

CHAUDFROID SAUCE:
1 tablespoon powdered gelatine
3 tablespoons water
200 ml (7 fl oz) thick mayonnaise
  (page 146)

TO GARNISH:
fresh chives
sprigs of chervil
sprigs of watercress

Preparation time: about 1½ hours,
  plus cooling and chilling
Cooking time: 2 hours, 20 minutes,
  allowing 20 minutes per 450 g (1 lb)
Oven: 190°C, 375°F, Gas Mark 5

This cooking time is based on the weight of the oven-ready turkey, not on its boned and stuffed weight. If you prefer not to eat game, use 3–4 skinned boneless duck pieces instead of the pheasant.

1. To bone the turkey, place it breast downwards on a board with the neck end facing away from you. Cut off the

wing tips, the parson's nose and the lower part of the legs below the drumsticks.

2. Slit the skin along the backbone from the neck to the parson's nose. Using a small sharp knife, gradually work the flesh away from the bones until you reach the leg joint. Cut through the joint, scrape down the leg bones, turning the legs inside out.

3. Continue working down the body to the wings, taking care at all times not to cut through the skin. When the wing bone is exposed, cut through the joint and work the flesh off the bones in the same way as for the legs, again turning them inside out.

4. Gently ease the flesh away from the breastbone. Remove any remaining pieces of gristle, tendon or bone from the flesh.

5. Cut the breasts from the pheasant, and then remove the flesh from the legs, carefully discarding the sinews. Remove the skin. (It is almost impossible to bone the wings of a pheasant.)

6. To make the stuffing, fry the onion and garlic in the oil until they are soft. Add the chicken livers and continue frying gently for 2–3 minutes, stirring frequently. Turn the mixture into a bowl and leave to cool.

7. Add the breadcrumbs, parsley, thyme, sausage meat and egg, with salt and pepper, and mix together thoroughly.

8. Lay the boned turkey flat on a board, skin side down. Cover with half the stuffing, then place the pheasant on top. Cover with the remaining stuffing and then pull the turkey together to enclose all the filling. Secure with skewers and, if necessary, sew together with string to keep the turkey a good shape. Leave the ends free for easy removal after cooking.

9. Place the turkey in a roasting tin into which it fits snugly. (If you are making two galantines, they can both be cooked at the same time in a large roasting tin.) Place the wine and water in a jug, season with salt and pepper then cover tightly with foil and cook in

a preheated oven for 2 hours 20 minutes.

10. Strain the stock and reserve, leaving the turkey in the tin until it is cold. Remove and chill thoroughly, preferably overnight.

11. Dissolve the gelatine in 3 tablespoons of water in a heatproof basin over a pan of gently simmering water. Pour in 150 ml ($\frac{1}{4}$ pint) of the reserved stock and stir until smooth, then add the mayonnaise and stir again until the mixture is smooth.

12. Remove the skewers and string from the turkey then stand it, join side downwards, on a wire rack over a plate. Brush with 100 ml ($3\frac{1}{2}$ fl oz) of the mayonnaise mixture then chill until set. Spoon the remaining mayonnaise evenly over the turkey and chill again until set.

13. Garnish the galantine with the chives and sprigs of chervil and arrange sprigs of watercress around the base. Serve in slices cut straight across the breast of the bird to reveal slices of turkey, stuffing and pheasant.

PLANKED BEEF

*5.5–6.5 kg (12–14 lb) sirloin of beef,
  boned and trimmed but not rolled
4 tablespoons oil or dripping*

MARINADE:
*600 ml (1 pint) red wine
salt
freshly ground black pepper
4 garlic cloves, crushed
3–4 bay leaves
2 onions, peeled and thinly sliced
4 strips orange rind
10 cloves
4 tablespoons wine vinegar*

TO GARNISH:
*spring onions
watercress
sliced cucumber*

Preparation time: about 20 minutes,
  plus marinating, cooling and chilling
Cooking time: about 2–2½ hours,
  allowing 10 minutes per 450 g (1 lb)
Oven: 220°C, 425°F, Gas Mark 7

1. Take the sirloin and fold the 'tail' end underneath to make an evenly shaped joint. Beat it slightly so that the meat is well pressed together, secure with string or skewers or a combination of the two.
2. Stand the joint in a container just large enough to hold it. Combine all the marinade ingredients in a bowl and pour them over the beef. Cover the beef and leave it to marinate for 24 hours, turning it over at least once.
3. Drain the joint and place it in a clean roasting tin. Reserve the marinade and all the ingredients. Season the joint lightly with salt and pepper and pour over the oil or dripping. Roast the joint in a preheated hot oven, allowing 10 minutes per 450 g (1 lb) for rare beef or 12 minutes per 450 g (1 lb) for medium cooked beef. Baste several times during cooking. This particular joint should not be well or over cooked.
4. Remove the joint from the tin and put it in a container into which it just fits or place it on a board. As it cools, cover it with a piece of foil and stand a weight or weights on it so it is lightly pressed and leave it in a cool place overnight. Several cans will do.
5. To serve, remove the weights from the beef and stand it on a large platter on a wooden board. Slice in long slices across the joint arranging the slices evenly on a plate or board. Gar-

nish with spring onions, watercress and slices of cucumber. Serve with Rosy béarnaise sauce.

ROSY BEARNAISE SAUCE

*300 ml (½ pint) red wine marinade
300 ml (½ pint) tarragon vinegar
12 egg yolks
500 g (1¼ lb) butter, slightly softened
salt
freshly ground black pepper*

Preparation time: about 50 minutes
Cooking time: about 20 minutes

If you find it easier, divide the ingredients in half and make this sauce in two batches.

1. Put the marinade from the Planked beef and the vinegar into a saucepan and boil hard. uncovered, until the mixture is reduced to 250 ml (8 fl oz). Strain it into a heatproof bowl or the top of a double saucepan and leave it to cool a little.
2. Beat the egg yolks into the vinegar mixture and cook them very slowly over a pan of barely simmering water, stirring or beating continuously until the mixture becomes very thick. Take care not to overheat or the sauce will curdle.
3. Remove the bowl from the heat and beat in the butter, a knob at a time, until it has melted completely and the sauce is smooth. Return the bowl to the pan of simmering water if it is getting too cool.
4. Taste and adjust the seasoning and transfer the sauce into two serving bowls or jugs. Cover with cling film and chill until required. Serve cold.

CHEESE, ONION AND ANCHOVY FLAN

SERVES 10 – MAKE 4
PASTRY:
*100 g (4 oz) plain flour
pinch of salt
100 g (4 oz) brown or granary flour
50 g (2 oz) butter or block
  margarine
50 g (2 oz) lard or white fat
cold water to mix*

FILLING:
*450 g (1 lb) onions, peeled and thinly
  sliced
3 tablespoons oil
3 eggs, beaten
1 teaspoon made mustard
1 teaspoon Worcestershire sauce
salt
freshly ground black pepper
150 ml (¼ ml) single cream or top of
  the milk
225 g (8 oz) mature Cheddar, grated
2 × 50 g (2 oz) cans anchovies,
  drained and soaked in milk for
  5–10 minutes
about 20 stuffed olives, halved
sprigs of sage, to garnish*

Preparation time: about 40 minutes
Cooking time: about 45 minutes
Oven: 220°C, 425°F, Gas Mark 7;
  then: 190°C, 375°F, Gas Mark 5

CLOCKWISE FROM THE LEFT: Rosy béarnaise sauce; Planked beef; Cheese, onion and anchovy flan

If you are going to serve four flans, make all the pastry in advance in one or two batches and chill until required. The onions can also be prepared, and fried ahead of time, then cooled, drained and chilled until needed.

1. To make the pastry, sift the plain flour and the salt into a bowl, mix in the brown or granary flour and rub in the fats until the mixture resembles fine breadcrumbs. Add sufficient cold water to mix to a pliable dough. Wrap and chill the dough while preparing the filling.
2. Fry the onions gently in the oil until they are soft and only lightly coloured, stirring occasionally. This should take about 15–20 minutes. Drain all the oil from the onions and leave them to cool.
3. In a bowl, beat the eggs with the mustard and Worcestershire sauce. Season with salt and pepper, then beat in the cream, followed by the grated cheese.
4. Roll out the pastry and use it to line a 28–30 cm (11–12 inch) flan ring, tin or dish. Spread the onions evenly over the base, then pour over the cheese custard.
5. Cook in a preheated hot oven for 20 minutes, then reduce the temperature to moderately hot for a further 20–25 minutes. [F]
6. Drain the milk from the anchovies, arrange them in a lattice design over the flan and put an olive into each square. Return to the oven for a few minutes. Remove from the oven and leave to cool. When cold wrap in foil and chill. Serve garnished with sprigs of sage.

[F] Cool, chill, wrap in foil and freeze for up to 1 week. Leave to thaw, wrapped, for 4 hours at room temperature, then garnish with the anchovies, olives and parsley sprigs.

POTATO, BROAD BEAN AND OLIVE SALAD

1.5 kg (3½ lb) potatoes
salt
750 g (1½ lb) frozen broad beans
150 ml (¼ pint) French dressing
 (page 121)
300 ml (½ pint) thick mayonnaise
 (page 146)
freshly ground black pepper
2 bunches spring onions, trimmed
 and thinly sliced
1 × 300 g (11 oz) jar or can black
 olives, drained, or pickled walnuts,
 drained and quartered
225 g (8 oz) streaky bacon rashers,
 very crisply fried or grilled and
 crumbled

Preparation time: about 40 minutes
Cooking time: 25 minutes

If you are using new potatoes do not peel them, but old ones may be peeled or not as you prefer.

1. Scrub or peel the potatoes and cook them in boiling salted water for about 10–15 minutes until they are just tender. Drain well.
2. Cook the beans in boiling salted water for about 5 minutes or according to the directions on the packet. Drain.
3. Cut the warm potatoes into dice and place them in a large bowl. Combine the dressing and the mayonnaise and season well with salt and pepper. Pour over the potatoes and toss until they are evenly coated.
4. Add the beans, spring onions and olives or pickled walnuts and toss again. Divide the salad between two or three large serving bowls and sprinkle with the crispy bacon. Cover the bowls with cling film and chill them in the refrigerator until required.

ITALIAN SALAD

3–4 firm round lettuces or 2 Webb's
 Wonderful or Iceberg lettuces
450 g (1 lb) tomatoes, quartered
10 hard boiled eggs, quartered
1 cucumber, sliced
3 green peppers, seeded and sliced
2 red peppers, seeded and sliced
3 tablespoons capers
350 g (12 oz) sliced salami, cut into
 narrow strips
150 ml (¼ pint) French dressing
 (page 121)

Preparation time: about 30 minutes

1. Roughly tear up the lettuces and divide them between two or three large bowls. Add the tomatoes, eggs, cucumber, green and red peppers, capers and finally the salami strips.
2. Just before serving add the dressing and toss lightly.

TABBOULEH WITH PEPPERS

1 kg (2 lb) bulgur or cracked wheat
2 green peppers, seeded and finely chopped
2 red peppers, seeded and finely chopped
350 g (12 oz) button mushrooms, sliced
3 tablespoons oil
2 bunches spring onions, trimmed and thinly sliced
300 ml (½ pint) French dressing (page 121)
2 tablespoons chopped fresh mint or parsley

Preparation time: about 30 minutes, plus soaking
Cooking time: about 10 minutes

1. Put the bulgur into a large bowl and cover with cold water. Leave to stand for at least 2 hours or overnight.
2. Drain the bulgur thoroughly, spread out on clean tea towels and leave to dry.
3. Put the green and red peppers into a saucepan of water, bring to the boil and boil for 1 minute. Drain, rinse under cold water and drain again.
4. Fry the mushrooms gently in the oil for 2–3 minutes. Mix with the peppers and onions and then add the dressing and mint or parsley.
5. Add the wheat and toss through the mixture evenly. Turn into 2 bowls, cover with cling film and chill until required.

TOMATOES WITH TARRAGON CREAM DRESSING

25–30 tomatoes

DRESSING:
4 tablespoons oil
2 tablespoons tarragon vinegar
finely grated rind of ½ lemon
1 teaspoon French mustard
1 teaspoon caster sugar
salt
freshly ground black pepper
4 tablespoons double or soured cream
2 tablespoons freshly chopped tarragon
chopped fresh tarragon, to garnish

Preparation time: about 20 minutes

1. The tomatoes may be quartered or sliced as preferred and arranged in two fairly shallow serving dishes or one

CLOCKWISE FROM TOP LEFT: Italian salad; Tabbouleh with peppers; Potato, broad bean and olive salad; Tomatoes with tarragon cream dressing

really large one.
2. Combine the oil, tarragon vinegar, lemon rind, mustard, sugar and salt and pepper to taste and whisk thoroughly, then whisk in the cream and tarragon and spoon over the tomatoes.
3. Sprinkle the tomatoes with tarragon, cover with cling film and chill until required.

RAYMOND'S GATEAU

SERVES 12 – MAKE 2
150 g (5 oz) plain flour
pinch of salt
100 g (4 oz) butter
300 ml (½ pint) water
4 eggs (size 3 or 4), beaten
450 ml (¾ pint) whipping cream
600 ml (1 pint) double cream
2 tablespoons brandy or rum
2 × 175 g (6 oz) cans sweetened
  chestnut purée
75 g (3 oz) plain chocolate, coarsely
  grated
4 pieces stem ginger, finely chopped

CARAMEL:
225 g (8 oz) granulated sugar
150 ml (¼ pint) water

TO DECORATE:
about 12 pink sugared rose petals
about 12 mauve sugared violets

Preparation time: about 1¼ hours
Cooking time: about 1 hour
Oven: 220°C, 425°F, Gas Mark 7

1. Sift the flour and salt into a bowl.
2. Place the butter and the water in a saucepan. Heat gently until the butter melts, then bring to the boil.
3. Add the flour to the pan all at once and beat until it is smooth and the mixture forms a ball leaving the sides of the pan clean.
4. Remove the pan from the heat, spread the paste out over the base of the saucepan and leave to cool for a few minutes.
5. Beat the eggs vigorously into the paste, a little at a time, to give a smooth, glossy paste. A hand-held electric mixer is best for this as it helps incorporate the maximum air.
6. Put the choux pastry into a piping bag fitted with a 1 cm (½ inch) plain nozzle and pipe out 55–60 walnut-sized balls on to greased baking sheets.
7. Cook in a preheated hot oven for about 25 minutes or until golden brown and firm to the touch. Pierce each bun to release the steam and cool on a wire rack.
8. Whip 300 ml (½ pint) of the whipping cream and use to part fill the buns using a piping bag fitted with a plain 5 mm (¼ inch) nozzle. Arrange a layer of filled buns on a serving dish to make a 20 cm (8 inch) circle.
9. Whip the remaining whipping cream and double cream together with the brandy or rum until stiff. Mash the chestnut purée until smooth, then fold it into the cream followed by the chocolate and ginger.
10. Spoon the cream mixture on to the circle of buns, piping it up into a pyramid.
11. Stick the buns in circles all around the pyramid, finishing with one at the top, covering as much of the cream as possible.
12. To make the caramel, place the sugar and the water in a saucepan and heat gently, stirring all the time until the sugar melts; then bring to the boil and boil hard without stirring until the syrup turns a light caramel colour. Remove the pan at once from the heat, let it cool a little until it begins to thicken, then drizzle all over the pyramid.
13. Arrange the pink and mauve sugared flowers over the gâteau. Leave to set.

LIME MOUSSE WITH FROSTED MINT LEAVES

SERVES 12 – MAKE 2
4 limes
6 eggs, separated
350 g (12 oz) caster sugar
2 tablespoons water
1 teaspoon lemon juice
5 teaspoons powdered gelatine
450 ml (¾ pint) whipping cream

FROSTED MINT LEAVES:
20 well-shaped mint leaves
little egg white, lightly beaten
little caster sugar

Preparation time: about 40 minutes,
  plus chilling
Cooking time: about 15 minutes

1. To make the frosted mint leaves, wash and dry the mint thoroughly. Brush with egg white, then coat with caster sugar. Place on a sheet of greaseproof paper and leave to dry.
2. Grate the rind from the limes and put it into a large warmed bowl with the strained lime juice. (You should get about 120 ml (4 fl oz) of juice from the limes.) Add the egg yolks and sugar. Put the bowl over a pan of gently simmering water and whisk until the mixture is thick and the whisk leaves a heavy trail when lifted.
3. Place the water and lemon juice in a small basin over a pan of gently simmering water, sprinkle on the gelatine and leave to dissolve. Stir to ensure that the gelatine is thoroughly dissolved.
4. Leave the gelatine mixture to cool a little, then stir it evenly through the mousse mixture.
5. Whip 300 ml (½ pint) of the cream until it is very thick but not too stiff, and fold it through the mixture.
6. Finally whisk the egg whites until they are very stiff and dry, then fold them quickly and evenly through the mousse. Pour the mixture into a 2.25 litre (4 pint) freezerproof glass bowl and chill until set. [F]
7. To serve, whip the remaining cream until stiff and, using a large star vegetable nozzle, pipe a row of stars around the top of the mousse. Arrange the frosted mint leaves between the stars.

[F] Open freeze, then wrap in a polythene bag. Thaw overnight in the refrigerator.

FROM THE TOP: Raymond's gâteau;
Lime mousse with frosted mint leaves

ALMOND CREAM CHARLOTTE

SERVES 12 – MAKE 2
175 g (6 oz) butter or margarine
175 g (6 oz) caster sugar
3 eggs
120 g (4¼ oz) self-raising flour, sifted
40 g (1½ oz) ground almonds
½ teaspoon baking powder
few drops almond essence
1 tablespoon cold water

FILLING:
200 g (7 oz) unsalted butter
100 g (4 oz) caster sugar
200 g (7 oz) full fat soft cream cheese
grated rind of 1 small orange
6 tablespoons fresh orange juice
6 tablespoons white wine

TO DECORATE:
300 ml (½ pint) double or whipping
  cream
1½–2 packets boudoir biscuits or
  sponge finger biscuits
segments of 2 mandarin oranges
strips of angelica
about 20 toasted whole blanched
  almonds
1 metre blue or orange satin ribbon

Preparation time: about 1 hour, plus
  chilling
Cooking time: about 20 minutes
Oven: 190°C, 370°F, Gas Mark 5

1. Cream the fat and sugar in a bowl until very light and fluffy. Beat in the eggs, one at a time, following each one with a spoonful of flour.
2. Fold in the remaining flour, followed by the almonds, baking powder, almond essence and cold water.
3. Grease three 20 cm (8 inch) sandwich tins and line the bases with greased greaseproof paper. Divide the cake mixture between the tins and level the tops.
4. Cook in a preheated moderately hot oven for 15–20 minutes until the cakes are well risen, golden brown and just firm to the touch. Turn out on to a wire tray and leave until cold.
5. To make the filling, place the butter in a mixing bowl and cream until soft. Beat in the sugar until the mixture is very light and fluffy, then beat in the cream cheese and orange rind until it is smooth.
6. Line a deep 20 cm (8 inch) round cake tin with non-stick silicone paper and place one of the cakes in the base.

7. Combine the orange juice and white wine and spoon 4 tablespoons over the cake. Cover with half the filling mixture and spread it out evenly.
8. Cover with the second cake, spoon over another 4 tablespoons of the orange juice and white wine mixture and then the rest of the filling. Top with the remaining cake and sprinkle over the rest of the orange juice and white wine mixture.
9. Cover the tin with a piece of non-stick silicone paper and place a light weight on top. Chill for at least 6 and up to 24 hours.
10. To serve, remove the cake carefully from the tin, strip off the paper and stand it on a serving dish. Whip the cream until it is stiff and use some of it to mask the whole cake.
11. Cut the boudoir biscuits so they stand 1 cm (½ inch) above the top of the cake and place them all round the outside.
12. Put the remaining cream into a piping bag fitted with a large star vegetable nozzle and pipe a series of stars all over the top of the cake to cover it completely. Decorate the charlotte with segments of mandarin orange, strips of angelica and toasted almonds and fasten a length of satin ribbon in a bow around the outside of the boudoir biscuits.

MULLED RED WINE

MAKES ABOUT 60 GLASSES
2 × 3 litre boxes or 8–9 bottles red
 wine
350 g (12 oz) raisins
450 g (1 lb) sugar
4 cinnamon sticks
thinly pared rind of 1 lemon
thinly pared rind of 1 orange
20 whole cloves
2.25 litres (4 pints) boiling water
450 ml ($\frac{3}{4}$ pint) brandy
2 lemons, thinly sliced
2 oranges, thinly sliced

Preparation time: about 15 minutes
Cooking time: about 40 minutes

1. Put the wine into a large saucepan or preserving pan. Add the raisins, sugar, cinnamon sticks, lemon and orange rinds and cloves.
2. Bring slowly up to the boil, stirring continuously until all the sugar has dissolved. Simmer very gently for 20–25 minutes, stirring occasionally.
3. Add the water and brandy and bring just back to the boil. Add the slices of lemon and orange. At this stage the cup may be cooled and reheated when you are ready to serve.
4. Ladle into glasses, putting a silver spoon into each glass before you pour in the wine. (Pouring the hot liquid over silver prevents glasses from cracking or breaking.) Extra bottles of wine can be added as the brew is drunk but for the best flavour, it is better to make another one.

BELOW: Almond cream charlotte; Mulled red wine

THREE TIER WEDDING CAKE

1 × 15 cm (6 inch), 1 × 20 cm (8 inch) and 1 × 25 cm (10 inch) round fruit cakes (chart, right)
2.25 kg (5 lb) Marzipan or Almond paste (below)
3 recipe quantities Apricot glaze (page 222)
Royal icing (page 223)
thick silver cake drums, of 20 cm (8 inch), 25 cm (10 inch), and 33 cm (13 inch) in diameter
7 or 8 round cake pillars

To make the cakes:
Preparation time: about 3 hours
Cooking time: about 4¾ hours for the large cake, about 3½ hours for the middle cake and 2¼ hours for the small cake
Oven: 150°C, 300°F, Gas Mark 2

It is best to make up the cake mixture in two batches. Make sufficient for the large cake first and then enough for the two smaller ones. Cook the large cake first and then, if your oven is large enough, you can cook the other two at the same time.

1. Grease and line three 15, 20 and 25 cm (6, 8 and 10 inch) round cake tins with double greased greaseproof paper.
2. Combine the currants, sultanas, raisins, mixed peel and ground almonds. Quarter the cherries. Wash off all the sticky syrup and dry them thoroughly on paper towels, then mix into the dried fruits with the lemon and orange rind.
3. Cream the butter until it is soft, then add the sugar and continue creaming until the mixture is very light, fluffy and pale in colour.
4. Weigh the self-raising and plain flours and sift them into another bowl with the spices.
5. Beat the eggs, one at a time, into the creamed mixture following each one with 1 tablespoon of the flour. Fold in the rest of the flour alternating with the sherry, treacle and gravy browning.
6. Mix in the dried fruit mixture evenly and turn it into the prepared tins.
7. Level the tops – do not make a hollow in the centre.
8. Tie several thicknesses of brown paper round the outside of the tins for protection during the cooking and cook the cakes in a preheated cool

oven. To test that they are done insert a metal skewer in the centre of the cakes – it should come out clean. If the skewer is at all sticky, return the cake to the oven for 10 minutes and then test it again.
9. Remove the cakes from the oven and leave to cool in the tins.
10. Prick the surface of the cakes all over with a skewer and pour 2 tablespoons of the brandy over the surface of the small cake; 3 tablespoons over the middle cake and 4–5 tablespoons over the large one. Wrap the cakes securely in foil and leave for 1 week, then add the remaining brandy in the same way and wrap up securely again. Store in a cool, dry place.

MARZIPAN OR ALMOND PASTE

MAKES 450 G (1 LB)
100 g (4 oz) caster sugar
100 g (4 oz) icing sugar, sifted
225 g (8 oz) ground almonds
1 teaspoon lemon juice
few drops of almond essence
1 egg or 2 egg yolks, beaten

Preparation time: about 10 minutes

About 2–3 weeks before the wedding is the right time to marzipan the cakes. The 15 cm (6 inch) cake requires about 350 g (¾ lb) marzipan, the 20 cm (8 inch) requires about 575 g (1¼ lb) and the 25 cm (10 inch) cake

1. Mixing all the ingredients to make a fairly firm dough

about 1 kg (2 lb), so make up the quantity you require.

Make up marzipan in quantities of not more than 900 g (2 lb) at a time, otherwise it becomes unmanageable. You can make up small quantities by using 50 g (2 oz) ground almonds, for example, and scaling down the other ingredients accordingly. The remainder, if securely wrapped in polythene will keep for up to a month or so. Remember that marzipan does not freeze.

To make a natural-coloured marzipan, use 2 lightly beaten egg whites instead of the egg or egg yolks for mixing.

If you do not have time or do not want to make your own marzipan, then commercial marzipan is available, ready to roll, in the traditional yellow or 'white', which is in fact natural-coloured. They are both good and easy to use and the natural one is ideal for adding colours to and for moulding as it gives truer colours than the yellow version.

1. Combine the sugars and ground almonds in a mixing bowl and make a well in the centre.
2. Add the lemon juice, almond essence and sufficient egg or egg yolks to mix to a firm but manageable dough.
3. Turn on to a lightly sugared surface and knead until smooth. Take care not to overknead or the marzipan may begin to turn oily. (There is no remedy for this and it then becomes difficult to use.) It can be wrapped in polythene or foil and stored for up to 2 days.

2. Kneading the marzipan until it is light and even

QUANTITIES OF CAKE MIXTURE REQUIRED

CAKE MIXTURE:	FOR THE 25 CM (10 INCH) CAKE	FOR THE 20 CM (8 INCH) CAKE	FOR THE 15 CM (6 INCH) CAKE
Currants	625 g (1 lb 6 oz)	300 g (11 oz)	165 g (5½ oz)
Sultanas	625 g (1 lb 6 oz)	300 g (11 oz)	165 g (5½ oz)
Raisins	350 g (12 oz)	200 g (7 oz)	75 g (3 oz)
Mixed peel	175 g (6 oz)	75 g (3 oz)	50 g (2 oz)
Ground almonds	100 g (4 oz)	50 g (2 oz)	25 g (1 oz)
Glacé cherries	225 g (8 oz)	100 g (4 oz)	75 g (3 oz)
Lemon rind	2 lemons	1 lemon	½ lemon
Orange rind	1 orange	½ orange	½ small orange
Butter	400 g (14 oz)	200 g (7 oz)	90 g (3½ oz)
Dark soft brown sugar	400 g (14 oz)	200 g (7 oz)	90 g (3½ oz)
Self raising flour	100 g (4 oz)	65 g (2½ oz)	40 g (1½ oz)
Plain flour	375 g (13 oz)	175 g (6 oz)	90 g (3½ oz)
Ground cinnamon	1½ teaspoons	¾ teaspoon	¼ teaspoon
Mixed spice	1¼ teaspoons	½ teaspoon	½ teaspoon
Ground nutmeg	½ teaspoon	large pinch	pinch
Eggs	6	4	2
Sherry	4 tablespoons	3 tablespoons	1 tablespoon
Black treacle	2 tablespoons	1 tablespoon	1 teaspoon
Gravy browning	1½ teaspoons	1 teaspoon	1 teaspoon
Brandy (approx)	150 ml (¼ pint)	6 tablespoons	4 tablespoons

To marzipan the cakes:
Preparation time: about 2 hours

1. Brush over the tops of the cakes with apricot glaze (see below).
2. Roll out the marzipan and cut three circles to fit the tops of the cakes. Invert each cake on to the marzipan, then carefully turn them up the right way and place on the cake boards. Trim off any excess marzipan. Alternatively lift the marzipan shape on to the top of the cake keeping it even. Trim off any excess and smooth the edges with a small palette knife.
3. Cut 2 pieces of string for each cake, one the exact height of the cake and the other the complete circumference. Roll out the excess marzipan and, using the string as a guide, cut out a strip the height and circumference of the cake. Two shorter lengths can be cut for each cake if this is easier.
4. Loosely gather the marzipan strip(s) into a coil and roll around the sides of the cakes moulding the marzipan to the cakes and smoothing the joins with a palette knife. Make sure the marzipan touches the board all round. Rub the marzipan lightly all over with icing sugar, brush off the surplus and leave to dry, uncovered, in a warm, dry, but not too hot a place for 1 week otherwise the oils from the marzipan will seep through into the royal icing and leave unsightly marks of discoloration.

Note: Some people prefer to add the marzipan to the sides of the cake before the top; it doesn't really matter which way you do it as long as it is kept neat and even and you fill any holes or dents before your start.

1. Inverting the cake on to the rolled-out marzipan

2. Shaping the marzipan round the top edge of the cake

3. Unrolling the marzipan strip cut to fit the side of the cake

4. Smoothing out all the joins in the marzipan

APRICOT GLAZE

Preparation time: about 5 minutes
Cooking time: about 5 minutes

175–225 g (6–8 oz) apricot jam
2–3 tablespoons water

Make up one recipe quantity of Apricot glaze for each cake. The cooled, sieved glaze can be stored in an airtight container in the refrigerator for up to a week, but it must be boiled and cooled again before applying it to the cake. The smallest quantity you can make up is 2 tablespoons jam and 1 teaspoon water, any less is difficult to handle.

Apricot glaze is also good for joining different shaped pieces of cake together before covering them with icing.

1. Put the apricot jam into a small saucepan with the water and heat gently until the jam has completely melted, stirring occasionally.
2. Rub through a sieve and return the purée to a clean saucepan.

1. Levelling the cake with marzipan, before adding the glaze

3. Bring back to the boil and simmer for at least 1 minute or until the required consistency is obtained. Allow to cool before use.

ROYAL ICING

17 egg whites
about 3.75 kg (8½ lb) icing sugar,
sifted twice
17 teaspoons strained lemon juice
1 teaspoon glycerine per 450 g (1 lb)
icing sugar
liquid food colouring of your choice

Make up the royal icing in batches using 4 egg whites and 900 g (2 lb) sugar each time. Although royal icing can be made in any quantity as long as you allow 1 egg white to each 225 g (8 oz) icing sugar, it is better to make up not more than a 900 g (2 lb) quantity of icing at a time because the icing keeps better if made in small quantities. It is difficult to make up much less than 1 egg white quantities, although it is possible to use ½ egg white and 100 g (4 oz) icing sugar.

The icing can be stored in an airtight container in a cool place for about 2 days. However, it must be stirred very thoroughly before use, and if necessary a little extra sifted icing sugar added to correct the consistency which often seems to soften if the icing is left to stand for more than a few hours.

While using the icing, cover the bowl with a damp cloth to prevent a skin forming. Egg albumen powder, available from specialist cake decorating shops, can be made up according to the instructions on the packet and used in place of fresh egg whites.

Glycerine can be added to help soften the icing and make cutting easier. It should be omitted from the icing for the first 2 coats on the top surface of the bottom tier of a wedding cake and the first coat on the top surface of the middle tier, as a hard surface is needed to take the weight of other tiers. It should be used carefully as too much glycerine will make a very soft icing.

1. Put the 4 egg whites into a clean, greasefree bowl and beat until frothy. Using a wooden spoon, gradually beat in 450 g (1 lb) icing sugar. Add the lemon juice (and the glycerine, when necessary), then beat in another 225 g (8 oz) icing sugar. Continue to beat in sufficient sugar so that the egg whites stand in soft peaks.
2. Cover the bowl with a damp cloth and leave for about 20 minutes to let the air bubbles come to the surface.

1. Making up the royal icing mixture

3. Spreading the icing over the top of the cake with a paddling movement

2. Using an icing comb to smooth the sides of the cake

4. Smoothing the icing over the top of the cake with an icing ruler

To ice the cakes:

Preparation time: 4–5 hours over several days for the base icing: and time for making the roses and leaves for decorating

To flat ice the cakes:

Some people prefer to ice the top of the cake first, then the sides; others do it the other way round. It doesn't really matter, so long as you add several thin coats rather than one thick coat, since this gives the smoothest surface. It is wise to apply the icing to one surface at a time rather than all in one go, allowing each application time to dry before continuing or you may spoil the surface already put on the cake.

After each coat to the top or sides, it is important to pare or cut off any lumps or bumps in the icing, using a finely serrated-edge knife.

An ordinary royal-iced cake requires 2 coats on the top and sides. Sometimes an extra coat on the top is necessary, if it is not as smooth as you

would like. A wedding cake, however, requires 3 coats all over, with an extra coat on the top for the lower tiers, to help them hold the weight of the other cakes.

1. Attach the cakes to the boards with a dab of icing.
2. To flat ice the cakes, put a quantity of icing in the centre of each cake and smooth it out with a palette knife, using a paddling action to push out as many air bubbles as possible. Take an icing ruler or long palette knife and draw it across the cake towards you, carefully and evenly, keeping the ruler at a 30° angle. Take care not to press too heavily or unevenly. Remove the surplus icing by running the palette knife around the top edge of the cake, holding it at right angles to the cake. If the surface is not sufficiently smooth, cover it with a little more icing and draw the knife across again. Repeat on the other 2 cakes and leave to dry.
3. To flat ice the sides of the cakes, stand them on an icing turntable or

upturned plate and spread a thin but covering layer of icing all round the sides, keeping it fairly even. Hold an icing comb at an angle of about 45° to the cake. Starting at the back of the cake, with your free hand slowly rotate the cake, and at the same time move the comb slowly and evenly round the sides of the cake. Remove the comb at an angle and fairly sharply, so the join is hardly noticeable. Lift any excess icing from the top of the cake with a palette knife or icing ruler.. If it is not sufficiently smooth, wipe the comb and repeat. Leave to dry.

4. When each layer is dry, add further coats to the top and then to the sides until the cakes are perfectly smooth. Giving 3 coats to the sides and 4 to the tops should take about 3 days. If the layers dry unevenly, pare off the excess dry icing with a finely serrated knife, before adding the next layer. Leave the cakes for 24 hours to dry completely before beginning the decoration.

ROYAL ICING ROSES

All icing takes practice, but making flowers take a lot of practice and patience. Roses are probably the most popular flower of all to make and are a good start if you are a beginner. Make the roses in any colour you like but remember that royal icing dries a shade darker.

1. Half fill a piping bag with a petal nozzle with coloured icing; keep the remainder in an airtight container.
2. Cut out 2.5 cm (1 inch) squares from non-stick silicone paper and fasten one on an icing nail (or use a cork stuck onto a short skewer) with a tiny dab of icing.
3. Hold the icing bag so the thin edge of the nozzle is pointing upwards, then squeezing evenly and twisting the nail at the same time, pipe a tight coil for the centre of the rose. Continue to add 4 or 5 more petals piping the icing and twisting at the same time, but taking each petal only about three-quarters of the way round the flower. Begin each one in a different part of the flower. Make sure the base of the nozzle tips in towards the centre of the flower each time or the rose will look like a cabbage.
4. Remove to a tray and leave for 24–48 hours to dry. Make the other 69 roses in the same way.

1. Piping a tight coil for the centre of the rose

2. Adding the petals, beginning in a different part of the rose each time

3. One or two really open petals can be worked at the base of the rose

To decorate and assemble the cake

1. To make the template for the top of the cakes, cut three 4-point slightly concave star shapes out of thick card to fit the cakes. Trim a little to allow room to pipe round the cards. Position each one on the appropriate cake.
2. Fill a piping bag fitted with a small star nozzle with white icing and outline the templates with a row of shells.

Leave to dry, then remove the templates.

3. Make a mark on the sides of the cakes halfway between the points of the star. Cut an inverted 'V' shape from thick paper to fit between the marks. Position, attaching with a tiny dab of icing, and then pipe a row of shells to outline it. Remove the template and pipe a second 'V' below the first one taking it to the board directly below the first one. Continue to pipe these 'V's all around each tier of the cake. Leave to dry.

4. Using the same star nozzle, pipe a border of slightly slanting shells with the points facing the edge of the board around the base of each cake and leave to dry.

5. Put a little white icing into a piping bag fitted with a No. 1 writing nozzle and pipe a 'V' shape on top of each cake inside the points of the star, then pipe another one inside it. Leave to dry.

6. Put a little coloured icing to match the roses (or a shade darker) into a piping bag fitted with a similar writing nozzle and overpipe the white 'V' shapes. Pipe a coloured line beneath the 'V' shapes.

7. To make the lace pattern, fill a piping bag fitted with a fine No. 0 or No. 1 writing nozzle with white icing. Pipe a freehand lacy design to fill the space outside the star on top of the cakes and inside the top row of shells on the sides. Leave to dry.

8. Finally, attach the roses using a dab of icing for each one. Each tier has a cluster of 3 roses in the space on the sides of the cake; and one at each point of the star on top. The top two tiers have one rose on the board at the base of the 'V' shells, and the bottom tier has clusters of three roses at these points.

9. To assemble the cakes, stand the large tier on a cake stand and arrange 4 pillars in the star points. Put the middle cake on the pillars arranging the 'V's to line up with those on the larger cake. Place 3 or 4 pillars on the middle cake and stand the smallest cake on them. Top with a vase of flowers, if wished.

RIGHT: Three tier wedding cake

TEA & COFFEE PARTIES

A tea or coffee party can be formal or informal; an occasion to get out your prettiest china and tablecloths or to entertain on a large scale to raise funds for a worthy cause, but a children's party is always an occasion for a flight of fancy when you can let your imagination run riot. Our recipes, covering all these possibilities, range from homemade breads, sandwich fillings, cakes and cookies to delectable preserves.

CLOCKWISE FROM THE TOP: Black Forest cherry gâteau; High butter shorties; Marzipan spiced teabread; Nutty brown sugar meringues; Sandwiches and sandwich fillings

SWEET AND SAVOURY SUGGESTIONS

Cheese Scones

Green Tomato Chutney

Miniature Cornish Pasties

Bridge Rolls with Two Toppings

Quick Wheatmeal Bread

Sandwiches and Sandwich Fillings

Queen of Jams

Currant Berry Jam

Lemon Curd

High Butter Shorties

Coffee Kisses

Marzipan Spice Teabread

Nutty Brown Sugar Meringues

Chocolate Eclairs

Sticky Gingerbread

Madeira Cake

Farmhouse Sultana Cherry Cake

Black Forest Cherry Gâteau

Strawberry Cream Sponge

COUNTDOWN

These are the easiest parties to prepare ahead since the tea and the coffee are all that really require last minute attention. Cakes and biscuits can be made the day before and stored in airtight containers. Homemade breads are best eaten the day they are made, but sandwiches are better made with day old bread. Provided they do not contain salad vegetables, jam or hardboiled egg and mayonnaise, sandwiches can be made in advance, wrapped in cling film and kept overnight in the refrigerator or overwrapped in foil and frozen for up to 2 months. Spread the butter right up to the crusts so that the filling does not seep through. Most cakes, biscuits and bread will freeze very well for up to 6 months.

CHEESE SCONES

MAKES 8–10
225 g (8 oz) self-raising flour
½ teaspoon salt
50 g (2 oz) butter or margarine
75 g (3 oz) mature Cheddar cheese, finely grated
1 teaspoon dry mustard
pinch of cayenne pepper
150 ml (¼ pint) milk
milk, to glaze

Preparation time: 15 minutes
Cooking time: 12–15 minutes
Oven: 220°C, 425°F, Gas Mark 7

1. Place the flour and salt in a bowl. Add the butter or margarine, cut into pieces, and rub into the flour with the fingertips until the mixture resembles fine breadcrumbs. Mix in the grated cheese, mustard and cayenne.
2. Add the milk and mix lightly to a soft dough.
3. Turn out on to a floured surface and knead lightly. Do not overhandle: the less the mixture is handled, the lighter the result.
4. Roll out to 1 cm (½ inch) thickness and cut into rounds with a 6 cm (2½ inch) pastry cutter.
5. Place the scones on a baking sheet and brush with milk. Bake in a preheated oven for 12–15 minutes, until risen and golden brown.

GREEN TOMATO CHUTNEY

MAKES ABOUT 2.5 kg (5½ lb)
1.75 kg (4 lb) green tomatoes, roughly chopped
450 g (1 lb) cooking apples, peeled, cored and chopped
450 g (1 lb) onions, peeled and chopped
2 large garlic cloves, crushed (optional)
225 g (8 oz) sultanas
1 tablespoon salt
1 tablespoon pickling spice
25 g (1 oz) root ginger, roughly chopped
1 chilli
600 ml (1 pint) vinegar
450 g (1 lb) brown or white sugar

Preparation time: about 30 minutes
Cooking time: about 2¾ hours

1. Place the tomatoes, apples and onions in a large pan with the garlic (if using), sultanas and salt. Tie the pickling spice, ginger and chilli in a muslin bag and add to the pan. Add half the vinegar and bring to the boil. Reduce the heat, then simmer for 1 hour or until the vegetables are reduced to a pulp and the mixture is thick.
2. Dissolve the sugar in the remaining vinegar and add to the chutney. Simmer for about 1½ hours, stirring frequently, or until the chutney is thick.
3. Remove the muslin bag and, while still hot, spoon the chutney into the prepared jars. Seal with airtight, vinegar-proof covers.

MINIATURE CORNISH PASTIES

MAKES 12
FILLING:
225 g (8 oz) potatoes, peeled and diced
1 tablespoon oil
225 g (8 oz) minced beef
75 g (3 oz) onion, finely chopped
1 dessertspoon tomato purée
1 teaspoon Worcestershire sauce
few drops of Tabasco sauce
1 beef stock cube dissolved in 1 tablespoon hot water
salt
freshly ground black pepper

PASTRY:

225 g (8 oz) plain flour
1 teaspoon salt
75 g (3 oz) lard
50 g (2 oz) margarine
3 tablespoons water
1 egg or milk, to glaze (optional)

Preparation time: 1 hour, plus
  cooling
Cooking time: 30 minutes
Oven: 200°C, 400°F, Gas Mark 6

1. To make the filling, boil the potatoes in salted water for about 10 minutes. Drain and cool. Heat the oil in a frying pan and fry the mince and onion until brown. Add the tomato purée, Worcestershire and Tabasco sauces, beef stock, salt, pepper and potatoes and leave to cool for 1 hour.
2. To make the pastry, sieve the flour and salt into a bowl and rub in the fats until the mixture resembles fine breadcrumbs. Add sufficient water to make a dough.
3. Roll out thinly and cut into 10 cm (4 inch) rounds.
4. Dampen the edge of one half of each round. Place a heaped teaspoon of filling in the centre and flute the edges together. Place the pasties on a baking sheet and bake in a preheated oven for 30 minutes. Serve hot.

CLOCKWISE FROM TOP LEFT: Green tomato chutney; Miniature Cornish pasties; Cheese scones

BRIDGE ROLLS WITH TWO TOPPINGS

MAKES 24 OPEN ROLLS
12 bridge rolls, halved
75 g (3 oz) butter, softened

CREAM CHEESE AND PINEAPPLE
TOPPING:
225 g (8 oz) full fat soft cheese
1 × 215 g (7½ oz) can crushed
pineapple, drained
1 tablespoon mayonnaise

TO GARNISH:
cucumber slices, quartered
radish slices, halved

TUNA FISH AND MAYONNAISE:
1 × 200 g (7 oz) can tuna in oil,
drained and flaked
3 tablespoons mayonnaise
1 dessertspoon lemon juice
salt
freshly ground black pepper

TO GARNISH:
stuffed olives, sliced
lemon slices, quartered

Preparation time: 20 minutes

1. Cut the rolls in half and spread thinly with butter.
2. Mix together the ingredients for the chosen topping and spread on the rolls. Serve garnished with the olive, lemon, cucumber and radish slices.

QUICK WHEATMEAL BREAD

MAKES 1 LOAF
300 ml (½ pint) warm water
2 teaspoons sugar
2 teaspoons dried yeast
450 g (1 lb) wheatmeal flour
1½ teaspoons salt
15 g (½ oz) butter, margarine or lard
cracked wheat or oats, for sprinkling

Preparation time: 10 minutes, plus rising
Cooking time: 30 minutes
Oven: 230°C, 450°F, Gas Mark 8

This loaf can be made and on the table in just over an hour. It is very simply made with just one rising.

1. Measure the warm water into a jug. Sprinkle over 1 teaspoon of the sugar and the yeast and leave for about 10 minutes, until frothy.
2. Place the flour, salt and remaining sugar in a mixing bowl and rub in the fat.
3. Pour the yeast liquid, all at once, onto the flour and mix to a soft dough.
4. Place the dough on a floured surface and knead for 5 minutes, until smooth and no longer sticky.
5. Shape the dough into a round and place on a greased baking sheet. Cut a deep cross in the top with a sharp knife.
6. Cover with oiled polythene and leave until doubled in size, about 30 minutes.
7. Remove the polythene and brush with water. Sprinkle with the cracked wheat or oats.
8. Bake in a preheated hot oven for 30 minutes until brown and crisp and the bread sounds hollow when tapped on the base. Cool on a wire tray.

Variations:
Tin loaf: Shape the dough into an oblong and place in a greased 1 kg (2 lb) loaf tin. Leave to rise and bake as above.
Rolls: Divide the dough into 12 equal pieces. Shape into balls and place apart on a greased baking sheet. Leave to rise as above and bake for 12–15 minutes at the same temperature as above.

SANDWICHES AND SANDWICH FILLINGS

EACH FILLING MAKES 44 MINI
SANDWICHES, i.e. ENOUGH FOR 1
SLICED LOAF
1 sliced loaf
100 g (4 oz) butter, softened

EGG AND CRESS:
5 hard-boiled eggs, mashed
3–4 tablespoons mayonnaise
salt
freshly ground black pepper
2 punnets mustard and cress

LIVER PATE AND TOMATO:
350 g (12 oz) spreading pâté
225 g (8 oz) tomatoes, thinly sliced
salt
freshly ground black pepper

AVOCADO AND PRAWN:
2–3 ripe avocados, mashed with 1–2
tablespoons lemon juice
350 g (12 oz) peeled prawns, chopped
4 tablespoons mayonnaise

SALMON AND CUCUMBER:
1 × 225 g (8 oz) can red salmon,
drained and flaked, with 2–3
tablespoons mayonnaise
½ cucumber, skinned and thinly
sliced
salt
freshly ground black pepper

Preparation time: 20 minutes

To cut even sandwiches and remove the crusts, it is a good idea to pile several on top of each other and then cut through the pile.

1. Spread each slice of bread thinly with butter.
2. To make the egg and cress sandwiches, mash the eggs and mayonnaise together, adding salt and pepper to taste.
3. Spread the mixture on to the bread, add a sprinkling of mustard and cress, then cover with another slice of bread.
4. Cut the sandwiches into 4 triangles and cut off the crusts.

5. Make the other fillings in the same way using brown bread for the Liver pâté and tomato and Salmon and cucumber sandwiches and white bread for the Avocados and prawns.

CLOCKWISE FROM THE LEFT: Bridge rolls with two toppings; Quick wheatmeal bread; Sandwiches and sandwich fillings

QUEEN OF JAMS

MAKES ABOUT 2.75 kg (6 lb)
1.5 kg (3 lb) peaches
grated rind and juice of 4 large
lemons, pith and pips reserved
450 ml (¾ pint) water
1 cinnamon stick
1 × 2.5 ml spoon (½ teaspoon) cloves
1 × 2.5 ml spoon (½ teaspoon) allspice
berries
1.5 kg (3 lb) preserving sugar

Preparation time: 10 minutes
Cooking time: about 50 minutes

1. Skin the peaches by steeping in boiling water for 10 to 20 seconds; drain and skin them. Cut in half, through to the stone, twist to separate the two halves and remove the stones. Slice the peaches and place in a large pan. Crack open the peach stones with a hammer, remove the skins from the kernels, then add the kernels to the peaches. Add grated rind and juice of the lemons and pour over the water.
2. Tie the peach stones, lemon pith and pips, cinnamon, cloves and allspice in a muslin bag and add to the pan. Heat gently and simmer for about 30 minutes or until the peaches are soft but still retain their shape.
3. Remove the muslin bag, squeezing the juice back into the pan. Add the sugar and heat gently, stirring until the sugar is dissolved. Bring to the boil, then boil rapidly until setting point is reached. Remove the scum.
4. Cool slightly, stir, then pour into prepared jars. Place waxed discs over the jam, overwrap with cellophane, fasten and label.

CURRANT BERRY JAM

MAKES ABOUT 3 kg (7 lb)
1 kg (2 lb) red currants
1 kg (2 lb) strawberries or
raspberries, etc. hulled
grated rind and juice of 2 oranges
or lemons
1.75 kg (4 lb) granulated sugar

Preparation time: 10 minutes
Cooking time: 30 minutes

1. Strip the currants off the stalks by running a fork tine down each stalk. Place the currants and hulled berries in a large pan and add the rind and juice from the oranges or lemons. Heat

gently to extract the juice, then simmer for 15 minutes.
2. Add the sugar and heat gently, stirring until the sugar is dissolved. Bring to the boil, then boil rapidly until setting point is reached. Remove the scum. Cool slightly, stir, then pour into prepared jars. Cover immediately with waxed discs, overwrap with cellophane, fasten and label.

LEMON CURD

MAKES 750 g (1¾ lb)
4 medium lemons
100 g (4 oz) butter
350 g (12 oz) granulated or caster
sugar
4 eggs, lightly beaten

Preparation time: 5 minutes
Cooking time: about 20 minutes

1. Grate the lemon rind into a bowl, then add the squeezed juice. Cut the butter into pieces, and add it with the sugar. Strain the eggs into the bowl. Place the bowl over a pan of simmering water, then stir until the sugar has dissolved and the butter melted.

2. Continue to cook, stirring constantly, until the curd thickens enough to coat the back of a wooden spoon. Do not overcook, as the eggs may curdle. Pour into prepared jars and cover with a waxed disc and cellophane as for jam. Keeps for 1 month, or 3 months in the refrigerator.

FROM THE LEFT: Queen of jams; Currant berry jam; Lemon curd

HIGH BUTTER SHORTIES

MAKES 26
225 g (8 oz) butter, softened
50 g (2 oz) caster sugar
½ teaspoon vanilla essence
225 g (8 oz) plain flour, sifted
7 blanched almonds
3 glacé cherries, halved
50 g (2 oz) plain chocolate, broken into pieces

Preparation time: 15 minutes, plus cooling
Cooking time: 10–12 minutes
Oven: 190°C, 375°F, Gas Mark 5

This recipe makes a selection of rich butter biscuits. The mixture is piped into different shapes – some are chocolate-dipped fingers and others are stars decorated with almonds and cherries.

1. Put the softened butter and sugar into a bowl and cream with a wooden spoon until light and fluffy. Mix in the vanilla essence and the flour to form a soft mixture.
2. Place the mixture in a piping bag fitted with a large star tube and pipe thirteen 7.5 cm (3 inch) finger lengths on to a greased baking sheet. Place in a preheated oven and bake for 10 minutes until pale golden and cooked through. Transfer to a wire rack and leave to cool completely (about 15 minutes).
3. Meanwhile pipe the remaining mixture into 13 stars on a greased baking sheet. Top 6 of these with a blanched almond and the remaining 7 with a halved glacé cherry. Bake in a preheated moderate oven for 12 minutes, until pale golden and cooked through. Transfer to a wire rack and leave to cool completely (about 30 minutes).
4. Place chocolate pieces in a heatproof basin over a saucepan of hot but not boiling water until melted (do not stir chocolate). Dip the ends of the finger biscuits in melted chocolate and leave to set about 45 minutes on a wire rack before serving. [A]

[A] The biscuits can be stored for up to 2 weeks in an airtight container.

COFFEE KISSES

MAKES ABOUT 15
100 g (4 oz) butter or margarine
50 g (2 oz) caster sugar
150 g (5 oz) self-raising flour
3 tablespoons strong black coffee

ICING:
50 g (2 oz) butter, softened
100 g (4 oz) icing sugar, sifted
1 tablespoon strong black coffee
icing sugar, for dusting

Preparation time: 20 minutes
Cooking time: 10 minutes
Oven: 190°C, 375°F, Gas Mark 5

1. Place the butter or margarine and sugar in a bowl. Beat with a wooden spoon for 10 minutes, or in a mixer for 5 minutes, until light and fluffy.
2. Add the flour and coffee and mix to a stiff dough.
3. Place the mixture in a piping bag, fitted with a large star tube. Pipe an even number of small stars with the mixture, a little apart, on a greased baking sheet. The mixture will make about 30 stars.
4. Bake in a preheated oven for 10 minutes, until just beginning to colour. Cool on the baking sheet for 5 minutes, then remove and leave to cool completely on a wire tray.
5. To make the icing, beat together the butter, icing sugar and coffee until light and creamy.
6. Sandwich 2 stars together with a little icing, then dust with icing.

MARZIPAN SPICE TEABREAD

MAKES A 1 kg (2 lb) LOAF
450 g (1 lb) strong plain white flour
½ teaspoon salt
1 tablespoon caster sugar
50 g (2 oz) butter, diced
1 packet easy blend dried yeast (equivalent to 25 g (1 oz) fresh yeast)
75 g (3 oz) mixed dried fruit
200 ml (7 fl oz) tepid milk
1 egg, beaten

FILLING:
100 g (4 oz) ground almonds
100 g (4 oz) soft light brown sugar
1 teaspoon ground cinnamon
1 egg, beaten

TO GLAZE:
6 tablespoons icing sugar, sifted
1 tablespoon lemon juice

Preparation time: 15 minutes, plus rising and cooling
Cooking time: 40 minutes
Oven: 200°C, 400°F, Gas Mark 6

This easy-to-make teabread is filled like a Swiss roll with a mouthwatering almond, sugar and spice mixture that looks most attractive when the loaf is sliced. The tea bread is best eaten the day it is baked, with butter.

1. Sift the flour with the salt and sugar into a large mixing bowl. Rub in the butter with the fingertips until the mixture resembles fine breadcrumbs. Add the yeast and dried fruit and stir well to mix thoroughly.
2. Add the milk and egg and mix to form a soft dough, using a wooden spoon. Turn the dough on to a lightly floured board or work surface and knead by hand for about 10 minutes until the dough is smooth and elastic. (Or mix for 2–3 minutes in an electric mixer fitted with a dough hook.)
3. Shape the dough into a round ball, place in a large lightly oiled polythene bag and tie loosely. Leave in a warm place to rise for about 1 hour until the dough is doubled in size and springs back when pressed with a floured finger. [A]
4. To make the filling, mix all the filling ingredients in a bowl until thoroughly blended. [A]
5. Turn the risen dough on to a lightly floured board or work surface and knead for 1 minute. Roll the dough out to a rectangle, with a width equal to the length of a 1 kg (2 lb) loaf tin, and 30 cm (12 inches) long.
6. Spread the filling over the dough to within 1 cm (½ inch) of the edges. Roll up the dough, like a Swiss roll, starting from a short edge. Place, join side down, in a greased 1 kg (2 lb) loaf tin and ease the dough into the corners. Cover with lightly oiled cling film and leave to prove for about 30 minutes until doubled in size and almost reaching the top of the tin.
7. Place in a preheated oven and bake for 40 minutes or until golden brown and cooked through. (Cover with foil during cooking if necessary to prevent over-browning.)
8. Turn the loaf out of the tin on to a wire rack. Mix the icing sugar with the lemon juice and brush over the top

and sides of the hot loaf. ⏏ Leave to cool slightly before serving hot or cold, sliced and buttered.

🅐 The dough can be made in advance and left to rise overnight in the refrigerator in a large, lightly oiled polythene bag (tied loosely to allow room for expansion). Knead well to bring back to room temperature before using.

🅐 The filling can be made several hours in advance, covered with cling film and kept in a cool place.

🅕 When cold, freeze for up to 1 month. Thaw for 3–4 hours at room temperature to serve cold, or toast and serve hot with butter.

🅜 Or microwave on Defrost for 4–6 minutes before serving.

CLOCKWISE FROM THE LEFT: High butter shorties; Coffee kisses; Marzipan spice teabread

NUTTY BROWN SUGAR MERINGUES

MAKES 10
2 egg whites
100 g (4 oz) light soft brown sugar
25 g (1 oz) chopped mixed nuts
150 ml (¼ pint) whipping cream
1 teaspoon icing sugar
few drops of vanilla essence

Preparation time: 10–15 minutes, plus cooling
Cooking time: 6–8 hours, or overnight
Oven: 110°C, 225°F, Gas Mark ¼

1. Line a baking sheet with non-stick silicone paper or lightly greased greaseproof paper.
2. Whisk the egg whites in a bowl until stiff. Sprinkle over 50 g (2 oz) of the sugar and whisk again until very stiff and glossy.
3. Lightly fold in the remaining sugar, using a large metal spoon. Put the mixture into a piping bag fitted with a large star tube, and pipe 20 star-shapes on to the prepared baking sheet. Sprinkle with nuts.
4. Bake the meringues in a preheated very low oven for 6–8 hours, or overnight, until completely dried out. Transfer to a wire rack to cool for 15 minutes only, then store in polythene bags in an airtight tin until required. Ⓐ.
5. Whip the cream with the icing sugar and vanilla essence to taste until stiff peaks form. Use to sandwich the meringues together in pairs. Serve within 30 minutes of assembling.

Ⓐ The meringue shells can be kept successfully for up to 6 weeks. Store in a polythene bag in an airtight tin.

Variations:
White meringues: Use caster sugar instead of light soft brown sugar.
Choc and nut meringues: Mix whipped cream (without icing and vanilla essence) with 1½–2 tablespoons of chocolate hazelnut spread and use to sandwich the meringues together.

CHOCOLATE ECLAIRS

MAKES 20–24
150 ml (¼ pint) double or whipping cream, whipped

CHOUX PASTE:
50 g (2 oz) butter or margarine
150 ml (¼ pint) water
65 g (2½ oz) plain flour
pinch of salt
2 eggs (sizes 1, 2), beaten

TOPPING:
100 g (4 oz) plain chocolate
25 g (1 oz) butter

Preparation time: 20 minutes
Cooking time: 20–25 minutes
Oven: 220°C, 425°F, Gas Mark 7

For round éclairs simply pipe the choux paste into buns about the size of a large walnut.

1. To make the choux paste, melt the butter or margarine in the water in a saucepan, then bring to the boil. Remove from the heat.
2. Sift the flour and salt together and tip all at once into the pan. Beat with a wooden spoon to give a smooth paste which forms into a ball.
3. Spread out the paste over the bottom of the pan and leave to cool for several minutes.

4. Gradually beat in the eggs until the mixture is smooth and glossy and gives a piping consistency. A hand-held electric mixer is ideal for this task.
5. Put the choux paste into a piping bag fitted with a plain 1 cm (½ inch) nozzle. Pipe the paste into straight lines about 6 cm (2½ inches) long, spaced well apart, on greased baking sheets. Cut the ends of the paste from the nozzle with a knife.
6. Bake in a preheated hot oven for 20–25 minutes or until well risen, firm and a pale golden brown.
7. Make a slit in the side of each éclair to allow the steam to escape and return to the oven to dry out for a few minutes.
8. Transfer to a wire rack to cool.
9. If using cream to fill the éclairs, whip it until stiff. Slit each éclair in half carefully and fill with the cream.
10. Melt the chocolate in a heatproof bowl over hot water, then stir in the butter until melted. Remove from the heat and cool until beginning to thicken.
11. Dip the top of each éclair into the topping or spread with a palette knife. Leave to set.

STICKY GINGERBREAD

MAKES ABOUT 15 PIECES
275 g (10 oz) plain flour
2 teaspoons ground ginger
1 teaspoon bicarbonate of soda
100 g (4 oz) margarine
100 g (4 oz) light soft brown sugar
225 g (8 oz) golden syrup
100 g (4 oz) black treacle
2 eggs, beaten
150 ml (¼ pint) hot water

Preparation time: 15 minutes
Cooking time: 45 minutes
Oven: 180°C, 350°F, Gas Mark 4

1. Grease and line a 30 × 23 cm (12 × 9 inch) roasting tin.
2. Sift the flour, ginger and bicarbonate of soda into a large mixing bowl.
3. Place the margarine, sugar, syrup and treacle in a saucepan. Heat gently until the margarine has melted and the sugar has dissolved.
4. Make a well in the centre of the dry ingredients. Pour the mixture from the saucepan into the flour and beat well to mix.
5. Add the beaten eggs and hot water and mix to a smooth batter.
6. Pour the mixture into the prepared tin.
7. Bake in a preheated moderate oven for 45 minutes until the cake springs back when pressed with the fingers.
8. Turn out of the tin, remove the paper and cool on a wire tray. Keep for 2 days before eating, then cut into slices to serve. To store, wrap in greaseproof paper, then foil. The gingerbread will keep for up to 2 weeks.

FROM THE LEFT: Nutty brown sugar meringues; Chocolate éclairs; Sticky gingerbread

MADEIRA CAKE

MAKES A 15 cm (6 inch) CAKE
175 g (6 oz) butter
175 g (6 oz) caster sugar
3 eggs, beaten
225 g (8 oz) plain flour
1 teaspoon baking powder
grated rind of ½ lemon
strip of citron peel (optional)

Preparation time: 20 minutes, plus cooling
Cooking time: 1½ hours
Oven: 160°C, 325°F, Gas Mark 3

1. Grease and bottom line a 15 cm (6 inch) round cake tin.
2. Place the butter and sugar in a bowl. Beat with a wooden spoon for 10 minutes, or in a mixer for 5 minutes, until light and fluffy.
3. Beat in the eggs, a little at a time.
4. Sift the flour and baking powder into the bowl. Fold them into the mixture using a metal spoon. Fold in the lemon rind.
5. Place the mixture in the prepared tin. Smooth the top. If using, place the strip of citron peel in the centre of the cake.
6. Bake in a preheated moderate oven for 1½ hours until the cake has risen and is light golden in colour. When cooked the cake should spring back when pressed with the fingers.
7. Turn out and cool on a wire tray.

FARMHOUSE SULTANA CHERRY CAKE

MAKES A 1 kg (2 lb) LOAF-SHAPED CAKE
225 g (8 oz) plain flour
1¼ teaspoons baking powder
175 g (6 oz) soft margarine
175 g (6 oz) caster sugar
2 eggs
75 g (3 oz) glacé cherries, washed, dried and quartered
75 g (3 oz) sultanas
1 tablespoon milk
8 sugar lumps, roughly crushed, to decorate (optional)

Preparation time: 10 minutes, plus cooling
Cooking time: 1¼–1½ hours
Oven: 160°C, 325°F, Gas Mark 3

1. Grease a 1 kg (2 lb) loaf tin and line the base and sides with greased grease-proof paper.
2. Sift the flour with the baking powder into a mixing bowl. Add the margarine, sugar and eggs and beat well for 2–3 minutes with a wooden spoon, or for 1 minute in an electric mixer, until thoroughly mixed.
3. Stir in the cherries, sultanas and milk, then turn the mixture into the prepared tin. Smooth the surface with a spoon and sprinkle with the crushed sugar lumps, if using.
4. Place in a preheated moderate oven and cook for 1¼–1½ hours until well risen, golden brown and cooked through. To test: insert a fine warmed skewer into the centre of the cake; if when removed the skewer is clean, the cake is cooked; if not, return it to the oven and bake for a further few minutes before testing again.
5. Turn the cake out of the tin on to a wire rack, remove the lining paper and leave for 1½–2 hours to cool com-

FROM THE LEFT: Madeira cake; Farmhouse sultana cherry cake

pletely. F When cold, wrap up the cake in greaseproof paper and store in an airtight tin.

F Freeze for up to 3 months. Thaw for 2–3 hours at room temperature.

M Or microwave on Defrost for 5–8 minutes, then stand for 15 minutes before serving.

Variation: Add $\frac{1}{2}$ teaspoon finely grated orange or lemon rind to the mixture.

BLACK FOREST CHERRY GATEAU

MAKES A 20 cm (8 inch) ROUND
  CAKE
6 eggs
175 g (6 oz) caster sugar
175 g (6 oz) plain flour
50 g (2 oz) cocoa
*8 tablespoons Kirsch or cherry
  brandy*
*2 × 450 g (15 oz) cans black cherries,
  drained, stoned and halved, juice
  reserved*

FILLING:
*600 ml (1 pint) double cream,
  whipped*
2 teaspoons arrowroot
*150 ml (¼ pint) juice from the
  cherries*
*75 g (3 oz) plain dark chocolate,
  grated, or chocolate scrolls, to
  decorate*

Preparation time: 50 minutes, plus
  overnight soaking
Cooking time: 30–40 minutes
Oven: 190°C, 375°F, Gas Mark 5

1. Grease and flour two 20 cm (8 inch)
round cake tins.
2. Place the eggs and the sugar in a
bowl and set over a pan of simmering
water.
3. Whisk the eggs and sugar until they
are pale and thick enough to leave a
trail. Remove the bowl from the pan of
water and continue to whisk until the
mixture is cool.
4. Sift in the flour and cocoa powder
and fold them gently into the egg
mixture.
5. Divide the mixture between the 2
tins and bake them in a preheated
moderately hot oven for 30–40
minutes or until firm and spongy.
6. Leave the cakes to cool in the tins.
Turn them out on to wire trays. When
they are completely cold, split the
cakes in half horizontally.
7. Sprinkle 2 tablespoons of Kirsch
and 4 tablespoons of cherry juice on
each layer. Soak overnight.
8. Sandwich a third of the cream and
half the black cherries between each
layer of chocolate cake.
9. Spread half the remaining cream
around the sides of the cake. Arrange
the remaining cherries in concentric
circles on top of the cake, leaving a
border for rosettes of whipped cream.
10. Slake the arrowroot with a little

water and stir it into the reserved
cherry juice. Bring the juice gently to
the boil, stirring continuously until it
clears and thickens.
11. Pour the cherry sauce over the
cherries on top of the cake.
12. Pipe a border of cream rosettes
round the edge of the cake and cover
the sides of the cake with grated
chocolate or chocolate scrolls. [F]

[F] Can be frozen for up to 3 months.
Open freeze until solid, then pack
carefully in a rigid container. To thaw,
remove from the container, place on a
serving dish and leave in the refrigerator overnight.

STRAWBERRY CREAM SPONGE

MAKES A 20 cm (8 inch) ROUND
  CAKE
3 eggs
75 g (3 oz) caster sugar
75 g (3 oz) plain flour
25 g (1 oz) butter, melted

TO SERVE:
150 ml (¼ pint) double cream
250 g (8 oz) strawberries, sliced
little icing sugar, to taste

Preparation time: 20 minutes
Cooking time: 20–25 minutes
Oven: 180°C, 350°F, Gas Mark 4

1. Grease and line two 20 cm (8 inch) sandwich tins.

2. Place the eggs and sugar in a bowl over hot water and whisk with an electric whisk for about 10 minutes until the mixture is light and thick and leaves a trail when the whisk is lifted.

3. Sift the flour into a bowl and fold in lightly, using a metal spoon, until evenly mixed. Pour the melted butter slowly into the mixture and fold in.

4. Pour the mixture into the prepared tins and level the surface. Bake in a preheated moderate oven for 20–25 minutes until the cakes are golden brown and firm to the touch. Turn out on to a wire tray and leave to cool. F

5. To serve, whip the cream, then place one cake on a serving plate and spread with the cream. Cover with the strawberries. Place the second cake on top and sift over the icing sugar.

F Pack in a polythene bag, seal, label and freeze for up to 3 months. To thaw, leave in wraps at room temperature for about 1 hour.

FROM THE LEFT: Black Forest cherry gâteau; Strawberry cream sponge

CHILDREN'S PARTY FOR TWELVE

Deck of Cards Open Sandwiches

Turkey Goujons with Tomato Dip

Cheese and Celery Boats

Gog-a-Dogs

Potato Crisp Cookies

Mouse and Rabbit Faces

Marzipan Dominoes

Ladybirds

Meringue Caterpillars

Cinderella's Coach

COUNTDOWN

2–3 days before the party

Make and decorate Cinderella's coach. Cover and chill.
Make the Meringue caterpillars and store in an airtight container.

The day before

Make the Mouse and rabbit faces. Store in an airtight container.
Make the Ladybirds and store in an airtight container.
Make the Marzipan dominoes and store in an airtight container.

In the morning

Make the Potato crisp cookies and store in an airtight container.
Complete step 1 of the Turkey goujons.
Cook the goujons if you are going to serve them cold. Cover and chill.
Make the dip for the Turkey goujons. Cover and chill.

About 2 hours before the party

Make the Deck of cards sandwiches. Cover with cling film.
Make the Cheese and celery boats. Harness the horse to Cinderella's coach.

30 minutes before the party

Cook the Gog-a-dogs
Cook the Turkey goujons if you are going to serve them hot.

DECK OF CARDS OPEN SANDWICHES

MAKES 16–20
8–12 slices brown or granary bread
butter for spreading
10 slices processed cheese
small piece cucumber, thinly sliced
about 6 cherry tomatoes
3–4 radishes
tiny sprigs of celery
tiny sprigs of parsley

Preparation time: about 30 minutes

The easiest way to cut out these sandwiches is with 'deck of cards' cutters, i.e. heart, diamond, club and spade shapes. They are made in both metal and plastic and are about 6 cm (2½ inches) high. If you are unable to find them, cut out your own pattern on a piece of thick card and use it as a template.

1. Cut out 4 of each of the deck of card shapes from the slices of bread – you should get 2 out of each slice. Spread each shape lightly with softened butter.
2. Using the same cutters, cut out 4 of each shape from the slices of processed cheese and place them evenly on the bread.
3. Cut the slices of cucumber into quarters and thirds, thinly slice the tomatoes and radishes and break the celery leaves and sprigs of parsley into tiny pieces.
4. Arrange the vegetable pieces over the cheese and top with a sprig of celery or parsley. Make a different topping for each shape of sandwich.
5. Place the sandwiches on a flat plate or board and cover with cling film until you are ready to serve.

TURKEY GOUJONS WITH TOMATO DIP

3 turkey breast fillets, total weight about 450 g (1 lb)
little seasoned flour
1 egg, beaten
about 100 g (4 oz) fresh white breadcrumbs or 1 packet golden breadcrumbs
deep oil or fat for frying

TOMATO DIP:
4 tablespoons chunky tomato pickle
4 tablespoons tomato ketchup
2 tablespoons soured cream

Preparation time: about 20 minutes
Cooking time: about 20 minutes

1. Cut the turkey fillets into narrow strips about 5 × 1.5 cm (2 × ½ inches). Toss them in seasoned flour, then dip in beaten egg and coat thoroughly with the breadcrumbs.
2. Heat the deep fat to 180°–190°C/ 350°–375°F or until a cube of bread browns in 30 seconds. Fry the goujons, a few at a time, for 3–4 minutes until they are golden brown and crisp. Drain on absorbent paper towels. If you are going to serve the goujons hot, keep the first batch warm while frying the rest; otherwise leave them to cool.
3. Combine all the ingredients for the dip and put them into a small serving bowl. Cover with cling film until required.
4. Serve the goujons on a plate with the bowl of tomato dip. They are equally good hot or cold.

FROM THE TOP: Deck of cards open sandwiches; Turkey goujons with tomato dip

CHEESE AND CELERY BOATS

MAKES 18

225 g (8 oz) full fat soft cream cheese
50 g (2 oz) dry roasted peanuts,
  finely chopped
6 green celery sticks, about 20 cm (8
  inches) long
9 slices processed cheese
18 cocktail sticks

Preparation time: about 20 minutes

1. Combine the cream cheese and chopped peanuts and use to fill the celery sticks.
2. Cut each celery stick into 3 even-sized pieces to make boats.
3. Cut each slice of cheese in half diagonally to give 2 triangles. Thread each triangle on to a cocktail stick, and stick it firmly into the boat to represent a sail. Complete the others in the same way and arrange on a flat plate.

GOG-A-DOGS

MAKES 16

2 × 225 g (8 oz) packets pork, or
  pork and beef chipolata sausages
16 long slices streaky bacon, rinded
wooden cocktail sticks
coloured cocktail sticks (optional)
tomato ketchup, to serve

Preparation time: 15 minutes
Cooking time: about 15 minutes

1. Separate the sausages and prick them lightly. Roll them with your hand so they are evenly shaped.
2. Stretch out the bacon rashers with the back of a knife and then carefully wind one rasher right along the length of each sausage. Secure the ends by sticking a wooden cocktail stick through the sausage. (If you can only get short rashers, you will need two for each sausage.)
3. Stand the sausages in a grill pan and cook them under a preheated mod-

erate grill for about 7–8 minutes on each side.
4. To serve, allow the sausages to cool a little, then, if wished, remove the wooden cocktail sticks and replace them with coloured ones. Serve with a bowl of tomato ketchup for a dip.

POTATO CRISP COOKIES

MAKES 9–10

90 g (3½ oz) Gruyère cheese, grated
2 × 25 g (1 oz) packets cheese and
   onion flavoured potato crisps, lightly
   crushed
2 teaspoons sesame seeds
65 g (2¼ oz) plain flour
¾ teaspoon dry mustard
good pinch of garlic powder
pinch of cayenne pepper
65 g (2¼ oz) butter or margarine,
   melted

Preparation time: about 20 minutes
Cooking time: about 15 minutes
Oven: 190°C, 375°F, Gas Mark 5

These cookies should be eaten the day
they are made and are at their best if
served warm. Do not be tempted to
freeze them.

1. Put the cheese into a bowl and mix
in the crushed crisps, sesame seeds,
flour, mustard, garlic powder and
cayenne.
2. Add the butter and mix lightly to
form a dough.
3. Divide the mixture into 9 or 10
even-sized pieces and put them in
rough heaps on a greased baking
sheet.
4. Bake in a preheated moderately hot
oven for about 15 minutes until lightly
browned. If the cheese spreads during
cooking, mould it back into shape with
a small palette knife.
5. Cool the cookies on the baking
sheet for 3–4 minutes, then carefully
remove them to a wire tray. Serve warm
or cold.

*CLOCKWISE FROM TOP LEFT: Cheese
and celery boats; Potato crisp cookies;
'Gog-a-dogs*

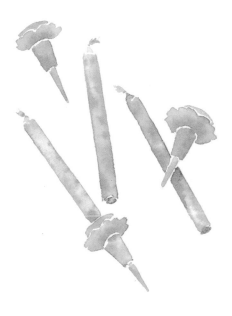

MOUSE AND RABBIT FACES

MAKES 24
100 g (4 oz) butter or margarine
75 g (3 oz) caster sugar
1 egg yolk
few drops of vanilla essence
225 g (8 oz) plain flour
50 g (2 oz) malted milk powder
2 tablespoons milk

GLACÉ ICING:
350 g (12 oz) icing sugar, sifted
1 tablespoon lemon juice
1–2 tablespoons hot water

TO DECORATE:
pink or silver balls
pink jelly sweets
angelica
chocolate dots

Preparation time: about 1 hour, plus
   cooling and setting
Cooking time: about 20 minutes
Oven: 180°C, 350°F, Gas Mark 4

1. Cream the fat and sugar together
until light and fluffy, then beat in the
egg yolk and vanilla essence.
2. Sift together the flour and malted
milk powder and work into the mixture, followed by the milk.
3. Knead the mixture until it is
smooth, then roll it out on a lightly
floured surface. Using a 6 cm (2½ inch)
plain cutter, cut out 24 circles.
4. Place the circles on lightly greased
baking sheets and cook in a preheated
moderate oven for 15–20 minutes until
a light golden brown. Allow to cool
briefly, then transfer to a wire tray and
leave until cold.
5. To make the glacé icing, mix together the icing sugar and lemon juice
and add sufficient hot water to make a
smooth icing thick enough to coat the
back of a spoon easily.
6. Spoon a little of the icing on each biscuit and spread it almost to the edges.
7. To make the mice, take half the
biscuits, add two pink balls for eyes, a
round piece of pink jelly sweet for a
nose and two small triangular pieces
for ears. Add very thin strips of angelica
for whiskers.
8. To make the rabbits, take the remaining biscuits and add pink balls for
eyes, a brown chocolate dot for a nose,
thin angelica for whiskers and a large
diamond jelly sweet cut to shape for
ears. Leave to set.

MARZIPAN DOMINOES

MAKES 16–18
100 g (4 oz) butter or margarine
100 g (4 oz) light soft brown sugar
2 eggs
90 g (3½ oz) self raising flour
15 g (½ oz) cocoa
¼ teaspoon baking powder
*2 teaspoons cold black coffee or
   water*
little apricot jam
175 g (6 oz) white marzipan
red liquid food colouring
green liquid food colouring

BUTTER CREAM:
50 g (2 oz) butter
100 g (4 oz) icing sugar, sifted
few drops of vanilla essence

Preparation time: about 45 minutes
Cooking time: 25–30 minutes, plus
   cooling
Oven: 180°C, 350°F, Gas Mark 4

1. Cream the fat and sugar together in
a bowl until very light, fluffy and pale in
colour.
2. Beat in the eggs, one at a time,
following each one with a spoonful of
the flour. Sift the remaining flour with
the cocoa and baking powder and fold
it into the mixture, followed by the
coffee or water.
3. Line a rectangular 28 × 18 × 4 cm
(11 × 7 × 1½ inch) tin with greased
greaseproof or non-stick silicone
paper. Pour in the mixture, spreading
it out evenly, especially into the corners
of the tin.
4. Cook in a preheated moderate oven
for 25–30 minutes until well risen and
firm to the touch. Turn out on to a wire
tray and leave until cold, then peel off
the paper.
5. Spread the top of the cake with
apricot jam, then cut it in half lengthways to give two long strips.
6. Divide the marzipan in two, and
colour one piece red and the other
green by kneading in liquid food
colourings.
7. Roll out each piece of marzipan into
a long strip to fit the pieces of cake.
Carefully place the cakes, jam side
downwards, on to the marzipan and
trim the edges.
8. Cut each slab of cake into 8 or 9
slices and turn them over so that the
marzipan side is on the top.
9. To make the butter cream, cream

the butter until soft, then beat in the
sifted icing sugar followed by the vanilla essence.
10. Put the icing into a piping bag
fitted with a medium to thick plain
writing nozzle. Pipe a line across the
centre of each domino, then pipe dots
on each side of the line to represent
the numbers on the dominos.

LADYBIRDS

MAKES 18
100 g (4 oz) soft margarine
100 g (4 oz) caster sugar
2 eggs
100 g (4 oz) self raising flour, sifted
1 teaspoon baking powder
grated rind of 1 small orange
*little orange jelly marmalade or
   apricot jam, sieved*
*225–350 g (8–12 oz) fondant icing
   or white marzipan*
red food colouring
50 g (2 oz) plain chocolate, melted
36 chocolate buttons
chocolate dots
36 silver balls

Preparation time: about 1 hour
Cooking time: 15–20 minutes, plus
   cooling and setting
Oven: 180°C, 350°F, Gas Mark 4

1. To make the cakes, put the margarine, sugar, eggs, sifted flour, baking
powder and orange rind into a bowl
and mix until blended, then beat hard
for 2 minutes.
2. Divide the mixture among 18
greased and floured patty tins, level the
tops and cook in a preheated moderate oven for 15–20 minutes until well
risen and firm to the touch.
3. Turn out on to a wire tray and leave
until cold. If necessary trim the cakes
so they stand evenly. They need to be
upside down.
4. Colour the fondant icing red by
kneading in the red colouring. Add a
touch of icing sugar if it becomes too
soft.
5. Roll out the fondant icing thinly
between two sheets of polythene and
cut it into 8 cm (3¼ inch) rounds. Roll
the trimmings to make a total of 18
rounds.
6. Brush the rounds of icing with marmalade and press one evenly over each
cake.
7. Put the melted chocolate into a
paper icing bag and cut off just the very

tip. Stick the chocolate buttons together in pairs for heads, then fasten one on to one end of each cake.

8. Pipe a straight line of melted chocolate down the centre back of each ladybird. Use melted chocolate dots to stick three or four chocolate dots to each one. Using melted chocolate attach two silver balls for eyes to the chocolate heads. Leave to set.

FROM THE TOP: Mouse and rabbit faces; Marzipan dominoes; Ladybirds

MERINGUE CATERPILLARS

MAKES 12–14
2 egg whites
100 g (4 oz) caster sugar
few drops green liquid food
  colouring
silver or coloured balls

Preparation time: about 20 minutes
Cooking time: 1¾–2 hours
Oven: 110°C, 225°F, Gas Mark ¼

1. Cover 1 large baking sheet or 2 smaller ones with non-stick silicone paper.
2. Place the egg whites in a clean grease-free bowl and whisk until they are thick, dry and stand in stiff peaks.
3. Whisk in the sugar, a dessertspoon at a time, making sure the meringue is stiff again before adding further sugar.
4. Add a few drops of green food colouring and mix it in quickly and evenly.
5. Put the meringue into a piping bag fitted with a plain 1 cm (½ inch) nozzle. Pipe caterpillars by making 5 or 6 twists with the nozzle while keeping the shape straight and finishing off quickly. If necessary, trim off the tip for the nose.
6. Add 2 silver or coloured balls to each caterpillar for eyes.
7. Cook in a preheated very cool oven for 1¾–2 hours until the meringues are firm and dry and will easily peel off the paper. (If you are using two baking sheets it is a good idea to reverse them after 1 hour in the oven.) Leave the meringues on the paper until cold, then remove and store in an airtight container. They will keep for up to 10 days.

CINDERELLA'S COACH

CAKE:
175 g (6 oz) butter or margarine
175 g (6 oz) caster or light soft
  brown sugar
few drops of vanilla essence
3 eggs
150 g (5 oz) self raising flour
25 g (1 oz) cocoa
½ teaspoon baking powder
1 tablespoon water
450 g (1 lb) white marzipan or
  fondant icing
green liquid food colouring
1 chocolate mini Swiss roll

BUTTER CREAM:
175 g (6 oz) butter
350 g (12 oz) icing sugar, sifted
few drops vanilla essence
2–3 teaspoons milk

TO DECORATE:
chocolate buttons
lemon slices
silver balls
2 bamboo skewers
1 china horse about 8 cm (3 inches)
  high
coloured ribbon or wool
2 plaster or icing rabbits

Preparation time: about 2 hours
Cooking time: about 50 minutes
Oven: 180°C, 350°F, Gas Mark 4

1. To make the cake, cream together the fat and sugar until light, fluffy and pale in colour. Beat in the vanilla essence and the eggs, one at a time, following each one with a spoonful of flour.
2. Sift the remaining flour with the cocoa and baking powder, then fold it into the mixture followed by the water.
3. Grease two 1.2 litre (2 pint) pudding basins, place a disc of greased greaseproof paper in the base of each one and dredge lightly with flour.

FROM THE LEFT: Meringue caterpillars; Cinderella's coach

4. Divide the cake mixture between the two basins and level the tops. Cook in a preheated moderate oven for about 50 minutes or until well risen and firm to the touch. A skewer inserted into the centre of the cake should come out clean.

5. Turn out the cake on to a wire tray and leave until quite cold.

6. To make the butter cream, cream the butter until soft. Place the icing sugar in a bowl and pour the vanilla essence into the milk. Beat in alternate spoonfuls of the two mixtures until the butter cream has a spreading consistency.

7. Trim the cakes so they fit together neatly, then sandwich them together with the butter cream. Spread the butter cream thinly all over the top and sides of the cake.

8. Tint the marzipan pale green by kneading in the liquid food colouring. Roll out the marzipan thinly between two sheets of polythene to make a circle large enough to enclose the whole cake.

9. Stand the cake upside-down on the marzipan and spread the rest of the cake with the butter cream. Fold the marzipan round the cake, cutting if necessary so that it covers it neatly.

10. Carefully position the coach to one side of a 30 cm (12 inch) round cake board, attaching it with a dab of butter cream and keeping the joins underneath.

11. Put the butter cream into a piping bag fitted with a star nozzle and pipe in a door with a window on each side of the coach. Fill in the lower half of the door, and pipe decorations round the windows.

12. Pipe a seat at the front of the coach with lines of butter cream and add 2 chocolate buttons for the cushions. Add another seat at the back of the coach for the coachmen. Place 2 chocolate buttons at the bottom of each door for steps.

13. Pipe an 11 × 7.5 cm (4½ × 3 inch) rectangle of shells on the roof of the coach. Pipe 3 lines along the length of the rectangle, pipe another 2 lines on top of them and a third line along the centre. Decorate the panel with lemon slices and silver balls. Pipe lines of shells at each corner of the coach from the top to the wheels. Add extra lines of shells, squiggles and stars, as liked, to complete the decoration.

14. Cut the mini Swiss roll into pieces and place at each corner of the coach to represent the wheels.

15. Cover the ends of 2 bamboo skewers with ribbon and stick them into the front of the coach below the seat for shafts, then stand a china horse between them. Tie in with ribbon and make a bridle and reins of ribbon.

16. Finally sit a rabbit on the front seat for the driver and another one on the back seat for the coachman. Leave the cake to set.

INDEX

ACKNOWLEDGEMENTS

The publisher would like to thank the following for their kind contribution to the food photography:

The Cranberry Information Bureau:
Christmas Day Lunch or Dinner, page 156–7;

Drambuie, The After Dinner Liqueur:
Birthday Dinner, page 84;

Marks and Spencer PLC:
French Bistro Supper, page 128–9;

Total Yoghurt:
Midsummer Night's Dream Dinner, page 146–7.

The publishers would also like to thank the following people and organizations who were involved in the preparation of this book:

Photographer James Murphy with stylist Marian Price for the photographs on pages 4, 8–9, 58–219, 226–49.
Food prepared for photography by Allyson Birch and Dolly Meers.
Colour illustrations in the recipe pages by Anne Ormerod.
The International Wine and Food Society for kind permission to reproduce the vintage chart on page 36.

Photography credits:
The Anthony Blake Photo Library: page 6;
Octopus Books Ltd: (Theo Bergstrom) page 37; (Martin Brigdale) 30, 40–42; (Laurie Evans) 46–47; (James Jackson) 11, 50–51; (Ian O'Leary) 12–13; (Duncan McNicol) 34–35; (Colin Maher) 33; (Vernon Morgan) 52 left and right, 53 above left, centre left, right, 220 right and centre, 223 above left and right, centre left and right, 224 above, centre and below; (James Murphy) 45, 48–49, 225; (Clive Streeter) 39, 222 above left and right, centre left and right, below right; (Paul Webster) 57.

Some of the material published in this book previously appeared in the following books published by Octopus Books Ltd:

American Cooking; Appetizing Starters; Barbecues and Summer Food; Cooking for the Family; Encyclopaedia of Asian Cooking: Encyclopaedia of Desserts; Encyclopaedia of Herbs, Spices and Flavourings; Finger and Fork Food; Four Seasons Salads; French Bistro Cookery; Good Home Baking; Home Preserves; Hostess Cookbook; Hot and Spicy; Mediterranean Cooking; Midday Meals; Salads and Vegetables; Slimmer's Year; St. Michael Cookery Course; Vegetarian Feast.